P9-DWX-468

DATE DUE

JA 4 '93			
NO 10 '94			
NO 21 '97			
RENEW			
DE 16 '97			
AP 10 '98			
MY 8 '98			
JY 30 '98			
AU 2 '00			
JE 11 '01			

DEMCO 38-296

ECONOMICS IN AMERICA

IN AMERICA

OPPOSING VIEWPOINTS*

Other Books of Related Interest in the Opposing
Viewpoints Series:

American Foreign Policy
American Government
American Values
America's Defense
America's Future
Civil Liberties
The Homeless
Immigration
The New World Order
Politics in America
Poverty
Social Justice
Trade

ECONOMICS IN AMERICA

OPPOSING VIEWPOINTS®

David L. Bender & Bruno Leone, *Series Editors*

Terry O'Neill, *Book Editor*
Karin L. Swisher, *Book Editor*

OPPOSING VIEWPOINTS SERIES ®

Riverside Community College
Greenhaven Press, Inc.   PO Box 289009   San Diego, CA 92198-0009
Library
4800 Magnolia Avenue
Riverside, California 92506

MAR '92

HO 2051
E34 1992

No part of this book may be reproduced or used in any form or by any means, electrical, mechanical, or otherwise, including, but not limited to, photocopy, recording, or any information storage and retrieval system, without prior written permission from the publisher.

Library of Congress Cataloging-in-Publication Data

Economics in America : opposing viewpoints / Terry O'Neill & Karin L. Swisher, book editors.
    p.   cm. — (Opposing viewpoints series)
  Includes bibliographical references and index.
  ISBN 0-89908-187-8 (lib. bdg. : alk. paper). — ISBN 0-89908-162-2 (pbk. : alk. paper).
  1. Budget deficits—United States.   2. Taxation—United States.   3. Banks and banking—United States.   4. United States—Economic conditions—1981-   5. United States—Economic policy—1981-   I. O'Neill, Terry, 1944- . II. Swisher,   Karin, 1966- . III. Series: Opposing viewpoints series (Unnumbered)
HJ2051.E34   1992
338.973—dc20   91-42802
                                                         CIP

Copyright © 1992 by Greenhaven Press, Inc.

"Congress shall make no law . . .
abridging the freedom of speech,
or of the press."

First Amendment to the U.S. Constitution

The basic foundation of our democracy is the first amendment
guarantee of freedom of expression. The Opposing Viewpoints
Series is dedicated to the concept of this basic freedom and the
idea that it is more important to practice it than to enshrine it.

Contents

Why Consider Opposing Viewpoints?

"It is better to debate a question without settling it than to settle a question without debating it."

Joseph Joubert (1754-1824)

The Importance of Examining Opposing Viewpoints

The purpose of the Opposing Viewpoints Series, and this book in particular, is to present balanced, and often difficult to find, opposing points of view on complex and sensitive issues.

Probably the best way to become informed is to analyze the positions of those who are regarded as experts and well studied on issues. It is important to consider every variety of opinion in an attempt to determine the truth. Opinions from the mainstream of society should be examined. But also important are opinions that are considered radical, reactionary, or minority as well as those stigmatized by some other uncomplimentary label. An important lesson of history is the eventual acceptance of many unpopular and even despised opinions. The ideas of Socrates, Jesus, and Galileo are good examples of this.

Readers will approach this book with their own opinions on the issues debated within it. However, to have a good grasp of one's own viewpoint, it is necessary to understand the arguments of those with whom one disagrees. It can be said that those who do not completely understand their adversary's point of view do not fully understand their own.

A persuasive case for considering opposing viewpoints has been presented by John Stuart Mill in his work *On Liberty*. When examining controversial issues it may be helpful to reflect on this suggestion:

9

The only way in which a human being can make some approach to knowing the whole of a subject, is by hearing what can be said about it by persons of every variety of opinion, and studying all modes in which it can be looked at by every character of mind. No wise man ever acquired his wisdom in any mode but this.

Analyzing Sources of Information

The Opposing Viewpoints Series includes diverse materials taken from magazines, journals, books, and newspapers, as well as statements and position papers from a wide range of individuals, organizations, and governments. This broad spectrum of sources helps to develop patterns of thinking which are open to the consideration of a variety of opinions.

Pitfalls to Avoid

A pitfall to avoid in considering opposing points of view is that of regarding one's own opinion as being common sense and the most rational stance, and the point of view of others as being only opinion and naturally wrong. It may be that another's opinion is correct and one's own is in error.

Another pitfall to avoid is that of closing one's mind to the opinions of those with whom one disagrees. The best way to approach a dialogue is to make one's primary purpose that of understanding the mind and arguments of the other person and not that of enlightening him or her with one's own solutions. More can be learned by listening than speaking.

It is my hope that after reading this book the reader will have a deeper understanding of the issues debated and will appreciate the complexity of even seemingly simple issues on which good and honest people disagree. This awareness is particularly important in a democratic society such as ours where people enter into public debate to determine the common good. Those with whom one disagrees should not necessarily be regarded as enemies, but perhaps simply as people who suggest different paths to a common goal.

Developing Basic Reading and Thinking Skills

In this book, carefully edited opposing viewpoints are purposely placed back to back to create a running debate; each viewpoint is preceded by a short quotation that best expresses the author's main argument. This format instantly plunges the reader into the midst of a controversial issue and greatly aids that reader in mastering the basic skill of recognizing an author's point of view.

A number of basic skills for critical thinking are practiced in the activities that appear throughout the books in the series. Some of the skills are:

Evaluating Sources of Information. The ability to choose from among alternative sources the most reliable and accurate source in relation to a given subject.

Separating Fact from Opinion. The ability to make the basic distinction between factual statements (those that can be demonstrated or verified empirically) and statements of opinion (those that are beliefs or attitudes that cannot be proved).

Identifying Stereotypes. The ability to identify oversimplified, exaggerated descriptions (favorable or unfavorable) about people and insulting statements about racial, religious, or national groups, based upon misinformation or lack of information.

Recognizing Ethnocentrism. The ability to recognize attitudes or opinions that express the view that one's own race, culture, or group is inherently superior, or those attitudes that judge another culture or group in terms of one's own.

It is important to consider opposing viewpoints and equally important to be able to critically analyze those viewpoints. The activities in this book are designed to help the reader master these thinking skills. Statements are taken from the book's viewpoints and the reader is asked to analyze them. This technique aids the reader in developing skills that not only can be applied to the viewpoints in this book, but also to situations where opinionated spokespersons comment on controversial issues. Although the activities are helpful to the solitary reader, they are most useful when the reader can benefit from the interaction of group discussion.

Using this book and others in the series should help readers develop basic reading and thinking skills. These skills should improve the reader's ability to understand what is read. Readers should be better able to separate fact from opinion, substance from rhetoric, and become better consumers of information in our media-centered culture.

This volume of the Opposing Viewpoints Series does not advocate a particular point of view. Quite the contrary! The very nature of the book leaves it to the reader to formulate the opinions he or she finds most suitable. My purpose as publisher is to see that this is made possible by offering a wide range of viewpoints that are fairly presented.

David L. Bender
Publisher

Introduction

"I learned that economics was not an exact science and that the most erudite men would analyze the economic ills of the world and derive a totally different conclusion."

Edith Summerskill, British
politician, 1967

For many people, economics is a distasteful and forbidding topic. The esoteric terms and complex formulae economists seem to load their discussions with, even in their explanations to non-economists, discourage the average person. Prominent American economist John Kenneth Galbraith suggests that, like people in many professions, economists "protect" themselves from outsiders by using their own language. "All," he says, "like to see themselves as a priestly class with a knowledge, a mystique, that isn't available to the everyday citizen." Unfortunately, this reliance on professional jargon confuses and intimidates those who are not economists. British economist John Jewkes concurs, suggesting that "if economists had deliberately set out to confuse us they could hardly have been more successful."

To add to the confusion, articles about economics often present conflicting facts and conclusions. This is because economists base their theories and conclusions on statistics from various sources, often governments. In the United States, for example, the Bureau of the Census, the Bureau of Labor Statistics, the General Accounting Office, and various other government offices provide economists with much of their raw data. Unfortunately, these data are often flawed. For example, the Census Bureau collects its major data only once every ten years and takes many months, sometimes years, to process much of it. In addition, the Census Bureau has frequently come under fire for its inability to obtain complete and objective data. It is no wonder that economic projections based on this data are flawed and contradictory.

Another reason that economic conclusions are often contradictory is that, as American economist Robert Hamrin, author of *America's New Economy*, states, "Economics is not value free." In other words, economists, like other people, come to their work with preconceived ideas. Often these ideas influence their conclusions. Some have outright ideological biases that they attempt to support through their work. These preconceived ideas and biases are one reason that one economist can conclude that growing interest rates are good for the economy and another can conclude that they are bad.

Despite all the potential for confusion, a basic understanding of economics is of vital concern to everyone. As Leonard Silk, author of *Economics in Plain English*, writes, "The importance of economics to people in their daily lives . . . is too great for economics to be brushed aside as either irrelevant or too difficult." In fact, echoes John Kenneth Galbraith, "To have a working understanding of economics is to understand the largest part of life. We pass our years, most of us, contemplating the relationship between the money we earn and the money we need. . . . So an understanding of economics is an understanding of life's principal preoccupation." Economist and Nobel Prize Laureate Paul Samuelson has gone so far as to say that "survival itself can depend on economics."

Happily, understanding economics does not have to be impossible. The editors of this anthology have tried to contribute to this understanding by focusing on issues of immediate concern to readers. They have chosen authorities who communicate ideas in clear terms. They have selected viewpoints that represent a spectrum of economic analysis, for this is one of the challenges of the study of economics: to critically analyze many interpretations of the same "facts" and come to one's own conclusion about their value.

This all-new edition of *Economics in America: Opposing Viewpoints* replaces Greenhaven's 1986 book of the same title. The questions debated in this edition are What Is the State of America's Economy? How Serious Is the Budget Deficit? What Kind of Taxation Is Appropriate? How Can America's Banking System Be Strengthened? and What Is the Future of American Labor? The editors hope that as readers review the debates about issues that influence their daily lives, they will find understanding and inspiration for continuing study of America's economy.

What Is the State of America's Economy?

Chapter Preface

In 1989, the *New Republic* published an essay called "The Sky Is Always Falling" by writer Gregg Easterbrook. Only partly tongue-in-cheek, Easterbrook asserted that the subject of economics, long called "the dismal science," invariably inspires pessimism. Economists and those who report on the state of the economy, he states, rarely find something positive to say. One of the many examples Easterbrook cites relates to unemployment. He quotes a *Washington Post* headline for a story reporting a dip in unemployment after many months of concern about its high rate. The headline read "U.S. ECONOMY ADDS 400,000 JOBS IN MONTH: REPORT SPURS FEARS."

Easterbrook wondered why, after being concerned about *un*employment, reporters and economists would not be cheered by such an upturn. To add to the puzzle, only two months later, the *New York Times* headlined a story "APRIL JOB GROWTH EASED DECISIVELY, STIRRING CONCERN."

How, one wonders, is the public, which obtains most of its information about the economy from the mass media, supposed to make sense of such absurdity?

For one thing, people must look beyond the headlines. As Easterbrook points out and as most consumers of newspapers and television news know, the media thrive on bad news. It is more dramatic and compelling and, like an automobile accident, more likely to draw an audience than is the safe completion of an automobile trip. Therefore, it is often to the media's advantage to put a negative twist on a story.

Although the media can be partially blamed for the confusion about the state of the economy, this is not the whole story. The state of the economy is affected by a vast array of intertwining factors, such as the value of the dollar, the nation's debt, and gross national product. It is very possible, for example, that at one time high employment will be bad and at another be good. Other key economic factors, often called leading indicators, influence the overall analysis. For example, in the story cited above about the 400,000 added jobs, economists believed the increase in employment would cause interest rates to go up because people would be able to afford to pay more. The story evincing concern about unemployment's growth reflected concern that manufacturing growth was declining.

Economists must constantly evaluate a whole range of factors in determining whether the state of the economy is good or bad. And so must ordinary citizens.

In the following viewpoints, the authors debate the current state of the American economy.

"The most important thing . . . to know about the American economy is that it is very rich."

America's Economy Is Strong

Herbert Stein

Herbert Stein, a senior fellow at the conservative American Enterprise Institute in Washington, D.C., is an economist and coauthor of the forthcoming book *An Illustrated Guide to the American Economy*. In the following viewpoint, Stein asserts that America's economy, by any standard, is strong. Although problems exist, he says, history shows that America's wealth, size, and stability will allow its economy to endure.

As you read, consider the following questions:

1. List two pieces of evidence Stein offers to prove that America's economy is rich.
2. List two historical precedents that, according to the author, prove that America's economy will remain rich.
3. List two problems Stein acknowledges America's economy has. How important does he think it is to solve these problems?

Herbert Stein, "The U.S. Economy: A Visitor's Guide," *The American Enterprise*, July/August 1990. Copyright © 1990, Herbert Stein. Reprinted with permission from *The American Enterprise*.

The most important thing . . . to know about the American economy is that it is very rich. The best measure of that is the gross national product: the U.S. GNP is now running at $5,500 billion a year. This is a staggering figure. In 1940 when the GNP was first estimated, the figure was about $100 billion. It had been about the same in 1929. Of course, most of this increase was due to inflation. But in real terms after allowing for inflation, the GNP now is six times as high as it was in 1929 and three times as high per capita. Consider that in 1929 the United States was already the richest country in the world, and Americans were congratulating themselves on how well off they were.

Comparisons with other countries are difficult and possibly not very revealing. But by the best estimates, the GNP of the United States is probably two-and-one-half times that of Japan and five times that of Germany. On a per capita basis, GNP in America is probably one-third higher than in either of those countries. . . .

Implications of Being Wealthy

So the American economy is very rich, and there is every reason to think not only that it will continue to be rich but also that it will get richer. The basic reason for our prosperity is that 120 million Americans get up in the morning and go to work to do the best they can for themselves and their families and previous millions did the same thing for more than two centuries. America has always had a legal system that assures its people that they will enjoy the fruits of their efforts—their labor, their saving, their education, and their initiative. America's culture encourages people to benefit themselves economically and values their doing so. The country was populated by immigrants who wanted to live and work in such a legal system and culture. Moreover, the government has always been devoted to assisting and protecting people in these efforts. For example, the government has made available large amounts of capital in the form of land and education.

Events in America have to be understood in the perspective of the size of the economy. Almost everything we see happening turns out to be small relative to the size of the economy. Also, because of its size and diversity, the system seems to be stable and immovable in the aggregate while flexible in detail.

In earlier times, an event like the change of automobile models at the Ford Motor Company or a shortage of rain in Kansas could cause a national recession. The country is much more resistant to such things now. Even the loss of about $500 billion in the value of assets when the stock market crashed in 1987 was absorbed without much effect on the economy as a whole.

Actual or proposed policy changes also have to be seen in this perspective. For example, the Reagan defense buildup, which looked so huge at the time and was expected to be so disruptive economically, made hardly a ripple in the economy. . . .

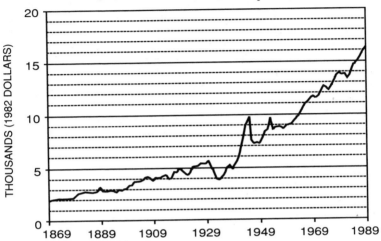

U.S. Real GNP Per Capita

Herbert Stein, *The American Enterprise*, July/August 1990.

For a country as rich as America is, getting richer faster is not a very important goal—or at least it is less important than it used to be and less important than it is in other countries. America's most important problems are not problems of the inadequacy of total national income but rather problems of inappropriate use of the national income the economy produces.

America's problems must also be seen in the perspective of American history. . . . It is useful to review some of the problems that have existed or have been alleged to exist in the past 60 years that no longer worry us. Looking back reminds us that the American society has the capacity to face its problems and deal with them.

The Stabilization Problem

The Great Depression gave rise to the fear that such catastrophes would recur or even that the economy would live in a state of permanent depression unless radical changes were made in the economic system. This fear is now gone, partly because that analysis was judged faulty; it underestimated the equilibrating features of the system. Changes in institutions and policies that stabilized the economy without weakening its free and efficient features dispelled those fears. Worry about the possibility of less severe, but still debilitating, recessions persisted, however. But the experience of the years since World War II has provided two lessons:

First, the only serious recessions, those of 1975 and 1982, in which unemployment rose to highs of 9 percent and 11 percent, respectively, came after fairly high inflation.

Second, even recessions of that depth turned out to be less painful than had been expected because they were short. This was because the average worker had substantial assets and was likely to be in a family with more than one worker, so that a period of unemployment was not disastrous.

What remains as the chief uncertainty about the stability of the economy is the possibility of inflation. This is seen as a political problem—whether the temptation of the short-term political advantages of inflationary policy can be resisted. The inflation rate in the United States is now about 4.5 percent. The economy is much better adapted to such a rate now than it was, for example, in 1971 when that rate caused the imposition of price controls. It is nevertheless a cause for concern.

Unemployment has been running near 5.25 percent. That is somewhat higher than used to be considered full employment, but it is not a serious figure in the aggregate. Half of the unemployed are out of work for periods of five weeks or less, and the average duration of unemployment is about 12 weeks. The unemployment problem today is serious in that it most affects black youths, who are not being brought into the work force.

The Mythical Freedom Problem

Around the end of World War II, there was a great deal of worry in this country that although the threat of Nazism had been withstood, the threat to freedom remained serious. The threat—best described in Friedrich Hayek's book, *The Road to Serfdom*—was seen to lie in the expansion of the role of government that had been going on here under the New Deal and in England and elsewhere even longer. Although the argument was mainly about England, the author made it applicable to the United States, and the book was a best-seller here.

This worry has not since been as acute as it was in the first years after World War II, but it remains a standard part of political rhetoric and rises in pitch from time to time. There is some evidence of growing concern now. In a curious parallel to the post-Nazi era, the champions of freedom in the postcommunist era are finding the enemy at home—or are at least looking for him there.

The threat to American freedoms has never been real. Americans are more free now than they have ever been. Individual options have been increased enormously by the growth of incomes; the improvement of education, information, and mobility; the expansion of competition, including the increased exposure to the world market; and the reduction of legal and cultural discriminations of all kinds, based on race, religion, ethnicity, and gender.

The government sector in the United States has expanded in the past 60 years, but it is still small by international standards. Relative to GNP, government expenditures and receipts in the United States are at about the same level as they are in Japan and lower than in any other large industrial country.

As a fraction of GNP, government expenditures in the United States rose from 10 percent in 1929 to 34 percent in 1989. By other measures the government share is smaller and has risen less. Receipts have risen from 10.9 percent to 32 percent, government purchases of goods and services from 8.6 percent to 19.8 percent, and government output, measured by payrolls, from 4.3 percent to 10.3 percent.

But the private sector has also expanded enormously. Even if the government share is estimated to have risen from one-tenth to one-third of GNP, the nongovernment GNP is four times as large today as it was in 1929 and twice as large per capita.

The total of government expenditures, however, is a poor measure of government's power to coerce individuals and limit their freedom, for several reasons. Forty percent of all government expenditures are for interest payments or transfers made according to objective formulas that do not enable the government to discriminate among individuals. The government is decentralized: the federal government makes only about 40 percent of government purchases of goods and services (less than 8 percent of GNP, three-fourths of which is for defense), the rest is made by states and localities. Moreover, the government's ability to exercise its influence in a coercive way is limited by the division of powers among the executive, legislative, and judicial branches, by the party system, and by public opinion. . . .

Other Worries

From time to time in American history, great concern has been expressed that the economy would be dominated by giant monopolies that would smother efficiency, prevent the achievement of full employment, and concentrate excessive power in a few private hands. Such concerns were heard in the 1930s and, to a lesser extent, in the 1950s. They are hardly heard any more. The American economy is seen to be highly competitive, more competitive than ever before. Government policy has helped avert a trend to monopoly. But the main lesson is that unless government positively enforces monopoly, there are strong natural tendencies for competition to emerge. Moreover, reduced costs of transportation and communication and lowered governmental barriers to international trade have greatly widened the markets within which enterprises must compete.

Given the common notion of the United States as the country of big business, it is significant to note that most American workers are employed in fairly small enterprises. In 1985, 55 percent were employed in establishments of 99 or fewer workers and only 13 percent in establishments of over 1,000 workers. There seems to be no trend for the proportion in large establishments to increase.

International Comparison of Real GNP Per Capita, 1989
(U.S. = 100 Percent)

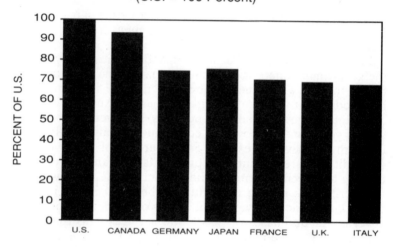

Herbert Stein, *The American Enterprise*, July/August 1990.

Parallel to this worry about monopoly but on the other side of the political spectrum, there has been concern about the power of labor unions. This was especially notable just after World War II. Membership in unions was increasing, and so, apparently, was their economic and political power. Some thought stronger unions would stifle productivity and generate inflation. But this fear also passed. The proportion of nonfarm employees enrolled in unions peaked at about 30 percent in 1955 and has declined since to about 20 percent. Even where unions exist, they are less powerful than they were. Again, public policy, expressed in the Taft-Hartley Act of 1947, had something to do with limiting the trend to unionization. But the primary force was competition: unionized enterprises could not compete with the nonunionized—even in the benefits they provided their workers.

There was never any evidence that the spread of unionism, while it was going on, yielded benefits for workers as a whole. During the period of declining unionism, the labor share of the national income has increased from 67 percent to 74 percent. This suggests that unions were not essential to improving the condition of labor.

A third worry that has arisen from time to time is that the economy was chaotic and erratic and would stagnate because the United States had no "economic plan." This worry naturally arose when difficulties appeared, most notably in the 1930s. It recurred around the end of the 1950s, when the launching of Sputnik raised the fear that the Soviets might be outdoing the United States and when many Americans were fascinated by comprehensive British and French economic plans. There was another wave of talk in favor of planning in 1975 and 1976 after the oil shock.

But the idea that the United States should have a national economic plan never had much popular appeal. Any push to develop one has now disappeared entirely, and given recent events in Eastern Europe, none is likely to reemerge soon.

The Adaptive Society

The American system has performed well. And it continues to do so, not because it is finished, perfect, and free of problems, on a model laid down by Adam Smith, but because it adapts to its problems and solves or at least ameliorates them. The American economic system today is a long way from the capitalism of 1929. The government has assumed responsibility for maintaining economic stability. America has become a substantial welfare state, and about 15 percent of all personal income consists of transfers from the government. The government greatly affects national saving by its fiscal policy. It regulates almost every industry a little. But still, the free market remains at the heart of the economic system.

What makes the American society so adaptable is that we have an economic system interacting with a political system, each independent and each competitive within itself. Each system disciplines the other, limits its excesses, and acts to correct its deficiencies.

"The U.S. economy remains in a depression."

America's Economy Is Weak

Economic Commission, Communist Party USA

The Communist Party USA maintains a small but active membership in the United States. Primarily concerned with the plight of workers and with eliminating the economic class system, the CPUSA promotes unions and legislation that it believes advance the causes of the poor in America. In the following viewpoint, the CPUSA states that far from being wealthy, many Americans suffer from deteriorating economic conditions. These conditions, it asserts, are due in large part to racist and antilabor actions on the part of legislators and corporate leaders.

As you read, consider the following questions:

1. What evidence do the authors provide to support their assertion that U.S. domestic policy is "cynical," "racist," and "antilabor"?
2. List two pieces of evidence the authors use to support the contention that the U.S. economy is failing?
3. What solution do the authors see to the problems they perceive in the American economy?

Economic Commission, Communist Party USA, "The Social and Economic Crisis in the USA," *Political Affairs*, September/October 1991. Reprinted with permission.

What happened to the American Dream?" queries [a 1991 issue of] *Business Week*. The article, illustrated by photos of handsome couples, white and Black, and their children, describes the plight of "the Under-30 Generation," the first, it believes, to be worse off than their parents:

> Troy Marshall and his wife, Linda, both work, caring for sons, Cameron and Cory, in shifts. After adjusting for inflation, their income is about half what Troy's father earned in his 20s—while Troy's mother stayed home.
>
> Curtis Smith works, but can't afford to live with his girlfriend, Lawanda, and their children. . . . Incomes have dropped . . . devastating minorities.

"Is Uncle Sam Shortchanging Young Americans?" *Business Week* further asks, and the charts answer with a dramatic *yes*.

But *Business Week* cannot be expected to put this grim picture in total perspective: the youth are at the leading edge of the capitalist-government offensive against the entire working class, against 90 percent or more of the population. And at the other extreme is the vast accumulation of wealth by the richest one-tenth of 1 percent of the population—those who control the government and the economy and set the social "standards" for the country.

Social Conditions

The social crisis in the United States is an ongoing phenomenon. . . . The accumulation of social problems . . . is in fact the necessary and planned consequence of a domestic policy that is sophisticated, comprehensive, and cynical. Its objective is to make the wealthy wealthier by making working people poorer. It is carried out through an anti-labor, anti-union offensive, and a concurrent racist offensive against African Americans and other oppressed peoples. It is carried out by the capitalist class through the industrial-military-financial complex and its governmental structures, initiated by Reagan and continued by Bush. Its economic aim, pursued with tragic success, has been to intensify the exploitation of labor, hike the superprofits gained as a result of discrimination against Blacks, Hispanics, and other downtrodden peoples. . . .

Wholesale deregulation [for example, of savings and loan associations], relaxation of anti-trust laws, tax cuts for the wealthy, encouragement of runaway plants, promotion of leveraged buyouts, junk bonds, accumulation of corporate debt and pension raiding, workfare, high interest rates, maintenance of a large reserve army of unemployed, promotion of union busting and give-backs, deep cuts in income maintenance programs, limited unemployment compensation, non-enforcement of laws against sweat shops, child labor and migrant labor deregulation, and mounting deficits (which redistribute income to the rich), were among the mechanisms responsible for the rich getting richer and the decline in the living standard of workers and their families.

As a result of these procedures, the concentration of extreme wealth has been unprecedented. In just six or seven years, from 1981-1982 to 1988, the number of millionaires proliferated from 600,000 to 1,500,000—two and a half times. The number of "centi-millionaires" (wealth of more than $100 million) tripled—from 400 to 1,200, and the number of counted billionaires quadrupled—from 13 to 51.

Huck/*People's Weekly World*. Reprinted with permission.

Approximate calculations show that the combined incomes of this upper crust of the capitalist class now exceed the combined incomes of all production or non-supervisory workers in manufacturing, mining, construction, transportation, and public utilities—the main creators of material value.

Declining Real Wages

Real wages in the private sector have declined 18 percent since 1973, despite the rising productivity of labor. Between 1970 and 1989, the median income gap between white and

Black families widened by 5 percentage points, from 39 percent to 44 percent. By 1989, the 44 percentage-point gap cost the 7.5 million Black families $120 billion, representing extra profits for employers. Also, the downward pull this factor exerted on the wages of all workers was the real cost of the lack of affirmative action, a cost conveniently overlooked by the racists who instigate misguided white workers to complain that Black workers take jobs from them.

The class and racial distortion of income policy is compounded by tax changes further reducing the disposable incomes of the working and middle classes. This is brought out on the federal level by a chart prepared by the House Ways and Means Committee showing that effective tax rates for low-income groups have gone up more than 20 percent, while rates for the top 1 percent of income recipients have declined by more than 20 percent. State and local tax changes have followed suit.

Losing ground in international competition, U.S. capital chose to compete not on quality but on accelerated transition to a two-tier economy: a low-wage union-purged service and decentralized manufacturing sector, and a high-salary parasitic sector, the source of the malodorous sewer of corruption that has become characteristic of the high-flying top echelons of capital.

Harm to the Working Class

For working Americans, the experience of families in Waterloo, Iowa, is typical. William Schmidt writes [in the *New York Times*]:

> Like millions of other working people around America, in the last decade . . . [they] were swept into a kind of economic free fall . . . casualties of the new and sometimes brutal order remaking the nation's workplaces.

The anti-labor, racist offensive has a number of facets, some overt, some hypocritically concealed.

The employer-Administration offensive against trade unions has to some extent turned the clock back to the 1920s when underground campaigns were necessary to organize unions. The network of labor laws and institutions, notably the National Labor Relations Board, have become part of the union-busting apparatus. Workers who want to join a union know that once they sign up, their jobs are in jeopardy—if the boss finds out, they may be fired. Only militant tactics, such as those that built the CIO in the 1930s, can turn the tide.

The racist decisions of the Supreme Court, the Bush diatribes against "quotas", the conversion of the Equal Employment Opportunities Agency into the architect for an unequal employment pattern are combined with the ruling class' own "quota" system of placing a few conservative Blacks in prominent corporate, government, and military positions. . . .

Not only are funds for education cut, every effort is made to destroy the nation's traditional public school system and convert it into a largely private, unregulated, caste system. The Ivy League colleges and their prep school clones cater to the ruling class. Financial and other kinds of perks are available to lesser capitalists and the middle strata so as to create a total system of privileged elementary and secondary schools. White workers are encouraged to exercise "freedom of choice," opting to send their children to better-endowed and well-equipped schools, virtually free of African Americans and Hispanics. The aim? To doom all poor children, including white, but especially Black and Hispanic, to third-rate education, "tracked" to a lifetime of unemployment, part-time employment, "temporary" employment at or near the legal minimum wage—a guarantee of a life of poverty. . . .

American Economy Needs Help

What's wrong with this picture?: a photograph of Michael Boskin, chairman of the Council of Economic Advisers, and a handful of other U.S. officials arriving in Warsaw, published in various newspapers at the end of November 1989. The aim of the delegation's visit was to encourage the Solidarity-led government of Poland to pursue a free-enterprise course—in other words, to emulate the U.S.—in dealing with the country's economic troubles. . . .

There is something almost comic about those responsible for U.S. economic policy presuming to have the solutions to the difficulties of another nation, even one as desperate as Poland. These are the people, after all, who preside over the economic management of a country that is now the world's largest debtor, a country suffering from chronic industrial decline, a country that says it cannot afford to eliminate afflictions like homelessness, inadequate health care, and pollution. It is also a country where, as is less well known, average wage levels (adjusted for inflation) have been stagnant for years and distribution of income grows increasingly unequal. As for economic advice, the U.S. belongs on the receiving rather than the giving end.

Philip Mattera, *Prosperity Lost*, 1991.

Millions of couples, white and Black, are forced to bring up their children while living with parents or existing in other unsatisfactory arrangements. The number of broken families rises yearly, and it is, by far, highest among African American couples—not only because they are at the bottom of the economic ladder, but also because they are most-excluded from access to

decent, moderate cost housing. There are professors and politicians who ignore this and blame the phenomenon of single parents among Blacks on "ethnic characteristics" or on being part
of an idle "underclass." Their racism is exposed by their refusal
to analyze the facts: by 1988, 17 million children lived with one
parent, an increase of 7 million since 1970—and 63 percent of
these children were white. The fact that more than half of all
Black children are not living in a two-parent home is well
known. The largely suppressed reality is that, among Black families with incomes over $50,000, 96 percent of the children live
with both parents, essentially the same as the 95 percent of Hispanic children and 97 percent of white children in families at
that income level. But among families with incomes under
$10,000, the majority of white children, as well as the majority
of Black children, are not living with both parents. . . .

Cyclical Crisis

The U.S. economy remains in a depression. A preliminary report of the Commerce Department stated that the gross national
product increased at an annual rate of 0.4 percent in the second
quarter of 1991, following two quarters of decline. . . .

To analyze the current economic situation, it is necessary to
understand the structure of the business cycle. To start with, the
terms used by Establishment economists are misleading. In
their lexicon, there are two phases—recession and recovery. The
term "recession" was introduced after World War II because it
sounded less serious than "crisis."

The economic cycle, in its classical definition, has four phases:
crisis, depression, recovery, and boom. . . . The long-lasting
structural crisis of the U.S. economy has been aggravated by the
cyclical crisis. The steel industry has entered a new phase of decline. The auto industry, its prices doubled over the last decade,
has priced most of the population out of the market. It depends
increasingly on sales to rental agencies, corporations, governments, and the upper-income fifth of the population. The Big
Three strive to survive as partners—and potentially junior partners—of their Japanese rivals.

The solution appeared to be in the high-tech, aerospace, missile and computer industries, which grew continuously and employed, directly and indirectly, millions of workers during the
1980s. But their continuous growth has ended, followed by a
weeding out of the weakest, and by declining overall employment. That the structural crisis of U.S. industry remains unre-
solved is illustrated by the fact that, in July 1991, man-hours of
production workers in manufacturing, seasonally adjusted, were
only 2 percent above the low of the 1982 crisis, and 1 percent
below that low in durable goods.

The *financial crises* have become more complex. Hundreds of commercial banks have failed or are about to fail, bankrupting the Federal Deposit Insurance Company and leading to new drains on taxpayers, who will have to finance the salvage of the elitists' banks that are "too big to fail." High-interest junk bonds, worth hundreds of billions of dollars, hang over financial markets, with many doomed to default. And the international debt crisis remains acute.

Recovery from economic depressions follows the destruction of values during the crisis. That is, surviving capitalists are able to obtain properties of bankrupt enterprises at far below their former value. They reap a high rate of profit and start a new round of expansion on that basis. The Resolution Trust Company—formed to administer the sale of S & L properties—is turning over half-billion dollar parcels of real estate to monopoly corporations at a fraction of their worth, for example. The virtual abolition of anti-trust restrictions and the mergers of giant banks, with layoffs of tens of thousands of workers, are other examples.

These and other specifics of the present cycle make it clear that the U.S. working class can expect no automatic participation in a prospective economic recovery, whenever it comes. Officially approved is the prospect for continued high levels of unemployment. . . .

The International Arena

However, even taking into account all of these factors, the main economic goals of the U.S. ruling class are not within the United States, but in the international arena, and this, in turn, has an important further impact on the conditions of the masses of the American people. . . .

The transfer of U.S. manufacturing operations to virtually all parts of the capitalist world has mushroomed, and involves not only the giant transnationals, but thousands of medium-sized companies as well. The impact on U.S. industrial employment has been devastating. . . .

Of all the international crisis developments, those in Eastern Europe and the Soviet Union hold the gravest danger for American labor. The potential opportunities for U.S. corporations to transfer production and service operations to the ex-socialist countries, with their vast pools of skilled, politically-crushed labor, at low (dollar) wages, are indeed enormous . . . .

The times call for refutation of the propaganda fabrications of the Establishment, for ideological struggle, and, above all, for militant, united action by all progressive forces.

"The U.S. has a larger proportion of its population in the top and bottom parts of the income spectrum . . . than other countries do. "

Disparities Between the Rich and the Poor Are Increasing

Isaac Shapiro and Robert Greenstein

Isaac Shapiro, a senior research analyst for the Center on Budget and Policy Priorities in Washington, D.C., specializes in issues related to employment. Robert Greenstein is the founder and director of the Center on Budget and Priority Studies and a former administrator in the U.S. Department of Agriculture. In the following viewpoint, the authors assert that the 1980s witnessed a frightening and continuing economic trend in which incomes of poor people are decreasing while the incomes of the rich are dramatically increasing. They conclude that this trend will lead to an ever more disparate and unfair society, with a growing percentage of the population in dire circumstances.

As you read, consider the following questions:

1. Shapiro and Greenstein say the rich are getting richer and the poor poorer. What do they say is happening to the large middle class?
2. List two reasons the authors give for the growing income disparities.
3. What do the authors suggest could stop the trend toward growing economic disparity?

Isaac Shapiro and Robert Greenstein, "Selective Prosperity Increasing Income Disparities Since 1977," 1991. Reprinted with permission of the Center on Budget and Policy Priorities, Washington, DC.

Data compiled by the Congressional Budget Office, and published in the 1991 *Green Book* issued by the House Committee on Ways and Means, provide fresh evidence of a growing trend toward greater income inequality in the U.S. During the period examined by CBO, the incomes of the wealthiest households shot up dramatically. But middle-income households received only a slight income gain, and low-income households became poorer.

• From 1977 to 1988, the average *after*-tax income of the poorest fifth of households fell 10 percent, after adjusting for inflation.

• The middle fifth of households experienced an average after-tax income gain of less than four percent over this period.

• By contrast, the top fifth of households realized an average gain in after-tax income of 34 percent. At the same time, the average after-tax income of the richest one percent of Americans more than doubled from 1977 to 1988, rising 122 percent after adjusting for inflation. The average after-tax income of these households reached $451,000 in 1988, up from $203,000 in 1977. (The dollar figures used here are expressed in 1992 dollars.)

Unequal Division of Economic Pie

Due to these developments, the division of the overall economic pie became much more unequal. An especially large share of income is now received by the richest one percent of Americans.

• In 1988, the total after-tax income of the richest one percent of all Americans was almost as great as the total after-tax income of the bottom 40 percent of Americans combined. In other words, *the richest 2.5 million Americans now have nearly as much income as the 100 million Americans with the lowest incomes.*

• This is in sharp contrast to 1977, when the total after-tax income of the bottom 40 percent of Americans was more than double the total after-tax income of the richest one percent.

The share of the national income going to the middle class also declined during this period. In 1977, the broad middle class—the 60 percent of U.S. households in the middle of the income spectrum—received 50.6 percent of all after-tax income. By 1988, its share had dropped to 46.3 percent.

This leads to another new development in the division of the nation's economic pie: the wealthiest one-fifth of the population received as much after-tax income in 1988 as the other 80 percent of the population combined.

The growth in income inequality shown by the CBO data is also reflected in Census data. The Census data show in 1989, the last full year of the recovery, *before*-tax income was more unevenly divided than at any time since the end of World War II. (As would be expected, most Americans did benefit from the long economic recovery in the 1980s, but upper-income households gained the most. Moreover, over the course of the full business cycle from 1979 to 1989, including the recessions of the early 1980s and the subsequent recovery, upper-income households were the only group to emerge with significant income improvements.)

Average After-Tax Income Gains and Losses Between 1977 and 1988, by Various Household Income Groups

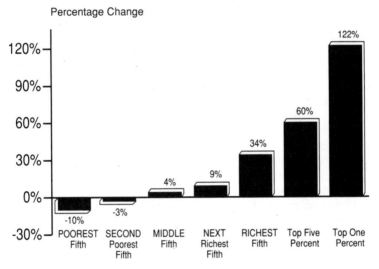

Percentage Change

Source: Congressional Budget Office.

Most of the growth in income disparities has resulted from increased inequality in *before*-tax incomes. One factor influencing the divergence in before-tax incomes is a growing wage and salary gap between high-earners and other Americans. The average wage and salary income of the richest one percent of Americans more than doubled from 1977 to 1988, after adjusting for inflation, rising by $130,000 per household. By contrast, the average wage and salary income of the bottom 90 percent of the population *fell* 3.5 percent or more than $800.

Very large increases in the capital gains income of wealthy households also contributed to the sharpening of income disparities.

• From 1977 to 1988, the average capital gains income of the wealthiest one percent of households more than doubled, rising from $72,000 to $156,000.

- For other Americans, the picture was very different. The average household in the bottom 90 percent of the population experienced a $47 *drop* in capital gains income from 1977 to 1988, after adjusting for inflation. Their capital gains income fell from $299 to $252.

For households in the lower parts of the income scale, reductions in government benefit programs contributed to the decline in their before-tax incomes. The data in the *Green Book* indicate that 43 percent of the increase in poverty between 1979 and 1989 was due to reductions in benefit programs at federal, state, and local levels.

Especially sharp reductions occurred in the Aid to Families with Dependent Children program, the nation's basic cash assistance program for poor single-parent families. From 1970 to 1991, the maximum AFDC benefit for a family of three with no other income declined 42 percent in the typical state, after adjusting for inflation. In fact, AFDC benefits have eroded so sharply that the average value of AFDC and food stamp benefits *combined* has now fallen to about the same level as the value of AFDC benefits *alone* in 1960, before the food stamp program was created.

The recent contraction of another part of the safety net—unemployment insurance—has had a detrimental effect on unemployed workers at various income levels. This contraction has been keenly felt in recent months; the proportion of the unemployed receiving benefits during the current recession has been smaller than in any other recession since the end of World War II.

Effect of Changes in Tax Burdens

While the bulk of the growth in inequality is due to increased disparities in *before*-tax incomes, changes in federal tax policy exacerbated these trends. CBO data indicate that in the period since 1977, the richest Americans received large tax reductions, while middle-income Americans did not.

- Between 1977 and 1992, the effective tax rate borne by the richest one percent of Americans—that is, the percentage of income they pay in all federal taxes combined—will decline 18 percent. . . . In 1977, the richest one percent of U.S. households paid an average of 35.5 percent of their income in federal taxes. In 1992, CBO estimates they will pay 29.3 percent.

- During this same period, the percentage of income that middle-income households pay in taxes is expected to tick up from 19.5 percent to 19.7 percent. If the wealthiest one percent of households paid the same percentage of their incomes in taxes in 1992 as they paid in 1977, they would owe $42 billion more in taxes in 1992.

In the 1950s and 1960s, income disparities narrowed in the United States. In the early 1970s, disparities began to grow. This trend then accelerated in the 1980s. The Census Bureau has noted that the growth in inequality from 1979 to 1989 was "about twice as large as the change between 1969 and 1979."

Rising Inequality

Some people did benefit greatly from recent economic policy. The richest 1 percent did exceedingly well, as reflected in their 74 percent pretax and 86 percent after-tax income growth from 1980 to 1990. Meanwhile, the after-tax income of the bottom 40 percent fell. This dramatic disparity has created the highest level of income inequality in the postwar period, reversing several decades of progress, and has left us with a poverty rate in 1989 (at the end of the recovery!) that surpassed that of any year in the 1970s. Between 1979 and 1989 the shares of income accruing to each of the bottom four-fifths declined, with the increase in the income share of the top fifth primarily rising among the upper 5 percent.

Lawrence Mishel and David M. Frankel, *Dissent*, Spring 1991.

In addition, an international comparison indicates that in other Western industrial countries, incomes are distributed less unevenly than in the United States. These data show that the U.S. has a larger proportion of its population in the top and bottom parts of the income spectrum—and a smaller portion in the middle—than other countries do.

This study, known as the Luxembourg Income Study, also examined child poverty rates in various Western countries, as well as the degree to which government policies reduced these rates. In each country, children living in families with incomes below 40 percent of that country's median disposable income, as adjusted by family size, were considered poor. The study found:

• In 1986, the U.S. child poverty rate before taxes and government benefits, stood at 22.3 percent. The average rate for all of the countries compared to the U.S. was 13.2 percent.

• When the effects of taxes and benefits were considered, the U.S. child poverty rate barely budged, dropping to 20.4 percent. In sharp contrast, policies in other countries reduced child poverty by nearly two-thirds, to 4.8 percent.

• After taxes and benefits are considered, the U.S. child poverty rate was *more than four times the average child poverty rate in the other nations in the study.*

Another recent study found that from 1979 to 1986, the poverty rate fell in Canada while rising in the United States even though the recessions of that period were more severe in Canada. The study found that the principal reason for the divergent trends was that Canada expanded public benefit programs while such programs were cut here. By the mid-1980s, the child poverty rate was twice as high in the U.S. as in Canada.

In short, it appears that alternative government policies can help yield different poverty and income distribution outcomes than those experienced in the United States.

"Spending of poor families grew nearly three times faster than that of wealthy families. "

Disparities Between the Rich and the Poor Are Not Increasing

Robert J. Myers and Ed Rubenstein

Robert J. Myers, former chief actuary of the Social Security Administration, is professor emeritus at Temple University in Philadelphia. Ed Rubenstein is economics analyst for *National Review*, a conservative monthly magazine. In the following viewpoint, the two authors argue that income for all Americans is increasing. In Part I, Myers asserts that the government's *Green Book*, which many analysts use to argue that incomes are decreasing, is inaccurate. He cites other data that show wages to be increasing. In Part II, Rubenstein points out that while the poor report reduced incomes, they actually have unreported and underreported incomes that when accounted for show an increase in wealth.

As you read, consider the following questions:

1. Why does Myers think the *Green Book* figures are misleading? Why does he believe Social Security wage data are more accurate?
2. On what basis does Rubenstein say the income of poor people is underreported?

Robert J. Myers, "Real Wages Went Up in the 1980s," *The Wall Street Journal*, August 21, 1990. Reprinted with permission of *The Wall Street Journal* © 1990 Dow Jones & Company, Inc. All rights reserved. Ed Rubenstein, "The Rich Poor," *National Review*, July 29, 1991, © 1991 by National Review, Inc., 150 E. 35th St., New York, NY 10016. Reprinted by permission.

I

It is often asserted that real wages have generally deteriorated since 1972. For ordinary wage-earners, the 1980s boom was no boom at all: Their condition stagnated while high-income people gobbled up the new wealth.

For example, the authoritative "Green Book," issued annually by the House Ways and Means Committee, claims that average yearly earnings in terms of constant 1987 dollars rose from $17,062 in 1970 to a peak of $18,109 in 1972. From then on, inflation-adjusted average earnings decreased to $16,699 in 1980 and then more slowly to $15,968 in 1989. The average rate of decrease in real average earnings from 1980 to 1989 was 0.5% per year.

The 1980s Boom

It is these figures that critics of the 1980s boom are relying on when they say there was no boom at all for most people who draw a paycheck. Happily, the figures are not correct.

In my opinion, the wage-indexing series developed by the Social Security Administration for various purposes in connection with the Social Security program is a better chronicle of wage movements than the Green Book. The Ways and Means statistics do not really reflect the amount that the average person earns in a year. Rather, they are average *weekly* earnings as reported by the Bureau of Labor Statistics of the Department of Labor times 52. Since some persons are not employed in all weeks of a year, this tends to overstate actual earnings.

At the same time, because BLS does not study the country's entire work force, but only production and nonsupervisory workers on non-agricultural payrolls, it tends to understate earnings.

In a final push toward error, BLS figures are obtained by survey sampling rather than by counting everybody.

The Social Security series is, by contrast, based on the total earnings of all employees in the first quarter of the year, annualized. The data involved in the computations are on a "complete count" basis and do not involve samples or surveys.

The Social Security wage data show the 1980s in quite a different light from the Green Book. While the two series agree about what happened in the 1970s, the Social Security data suggest that wages were in fact 4% to 7% lower than the BLS data in most of the 20 years from 1947 through 1966 and appreciably higher in the 10 years from 1980 through 1989. The Social Security average wage was 2.47% higher than the BLS average in 1980, and the differential steadily increased to as much as 14.3% for 1988 and 17.6% for 1989.

In constant 1987 dollars, the Social Security averages rose to a peak in 1972 of $18,147 and then slowly declined to $17,092 in 1980. But since 1980 after-inflation wages have grown by about 1.1% a year, to $18,778 in 1989.

So who's right, BLS or Social Security? One way to check is to match them both against a third wage series, average weekly wages in employment covered by the state unemployment insurance programs, as reported by the Office of Employment and Unemployment Statistics in the federal Department of Labor. (Because these data are based on only covered workers, they are affected by legislative changes in unemployment insurance coverage, and so data from before 1972 are not comparable with later data.)

How "Poor" Are the Poor?

Here is a sample of facts that [are] not mentioned in poverty reports:

- 38 percent of the persons whom the Census Bureau identifies as "poor" own their own homes with a median value of $39,200.

- 62 percent of "poor" households own a car; 14 percent own two or more cars.

- Nearly half of all "poor" households have air-conditioning; 31 percent have microwave ovens.

- Nationwide, some 22,000 "poor" households have heated swimming pools or Jacuzzis.

"Poor" Americans today are better housed, better fed, and own more property than did the average U.S. citizen throughout much of the 20th Century.

Robert Rector, Kate Walsh O'Beirne, and Michael McLaughlin, The Heritage Foundation *Backgrounder*, September 21, 1990.

Compare the unemployment insurance numbers to the Social Security and BLS numbers, and you find much greater correspondence with the Social Security numbers than with the BLS ones. Because the unemployment insurance numbers are based on weekly wages rather than quarterly ones, they tend to be higher than the Social Security numbers, but the relationship between them has been constant, while the relationship between them and the BLS numbers has not been.

Government Statistics Too Low

The ratio of the unemployment insurance average wage to the Social Security one has not deviated much from around 115% throughout the 1980s—the same relationship as obtained for the period from 1972 through 1979 as well. On the other hand, the ratio of the unemployment insurance average to the BLS numbers, after remaining level at about 115% from 1972 to 1979, deviated sharply afterward. It rose steadily to 131% in 1988—confirming the hypothesis that the BLS numbers are too low.

Although both the BLS and the Social Security series show a deterioration of wages totaling appoximately 7% from 1972 to 1980, the Social Security series shows an encouraging annual average rate of increase of 1.1% from 1980 to 1989, and the BLS series shows a dismaying decrease of 0.5%. The Social Security numbers are confirmed by a second major wage series; the BLS numbers are not. Democrats, Republicans—take your choice.

II

We are told that the poor got poorer during the Eighties. Virtually all sources show that the real income of poor families rose sharply until the mid Seventies, fell sharply under the Carter-engineered inflation of the late Seventies and early Eighties, rose again during the Reagan boom, but has not yet reached its Seventies peak.

But when economists look at what poor families actually *spend* rather than what they report as income, a very different story emerges, as a recent study by economists Susan E. Mayer of the University of Chicago and Christopher Jencks of Northwestern University shows:

Income v. Spending of the Rich and Poor

	1961	1973	1985	Percentage Change 1961-73	Change 1973-85
Per-Capita Income					
Poorest 10%	$ 1,243	$ 1,800	$ 901	44.8%	−50.0%
Richest 10%	18,688	29,240	32,382	56.5	10.7
All Families	6,504	10,017	10,313	54.0	3.0
Per-Capita Spending					
Poorest 10%	$ 1,653	$ 2,829	$ 4,545	71.1%	60.7%
Richest 10%	11,749	13,991	16,965	19.1	21.2
All Families	5,265	6,657	7,745	26.4	16.3

While the reported income of the poorest families plunged 50 per cent between 1973 and 1985, their real expenditures rose a whopping 60.7 per cent over the same period. Indeed, real per-capita spending of poor families grew nearly three times faster than that of wealthy families over both the 1961-73 and 1973-85 periods. Expenditure inequality shrank even as income inequality appeared to grow.

There may be perfectly legitimate reasons why poor families

40

spend more than their reported income. Many of them get money from sources which the federal surveys do not ask about, such as savings, loans, gifts, payments by boarders, subsidized housing, and Medicaid.

Most of the discrepancy, however, reflects the underreporting of income by poor families. People are increasingly reluctant to answer questions about income (response rates for federal economic surveys dropped from 95 per cent in 1948 to 72 per cent in 1985), and the volunteered answers are rarely honest. Mayer and Jencks cite a study of fifty Chicago welfare mothers that found not one was living entirely on her AFDC [Aid to Families with Dependent Children] benefit or was reporting all her outside income to the welfare department. The unreported income was as large as the welfare benefit.

Poverty Indicators

The link between reported income and living standards is tenuous, especially for the poor. More than half of the poorest tenth of all families owned a home in 1985, and decennial Census surveys show poor families were more likely to have a car, a telephone, an air conditioner, and a complete bathroom in 1980 than in 1970 despite stagnant or declining real income over this period.

The authors do not deny that material deprivation persists: survey data suggest that more families go hungry at some point in the year than lack a television. But this reflects the perverse priorities of consumers rather than the indifference of government.

"When a society fails to save, its members must ultimately pay the price for collective profligacy."

Lack of Savings Harms the Economy

B. Douglas Bernheim

Economist B. Douglas Bernheim, like many other economic analysts, is concerned about the level of savings in America. In the following viewpoint, he asserts that the amount of money saved by every citizen has a significant impact on the economy. Savings, in the form of bank accounts and financial investments, are used to fund personal and business loans, which are used to buy, build, and, in general, increase the nation's productivity. He claims that America's savings rate is declining at an alarming rate, thereby threatening America's economic growth.

As you read, consider the following questions:

1. According to the author, how does America's savings rate compare to that of other countries?
2. List two of the negative consequences Bernheim attributes to a low savings rate.
3. How does Bernheim link low savings to the trade deficit?

Excerpted, with permission, from B. Douglas Bernheim, *The Vanishing Nest Egg: Reflections on Saving in America*, a Twentieth Century Fund Paper, © 1991 by the Twentieth Century Fund, New York.

Rates of saving in the United States fell precipitously during the 1980s and are currently much lower than in any comparable period of our history. Although this disturbing phenomenon was not by any means confined to the United States, America has had the dubious distinction of leading the way. We currently save a much smaller fraction of national income than the rest of the industrialized world, and have done so throughout the postwar period. . . .

The Official Story

As illustrated in Figure A, official U.S. government statistics on saving paint a rather grim picture of the most recent decade. The rate of net national saving (expressed as a fraction of net national product, or NNP) remained relatively constant during the 1950s and 1960s. The preliminary indications of trouble appeared during the mid-1970s. Saving peaked at 10.8 percent of NNP in 1973, but then fell abruptly, matching its postwar low of 5.3 percent only two years later. Yet nascent concerns were short-lived, as saving rebounded to just under 8 percent of NNP—roughly its postwar average—in the last two years of that decade.

Unfortunately, national saving began to diminish once again in 1980. Two years later, the bottom fell out. Despite minor rallies in 1984 and 1989, the rate of net national saving has in every year since 1982 remained well below its previous postwar low. Overall, this rate plummeted from an average of 7.9 percent in the 1970s to a paltry 2.7 percent during the late 1980s. . . .

Widespread clamor over record-breaking federal deficits has created the impression that the government's lack of fiscal restraint is primarily responsible for the low rates of national saving—net and gross—witnessed during the 1980s. This is an exaggeration. Changing patterns of consumption and investment in the private sector have been quantitatively more important than public deficits. As noted earlier, the rate of net national saving fell by a staggering 5.2 percentage points between the 1970s and late 1980s. Roughly 3.3 percentage points, or nearly two-thirds of the total change, was attributable to declining rates of private saving (that is, the ratio of private saving to NNP). Of that amount, 2.7 percentage points—more than half of the total change—reflected plunging rates of personal saving. Even with skyrocketing federal deficits, government saving fell by only 1.8 percentage points. This breakdown attributes little more than one-third of the total decline in national saving to the public sector.

Rising Consumption

The fact that Americans save less than in previous decades means that our consumption of final goods and services has risen. Public consumption has actually changed little during the last few decades. Instead, private consumption has risen dramatically. This observation does not necessarily absolve lawmakers of responsibility for our current predicament. In particular, federal deficits have allowed the government to keep taxes low (relative to spending) and have therefore raised disposable income. Naturally, most people tend to spend more when their take-home pay rises.

Yet in practice, public deficits cannot account for most of the evident increase in private consumption. When an individual receives an additional dollar of disposable income, he usually spends some and saves some. Consequently, higher levels of disposable income should boost both private consumption and private saving as fractions of NNP. Yet private saving has fallen.

Figure A: Net National Saving for the U.S.

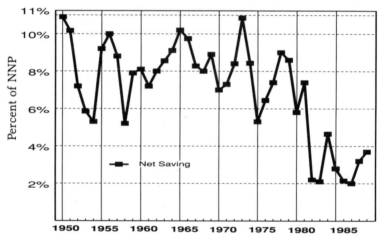

B. Douglas Bernheim, *The Vanishing Nest Egg*, 1991.

It is very difficult to explain the simultaneous decline of private saving and rise of private disposable income. Yet this issue is of paramount importance. Assuming that the propensity to save out of private income had not declined between the 1970s and 1980s, then national saving would have averaged about 6.2 percent of NNP during the late 1980s, rather than 2.7 percent. In contrast, the total elimination of all public deficits through increased taxes probably would not have raised the rate of national saving much beyond 3.7 percent. Clearly, neither skyrocketing federal budget deficits nor rising government consumption is primarily responsible for our current troubles. Surprisingly, the behavior of private individuals and businesses emerges as the principal cause of declining saving.

Comparison to Other Countries

Since most countries keep detailed national income accounts, official data are readily available for the purpose of making international comparisons of saving rates. Unfortunately, accounting conventions differ from country to country, and these differences can in principle render comparisons meaningless. Several international organizations, including the United Nations, the International Monetary Fund (IMF), and the Organization for Economic Cooperation and Development (OECD), collect extensive data on worldwide economic activity and compile national accounts based upon standardized accounting conventions. These efforts at standardization are not perfect, and therefore some problems of comparability remain.

Figure B, which is based upon OECD data, depicts rates of net national saving as percentages of gross domestic product (GDP) for the United States, Japan, and a collection of European countries. One conclusion is inescapable: the United States saves very little relative to other developed countries. . . .

When an individual fails to save, he jeopardizes his own economic security. Following retirement, serious illness, or involuntary job loss, he may well find that his resources are insufficient to maintain his accustomed standard of living, and at times he may experience significant hardship. Even if his luck holds out during his own lifetime, he will contribute little to the enrichment of his family line.

When a society fails to save, its members must ultimately pay the price for collective profligacy. For a time, a strong demand for consumer goods may buoy the economy, but robust economic performance simply masks the symptoms of a serious malady. Sooner or later, stagnation must displace prosperity as performance deteriorates.

Most individuals are not currently saving enough to provide themselves with adequate financial security. In addition, low rates of saving depress investment, thereby depriving the economy of new plant and equipment that are necessary for continued growth and prosperity. At the same time, inadequate saving renders the economy more vulnerable to external shocks, thereby raising the likelihood of a severe recession. . . .

The Social Consequences of Low Saving

Saving by Americans provides funds for new investments both at home and abroad. Similarly, a portion of foreign saving ultimately finances purchases of new plant and equipment in the United States. Total investment in the United States is therefore equal to domestic saving plus net inflows of capital from abroad. This simple observation has far-reaching implications. Specifically, lower rates of domestic saving must, of necessity, either depress domestic investment or boost net inflows of foreign capital. The relative importance of these two effects depends upon certain key features of the domestic and global economies.

To understand the link between saving and other macroeconomic aggregates, it is necessary to think in terms of the supply and demand for financial capital. When an individual saves, or when a foreign investor diverts resources to the American market, additional financial capital becomes available. In other words, the supply of new financial capital consists of domestic saving plus net inflows of foreign capital. When a business undertakes new investments in plant and equipment, it attempts to raise the necessary funds either internally or externally. Accordingly, the demand for new financial capital reflects the profitable investment opportunities of domestic businesses. As in other markets, the price of financial capital adjusts to bring supply and demand into balance. . . .

Reducing Supply of Capital

A decline in domestic saving at prevailing rates of interest reduces the supply of financial capital relative to demand. When demand exceeds supply, many businesses find themselves unable to raise funds for profitable investment opportunities. Some of these businesses are usually willing to bid for scarce funds by offering higher rates of return to potential investors. Thus, the price of financial capital, or rate of interest, rises in response to a supply shortage. Higher rates of interest provide more generous rewards to those who supply financial capital and consequently tend to stimulate supply. Rising interest rates also increase the cost of financial capital for domestic businesses, thereby reducing the number of potentially profitable investments. These two effects bring supply and demand back into balance at some higher price. If the supply of financial capital is very responsive to interest rates, then a small increase in these rates will restore balance, leaving investment largely unaffected. On the other hand, if supply is relatively unresponsive, then interest rates will have to rise substantially, producing a more pronounced decline of investment.

The weight of the available evidence indicates that domestic saving is rather unresponsive to interest rates. If foreigners were unable to invest in the United States, a sharp drop in the rate of saving would therefore produce significantly higher interest rates and lower investment. In practice, U.S. capital markets are open to foreign investors. As interest rates begin to rise in the

United States, foreigners divert funds from projects in their own countries to more profitable American opportunities. If foreigners are sufficiently responsive to rates of return in the United States, then declining rates of domestic saving should have very little impact on either interest rates or investment. However, larger net inflows of foreign capital would then result in greater foreign ownership of American assets. . . .

Figure B: An International Comparison of Net National Saving 1980-1987

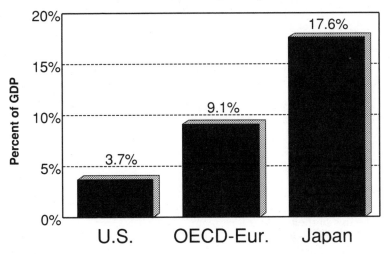

Source: Organization for Economic Cooperation and Development.

Aside from depressing domestic investment and promoting foreign ownership of American assets, inadequate saving also yields deteriorating current account balances. Indeed, these phenomena are two sides of the same coin. As a matter of national income accounting, the current account deficit is necessarily identical to the total net inflow of foreign capital. Since low saving stimulates foreign investment in the United States, it must therefore also contribute to the deterioration of the current account balance. Mechanically, this occurs as follows: When saving declines, the supply of financial capital falls short of demand, and interest rates start to rise. Higher returns attract foreign investors, who attempt to acquire dollars in order to purchase assets from American owners. This produces an increase in the relative demand for dollars and drives the real value of the dollar up relative to foreign currencies. Since foreign goods become relatively cheap for American consumers, the demand for imports rises. Likewise, the demand for exports declines as American goods become more expensive for foreign consumers. This imbalance contributes to the trade and current account deficits.

The current account is closely related to the better-known concept of the trade deficit. In particular, the current account deficit equals the trade deficit plus net outflows of capital income. The popular press has focused national attention on recent current account and trade imbalances, and has frequently interpreted these statistics as barometers for the international competitiveness of American industry. The preceding paragraph suggests that this interpretation is valid in only a very limited sense. A current account deficit arises when domestic saving falls short of domestic investment. This gap does not reflect a deterioration of the potential for our industry to compete at any given exchange rate. It does not measure productivity differentials, or the quality of productive inputs. Rather, the "loss of competitiveness" is exclusively attributable to appreciation of the dollar, which makes American goods relatively more expensive. Of course, the shortfall of saving may also depress investment, which would eventually affect the ability of American industry to compete at whatever rate of exchange ultimately prevailed. But that effect is not measured in any way by the current account balance.

Making Economy Vulnerable

Finally, inadequate saving renders the economy vulnerable to adverse events, and may as a result increase both the likelihood and expected severity of a recession. As has been noted, low rates of saving foster heavy dependence on foreign financial capital. A sharp decline in investment brought about by an interruption of the flow of capital from abroad would disrupt the U.S. macroeconomy in the short run and severely test the Federal Reserve's abilities to fine-tune aggregate performance. If the pace of economic activity slows sufficiently, many individuals and corporations are currently so highly leveraged that they might well find themselves unable to cover the carrying costs of accumulated debt. The repercussions from snowballing loan defaults and bankruptcies could produce a significant contraction of output and employment.

"The amount of US personal savings has increased dramatically."

Lack of Savings Is Not Harming the Economy

John P. Dessauer

A former international investment officer for Citibank, John P. Dessauer is also the author of *International Strategies for American Investors* and the publisher of a well-respected newsletter, *Dessauer's Journal of Financial Markets*. In the following viewpoint, Dessauer maintains that Americans are saving more than most experts believe. While the per capita rate may not be as high as would be ideal, Dessauer believes the total amount is impressive and contributes strongly to U.S. economic growth.

As you read, consider the following questions:

1. What relationship does Dessauer see between taxes and savings?
2. How does the author believe the government can encourage Americans to save?
3. Why does Dessauer think it unimportant that Americans' rate of savings is not quite as high as that of some other nations?

John P. Dessauer, "Surprise! Americans Are Saving More," *World Monitor*, August 1990. Reprinted with permission.

Buried under a landslide of frightening economic news, a rise in American personal savings has gone almost unnoticed. A growing federal deficit, a first-quarter burst of inflation, high interest rates, the savings and loan crisis, and a slowing economy captured the headlines. Feeling depressed about the future of the US economy is so popular that good news often seems unbelievable. But it is, in fact, true that the amount of US personal savings has increased dramatically. In 1989 the US personal savings pool increased by $204.4 billion. That is more than double the increase of $101.8 billion in 1987.

Key Building Block

Personal savings is a key building block for any economy. For this article, personal savings is defined as cash in the bank and investments in money market funds, stocks, and bonds. If the savings trend of 1988 and 1989 continues, the outlook for the US economy and financial markets will be much improved.

For years the United States has beaten its breast over Americans' low savings rate. Forgotten was the late Sen. Everett Dirksen's line: "A billion here, a billion there, and pretty soon you're talking about real money."

In 1987 the *rate* of US personal savings hit a low at 3.2% of disposable personal income. But even then the $101.8 billion added to savings was real money. This *amount* of money *added* to savings by Americans in 1987 was about twice the amount of *total* personal savings in 1972.

Americans probably should have saved more, but more than $100 billion wasn't all that bad.

The saddest thing is not Americans' persistence in looking at the dark side of every economic statistic; it is their refusal to modify their views when the situation improves. The 1989 total US personal savings was an all-time record, not in terms of the percentage rate but in terms of the total dollars accumulated. Savings continued to increase in early 1990.

Savings, especially personal savings, are essential not only to finance the federal deficit but also to support the overall health of the economy. The US needs capital to help make American business more competitive, to fix roads and bridges, and to finance other worthwhile long-term projects.

Look at Real Picture

It has become a part of the common wisdom that Americans don't save enough and that therefore the nation's economic future is less than bright. Investors should not jump to such conclusions. Instead they should take a close look at the story of US personal savings in the 1970s and '80s.

Sometimes ordinary common sense eludes people when they

focus too much on statistics. They complain about the federal deficit and argue that higher taxes are needed. At the same time they lament the low savings rate as if there were no connection between savings and taxes.

It should be obvious that people can save only if they have money left after taxes and living expenses. If taxes are increased, there will be less after-tax income available for living costs and savings. The deficit might go down, but so might the savings pool.

Don't Fret About Savings

We should stop fretting about the alleged dearth of US saving, about the alleged threat to our future living standards stemming from our current-account deficit, and about our alleged vulnerability to a withdrawal of foreign investment funds. Upon examination, these concerns seem either chimerical or inconsequential.

Henry N. Goldstein, *Cato Journal*, Winter 1990.

If we look at both taxes paid and savings accumulated as a percent of personal income, some startling facts emerge. In the 1970s the combined rate of taxes and savings remained fairly steady at roughly 20% of personal income. The savings rate declined in the 1970s. But, that was due to increased tax payments. The *combined* savings and tax rate in 1979 was 20.4% of personal income, exactly the same as in 1971.

The personal savings rate as published by the federal government fell from 8.1% in 1971 to 5.9% in 1979. That fact grabbed all the attention. Forgotten was the fact that personal tax payments to the government increased in the '70s.

The story of savings in the 1980s is somewhat different. Combined taxes and personal savings moved up above 21% in the first three years of the 1980s and then fell—first to 19% and finally to a low of 17.8% in 1987. The most likely explanation for first the higher combined rate and then a steep fall is the roller coaster interest-rate pattern of the 1980s.

Savings Tied to Taxes and Interest Rates

In the early part of the decade interest rates were extremely high, providing an incentive to save more of what was left after taxes.

Starting in 1984 US interest rates plunged. From a high of 10.5%, the interest on three-month treasury bills fell to a low of 5% in 1986.

Americans had come to enjoy high interest rates. When interest rates plunged, the incentive to save was reduced and spending increased.

The conclusion that the peculiar savings patterns of the 1980s are attributable to the wild fluctuations in interest rates seems to be confirmed by developments at the end of the decade. In 1988 the savings rate edged higher. It continued to climb in 1989. In the final year of the past decade the combined personal savings and tax payments came to 19.2% of total personal income.

The evidence is strong that Americans are returning to the financial patterns of the 1970s and early 1980s. Assuming that there are no extreme fluctuations in either interest rates or the economy in the next few years, the best estimate is that the rate of taxes plus savings will move back to the 20-21% level that prevailed in the 1970s and early '80s.

Will the savings pool keep growing rapidly? The answer depends on the rate of tax payments. If taxes rise to 15-16% of personal income, there will be only 5-6% left for savings.

The first sensible conclusion from this look at taxes, savings, and personal income is that there is no magic in reducing the federal deficit by raising taxes. As taxes go up, the amount of savings can be expected to go down, leaving the nation with the same problem: too little capital.

To Increase Savings

There are two ways to obtain a material change in the amount of personal savings. One is to cut government spending and allow tax payments to decline. The other is to have personal income grow significantly faster than government spending so that tax payments as a percentage of personal income can decline.

Pursuing a goal of rapid increase in personal income seems preferable to cutting the growth of government spending—until inflation is considered. The 1980s demonstrate quite clearly that inflation poses limits on the rate of growth in personal income.

In 1989, for example, personal income grew 8.9%. The result was rising inflation. Obviously, pushing the rate of growth of personal income carries real risks of producing an inflationary boom, followed by a bust.

Solving the nation's economic ills depends on staying within acceptable inflation limits. The limit appears to be 6-6.5% annual growth in personal income. Which means that government spending must grow at a rate significantly lower than that if the US savings pool is to grow large enough to meet all of the nation's needs.

The odds are that government spending and taxes will keep growing. The cost of welfare, Medicare, education, the war on drugs, and the savings and loan bailout leaves little room for cutting government spending.

At first blush this outlook would seem to lead to a dismal conclusion about the future for the American economy. However, that conclusion may not be right.

Overstated Savings Problem

Economist Robert J. Samuelson . . . provides authority for the assertion that there is no US savings problem that needs fixing. "The great savings debate," he declared in *The Washington Post*, "is mostly a political charade." Similarly, Robert Eisner, an economist at Northwestern University, referred in an article in *The New York Times* to a "phantom savings problem" that is "badly overstated."

Tom Wicker, *The New York Times*, March 5, 1990.

The two fastest growing categories of government spending in the 1980s were defense and interest on the national debt. Defense spending is likely to grow at a much slower rate, thanks to the reduced superpower conflict and the changed orientation of Eastern Europe. If Congress manages to reduce the annual deficit, the rate of growth of interest payments will also slow down. Keeping government spending growing at a reasonable rate may not be impossible after all. The amount of personal savings left after the deficit just might keep growing in the 1990s.

Savings Pool Should Grow

Reasonable, noninflationary growth in personal income makes more money available both for taxes and for savings. Even if the government takes a larger slice out of American paychecks as a part of efforts to reduce the federal budget deficit, the total annual US savings pool should grow.

• Using 6.5% for growth of personal income and 5% left over after taxes for savings, the annual savings pool will climb to $267 billion in 1992.

• If the federal deficit remains stuck at $100 billion, there still will be $167 billion left over to help finance things like improving business competitiveness.

The surprising fact about the US savings pool is that, almost no matter what the rate of savings may be, the dollars involved have become significant. In 1989 the increase in the savings pool of $204.4 billion was $52.4 greater than the federal deficit. That figure of $52.4 billion is about the same size as the total savings pool in 1972.

Size sometimes has its merits. When an economy as large as the United States' grows by 5%, the *additional* economic activity is greater than the total economic activity of many another nation.

Adding to US personal savings, albeit at a rate less than that of West Germany and Japan, does produce meaningful results.

Americans may continue to have a competitive problem for the next few years. However, if they keep the economy growing at a sustainable rate and personal income increases by 6.5% a year, their total available savings will be enough to keep America in the international game and buy time to make even greater improvement.

"America can no longer afford to live beyond its means."

The National Debt Threatens the Economy

Alfred L. Malabre Jr.

In 1987, Alfred L. Malabre Jr., a *Wall Street Journal* columnist and editor, wrote *Beyond Our Means*, a widely read exposition of his view that the United States for too long has been over-spending and consequently miring itself in perilous levels of debt. In 1991, his sequel, *Within Our Means*, asserted that America's spending and debt-incurring habits have not changed, but that it is possible to reverse this dangerous practice by cutting spending and reducing the deficit. In the following viewpoint excerpted from *Within Our Means*, he reiterates his view that the United States debt is threatening the nation's economy.

As you read, consider the following questions:

1. Why does the author believe it is vital for America to reduce its deficits and begin to live within its means?
2. How did the United States come to have its present economic difficulties, according to Malabre?
3. What negative effects does the author believe deficits have on an economy?

Excerpted, with permission, from *Within Our Means: The Struggle for Economic Recovery After a Reckless Decade* by Alfred L. Malabre Jr., © 1991 Alfred L. Malabre Jr.

When I wrote *Beyond Our Means* in 1987, the federal debt was $1.8 trillion, which at the time seemed an awesome sum, twice the total of only a half decade earlier. But now that figure appears almost puny, for the amount the government owes is nearing $3.5 trillion. It seems likely to push above $4 trillion by 1993—$16,000 for every man, woman, and child—and servicing may well cost over $300 billion in yearly interest, matching recent Pentagon budgets. And beyond this pileup there lies the government's staggering financial obligation for the various agencies that it backs, a sum approximating $6 trillion, more than five times the size of recent federal budgets. And while this debt continues to mount so does the share of the debt that's owed to foreigners. They hold some 20 percent of the federal debt, up from 15 percent in the mid-1980s, and one consequence is that more and more of the interest that American taxpayers must ultimately pay to service this debt winds up abroad—perhaps to be reinvested here, perhaps not. . . .

For perspective, net interest on the federal debt consumes about 15 percent of all government spending. This exceeds, for instance, the combined amounts that the government spends on health, science, space, agriculture, housing, the protection of the environment, and the administration of justice. Entitlement programs and other mandatory spending take up another 48 percent of the budget and defense outlays another 25 percent. This leaves only some 12 percent, which includes aid to such important programs as education and drug treatment. . . .

We Must Learn to Live Within Our Means

Nations and the people in them may live beyond their means for a considerable time—as we in America have clearly done—but sooner or later they must begin to live *within* their means. That time, for so long delayed, is at hand in America, I believe. But I also believe that it is within our means to restore our economy to reasonably sound health, though the task will entail some self-inflicted pain—higher taxes, less federal largess, tighter regulation of business activity. Especially painful is the prospect of higher taxes at the end of a prolonged economic expansion, when buying power is likely to be under increasing strain even without any tax rise. In other words, we Americans are going to have to spend some serious time at the gym and less time at the dinner table.

We are already beginning to experience some of this pain—for example, in swiftly mounting state and local tax bills, with much more of this to come, I suspect. To continue avoiding the hard choices would ultimately entail far greater distress. We can set about living within our means in a purposeful way, with sensible programs and courageous leadership in Washington, or be dragged into it in humiliating fashion through the forces of an increasingly interdependent world economy. We have a choice: Either we make our own rules and live by them or let our creditors make the rules for us.

Chuck Asay by permission of the *Colorado Springs Gazette-Telegraph.*

For a glimpse of the second possibility, consider what has befallen such once-profligate nations as Mexico and Brazil. Mexican living standards on the average have dropped by more than a third since the mid-1980s, surpassing even the slide in U.S. living standards during the Great Depression of the 1930s. In Brazil, where inflation rose 1,759 percent in 1989 and approached 5,000 percent by March 1990, business activity came nearly to a standstill while a new government laid off a quarter of its own bloated work force of 1.6 million and sought to remove from circulation some 70 percent of the nation's money supply through freezing interest on savings and various other holdings. For perspective, the U.S. money supply fell by about a third between 1929 and the low point of the Great Depression in 1933.

The United States will probably be spared such Draconian punishment, but something close to it is entirely possible, for the American economy, is far sicker than it should be after so many years of recession-free growth. Oppressive debt permeates all layers of the economy, though the real amount at the federal level is obscured by persistent smoke-and-mirror games in Washington. In global markets, the United States continues to lag behind as a competitor.

Foreign assessments of our situation range from saddened to appalled. For instance, Jacques Attali, a senior aide to French President François Mitterrand, told a recent interviewer that signs of America's decline are "unquestionable." The United States, he added, has become "a nostalgic nation, lacking foresight and turned sadly inward out of resentment over its diminishing weight in the world." His remarks followed such other disheartening examinations of America's prospects as *The Rise and Fall of Great Powers*, an exhaustive study in which Yale historian Paul Kennedy raises the possibility that the United States now faces the sort of decline that overtook such former world powers as Spain and Britain, and *Day of Reckoning*, in which Harvard economist Benjamin Friedman argues that excessive borrowing and anemic saving signal a prolonged erosion of American prosperity and global influence. . . .

Productivity Problem

There was nothing mysterious about what had harmed the economy during Reagan's years in the White House and posed such a challenge for Bush. It was well recognized in Washington as well as among business planners from New York to Los Angeles that the United States had a productivity problem, brought on by a combination of too much borrowing, too little saving, and too much spending on such nonproductive areas as defense, interest on debt, and various entitlements—as opposed to spending that would eventually strengthen the economy, such as for new plant and equipment, education, and the like. But habits of long standing are usually difficult to break, no matter how detrimental. This is especially so when a habit produces considerable temporary comfort.

An attempt to sustain the short-run comfort level was hardly unique to Reagan's presidency. But Reagan's complacency was reinforced by the dubious economics of a free lunch—the notion that lasting prosperity required little more than a fat cut in federal tax rates.

This idea, not surprisingly, was extraordinarily popular at the ballot box, promising increased prosperity at reduced expense. Business activity, spurred by tax-cutting, would generate such a surge in earnings that tax revenues would surge as well, even with reduced tax rates. Far from deepening, the budget deficit would narrow and disappear.

By the end of Reagan's two terms, the federal deficit remained enormous. Though down from the record $221 billion level of fiscal 1986, it was running at an annual rate of more than $160

58

billion when Reagan left office, still high and suggesting that the free lunch was proving to be somewhat less appetizing and less free than advertised. Yet, as the economic expansion rolled on and unemployment kept dropping, policymakers not surprisingly avoided the difficult steps, such as raising taxes and curbing spending, that would have brought the budget closer to balance. And they gained support from a number of prominent economists, both left and right of the political center, who argued that the perennial budget deficits, if not a boon, were at least irrelevant to the economy's good health.

One Solution: Make Deficits "Off-Budget"

A *Forbes* magazine editorial by M. S. Forbes, Jr., the late publisher's son and successor and, like his father, a staunch supporter of prosperity through tax cuts, noted that Washington, through legislative action, had already declared many spending items, from U.S. Postal Service losses to Farm Credit System costs, to be "off-budget"—that is, not a part of the regular federal budget whose well-publicized deficits were subject under the Gramm-Rudman-Hollings Act to yearly ceilings. "Why not go all the way," Forbes asked, only half in jest, "and proclaim the entire deficit an off-budget expense?"

Milton Friedman, who served as an informal adviser to Reagan, was by no means the only eminent economist to play down the deficit. Robert Heilbroner and Peter Bernstein, in other regards frequent critics of Reagan's economic policies, argued that perhaps Americans were overly concerned by the budget's chronic imbalances. "Reducing the deficit," they maintained, was far less urgent than supposed. In itself, the deficit was not particularly worrisome in their view, and it became so only when it reflected a frivolous use of federal revenues.

Robert Eisner, an economics professor at Northwestern University, argued in a similar vein that the federal budget was in far better shape than the government's numbers indicated. He partly blamed what he deemed to be inappropriate federal accounting procedures, which regarded investments as expenses and failed to account for the extent to which inflation eroded the value of what the government owed. . . .

Conservatives such as Friedman and Forbes and liberals such as Heilbroner and Eisner favored deficits for their own ideological reasons. To the conservatives, deficits meant protection against new federal spending initiatives by a government strapped for revenues. Meanwhile, many liberals viewed perennial deficits as a tolerable consequence of governmental efforts to maintain an expanding economy and to sustain needier folk through federal social programs; they regarded the Reagan deficits as less evil than a recession or cutbacks in aid.

But deficits do matter. Deficits encourage consumption and

depress aggregate savings, the very trends that weakened the American economy in the Reagan years. Deficits increase consumption, because, as government expenditures exceed revenues, federal money flows to consumers; the Treasury pays out more than it takes in. And deficits reduce savings, since they compel the government to borrow from a savings pool that would otherwise be more fully available for presumably more productive projects in private industry. Foreign savings inflows, it should be noted, have helped the government to fill its borrowing needs, but in the process, as we have seen, the United States has lost a good deal of economic independence. Federal outlays can be used to enhance productivity, to be sure, but this rarely happens and certainly did not under Reagan, as the woeful neglect of the nation's public infrastructure in those years testifies. In the main, the spending was for the military, various entitlement programs, and interest charges on the federal debt, which swelled with Reagan's deficits.

Debt Grows Wildly

While the national debt was only $43 billion in 1940, it has today grown to over $3.1 trillion, the interest on which amounts to $300 billion a year. Thus the national debt is today nearly two-thirds as large as our Gross National Product—the sum total annual output of the entire nation—and the interest on the debt amounts to almost one-third of the government's annual tax revenues. What is more, the national debt is growing by half a million dollars *every minute!* Averaged out across the entire population of America (not just amongst the taxpayers, although that would make a more precise illustration, since it is the taxpayers who are saddled with the entire burden) the national debt equates to a staggering debt of $50,000 for every U.S. family.

Clearly, the U.S. government has to obtain wealth from somewhere, to maintain this huge debt and to maintain its fruitless policy of massively redistributing wealth.

Anthony C. Fields II, *Conservative Review*, December 1990.

The argument was often made by the Reagan White House that large deficits were also evident in relatively vigorous economies abroad. In terms of overall economic activity, governmental deficit levels in 1988 were nearly as high in Japan and West Germany, for example, as in the United States. If such nations could retain their competitive vigor despite such deficits, why not the United States? One reason why not was that in the United States the rate of savings was generally far lower than overseas, and financing a deficit tends, of course, to weigh less heavily when savings are plentiful. Another factor was that in the United States, more than overseas, the deficits were largely used for purposes other than to improve productivity. Maintaining the infrastructure, for instance, was generally accorded a higher priority in the Japanese and West German budgets than in the U.S. budget. . . .

America Must Change

America can no longer afford to live beyond its means. . . .

Hope springs eternal, but it is difficult in such circumstances to believe that very deep trouble can in fact be avoided. The economy has grown increasingly fragile after nearly a decade of expansion prolonged by the buildup of debt, mainly in the Reagan years. The business cycle remains intact, with a new recession bearing down the road. . . . To try to cut the budget deficit at such a recessionary time is hazardous, since reduced government spending and higher taxes act to restrain economic activity. That's hardly the formula for keeping a recession in check. Lower interest rates could help spur the economy, of course, but nowadays U.S. rate levels depend on decisions made in Tokyo or Frankfurt as well as at the Federal Reserve in Washington. Coming at a horrible time, the S&L [savings & loan association] debacle only worsens matters. As 1990 unfolded, the credit quality of American corporations was falling at a "record pace," according to Moody's Investors Service Inc.

Even if there were clear solutions to such economic problems, the political setting—at home as well as overseas—presents an obstacle. The political system, as we have seen, lacks flexibility. Each party wants the other to make the moves. Legislators who decry the deficit at the same time resist any effort to cut wasteful federal programs within their own areas. Leadership is missing. As a nation, we have been partying, with such role models as Donald Trump. In a way, the whole country has been like Trump: Being rich was the fantasy of the 1980s, and Trump, best-selling author and casino entrepreneur, epitomized the dream. But now the party is over, and no one knows precisely how painful the developing hangover will turn out to be. It will be severe, a test of the nation's character. But it is not beyond our means to weather it and move on, through more sensible behavior to sounder prosperity.

"The facts show that [the nation's] deficits and debt are a greatly exaggerated problem, if they are a problem at all."

The National Debt Does Not Threaten the Economy

Robert Ortner

Robert Ortner was chief economist and under secretary of the Department of Commerce under the Reagan administration. Ortner has been a professor of economics and related fields, and his articles frequently appear in financial, economic, and general publications. In the following viewpoint, Ortner argues that concern about the nation's deficits are exaggerated. Looked at rationally, he asserts, the deficits represent a minor portion of the nation's assets.

As you read, consider the following questions:

1. Ortner acknowledges that the American government's debt level is huge—$2.2 trillion. Why does this amount not cause him concern?
2. Why does Ortner see foreign investment in the United States as a sign of the strength of America's economy?
3. What action does the author believe should be taken to reduce America's debt?

Excerpted from *Voodoo Deficits* by Robert Ortner, © 1990 by Robert Ortner. Reprinted with permission of Business One-Irwin. All rights reserved.

Now, don't get me wrong. I don't like budget deficits. I'm not advocating them for their own sake. Just like everyone else, I'd like a balanced budget. But here we are, with a $150 billion or so deficit and more than $2 trillion in federal debt held by the public. How serious is the deficit or the debt? How did we get there? What should we do about it?

Journalists, politicians, and Nobel Prize winners alike have proclaimed the federal budget deficits and debt to be America's most serious economic problems. And they assert that eliminating the deficit—by spending cuts, by tax increases, or preferably by both—must be our highest priority. But the facts show that these deficits and debt are a greatly exaggerated problem, if they are a problem at all. . . .

Heading for a Fall?

But we do have ongoing budget deficits. Do they mean that there is a serious problem lurking around the corner? Are we heading for a fall? A *Wall Street Journal* article in January 1989 headlined "The Budget Albatross" began, "The deficit hangs like an albatross around his [President Bush's] neck, hindering his movements in every direction." A more severe critic asks, "What can you say to a man on a binge who asks why it matters?" So Professor Benjamin Friedman began his book [*Day of Reckoning* (1988)] and, by analogy, concluded that borrowing is just as bad for the U.S. government. . . .

Mr. Friedman goes on: "We have enjoyed what appears to be a higher . . . standard of living by selling our and our children's economic birthright." Many others have also lamented the burden of debt we have allegedly hung on our economy and bequeathed to our children. But have we really burdened either our economy or our children? Or sold their birthright?

In 1989, total federal debt amounted to a little less than $3 trillion. But the federal government itself held about $675.0 billion, with about $2.2 trillion held by the public. With the 1989 population estimated at close to 245 million, the $2.2 trillion debt outstanding "amounts to roughly $9,000 for every man, woman, and child" as the doomsayers warn you. And this is the alleged burden we are supposedly passing on to our children for them to repay. A terrible burden indeed! . . .

Mind-Boggling Sums

Isn't $2.2 trillion in government debt so large that it may put a burden on our economy or impede its operation? Indeed, the sum is so large it is mind-boggling. Nonetheless, it can be viewed as an individual's debt can be, from the perspective of wealth and the economy's ability to carry it. Suppose Mr. Friedman's man suddenly takes on a $100,000 debt. Does this mean—as Mr.

Micawber might say—"misery?" So far, we do not know. This cannot be determined from the debt alone. At one extreme, if the new debt resulted from gambling losses and the man has no assets and little income to cover it, we can say with great confidence that he is in trouble. (Probably in more ways than one.)

U.S. Debt Is Inconsequential

The idea that the United States is the "world's biggest debtor nation" is a legacy of the 1980s. The phrase has become a staple of commentators and politicians everywhere, who automatically include it among the alleged sins of the past decade. And recently, the Commerce Department put the matter in numbers. It reported that the United States' "net international investment position" was a minus $412 billion in 1990. Strictly speaking, this means we owed foreigners that much more than they owed us.

Don't worry about it.

There are plenty of genuine economic problems without inventing artificial ones. The image of Uncle Sam as a giant global debtor implies that, like Mexico or Argentina, we have gone massively in hock with the rest of the world and are at the mercy of our overseas creditors. It just isn't true. Our future prosperity hasn't become hostage to foreigners. It still depends mostly on what we Americans do here at home.

Robert J. Samuelson, *Newsweek*, July 22, 1991.

Alternatively, suppose the new debt represented a mortgage against the purchase of, say, a $300,000 home and that the man has an annual income of $200,000 or more and no other indebtedness or extraordinary obligations. It would appear that the man, far from Mr. Micawber's state of misery, is in great shape.

Certainly we would not consider advising the man to sell his home in order to pay off his mortgage obligation. That would be nonsense. If his home were appreciating in value and his income growing, most reasonable financial analysts would advise him that he could, if he wished, take on and safely carry still more liabilities. At the other extreme, if the man is into his bookies and cannot pay, my advice to him would be to get out of town—today—and change his identity.

Similar, if not identical, relationships may be used in analyzing the federal debt. Did you know that the federal government owns vast amounts of assets? According to the Bureau of Economic Analysis (BEA), an arm of the U.S. Department of Commerce, at the end of 1988 the federal government held nearly $1.5 trillion worth of equipment and structures, not including normal operating inventories. In addition, the federal government owns vast amounts of land, mineral rights, oil reserves, gold reserves, and financial assets. The Federal Reserve banks, for example, hold well over $200 billion of treasury securities. In all, priced at current market values, these assets are worth more than the federal debt outstanding. Your government, in fact, has a positive net worth.

U.S. Debts Backed by Strong Assets

I suppose that adding up these assets and liabilities may give one a quieting sense of federal fiscal solvency, but it is a purely academic exercise (academic in the sense that Mark Twain would have used the term—irrelevant and useless). The federal government is not for sale, will not be liquidated, and will not be available for a leveraged buyout. Nor are its bonds in any danger of falling into "junk" status. On the contrary, its obligations are universally regarded as the highest standard of quality. And that is because its debt is moderate in relation to its assets and—more importantly—moderate in relation to the economy.

Government debt is also highly regarded because it is backed by two other assets not included in a customary balance sheet tally: the government's almost unlimited ability to tax (short of killing the goose that lays these golden tax eggs) and its almost unlimited ability to borrow (while its debt remains of moderate proportions). For these reasons, no business firm—not even the highest quality "Triple-A" borrower—can raise funds in the free market on terms as favorable as the U.S. treasury can.

Realistically, the government's debt and its annual deficits must be viewed on a going-concern basis. The more interesting and meaningful questions concern relationships between the debt and budget deficits on one side and the economy on the other. Can the economy carry this amount of debt? Will it be stifled by this debt or by the budget deficits? A little historical perspective should help to answer these questions and help to calm your fears.

Most economists use gross national product (GNP) to represent the economy. GNP is our best single measure of total economic output, and it is from this output that we earn our incomes. We also customarily refer to or imply GNP when we discuss economic growth. As large as the federal debt appears at 1989's $2.2 trillion, the figure has little meaning unless we consider it within the context of our economy—an economy that produced about $5.25 trillion in goods and services in 1989. That means that this "burdensome" debt amounts to about 42 percent of GNP.

While 42 percent is a more comprehensible figure, it still requires some historical perspective for its significance. The following chart shows this record since the early 1950s along with the same ratio to GNP for nonfinancial private debts. Financial institutions are not included, because they are in the business of borrowing and relending. Their inclusion would exaggerate and distort the totals. And before you become duly concerned about borrowing in the private sector, let's focus on the federal debt.

U.S. Government & Private Debt Outstanding (Relative to GNP)

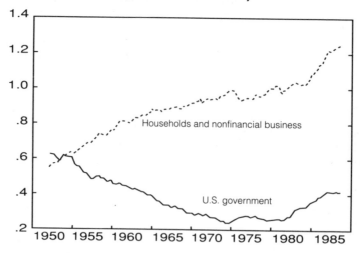

Robert Ortner, *Voodoo Deficits*, Dow Jones-Irwin, 1990.

Clearly, federal debt has grown faster than the economy since 1981. Three basic factors account for this acceleration: failure of the economy to begin to recover until the end of 1982; the tax cuts that were phased in from 1981 to 1983; and continued rapid growth in government spending. The low point in the ratio of debt to GNP was slightly over 24 percent in 1974. But note that in the early 1950s, federal debt was still about two thirds of GNP. I say "still" because toward the end of World War II, federal debt *exceeded* GNP—that is, it was more than 100 percent of GNP. Certainly, the "heavy debt burden" did not destroy the economy then. In fact, many economists and critics of the Reagan administration point out that the country enjoyed faster growth in the 1950s than it did during the recovery years of the 1980s.

If today's U.S. debt, at 42 percent of GNP, raises concerns, it is understandable that the huge federal borrowing of World War II caused great anxiety. Professor Evsey D. Domar, then a member of the Federal Reserve Board's division of research and statistics, wrote:

On November 30, 1945 the federal debt reached 265 billion dollars, a magnitude without precedent in the history of the country. . . . It is quite understandable that a debt of this magnitude should cause considerable apprehension, and that a policy of repaying at least a part of it should be advocated so often.

But rather than join the crowd in a knee-jerk reaction demanding higher taxes, Domar advocated a gradual solution in a broader economic context:

The greater is the rate of growth of income, the lower will be the ratio of debt and of interest charges to income. . . . Repayment of the debt is *not* the only available method of reducing the debt burden. This aim can also be achieved, and in a much safer way, by promoting a more rapid growth of income. That the latter is desirable of itself is evident.

These comments, which proved accurate then, are just as relevant today.

Today's debt at 42 percent of GNP is about average for the postwar period, and it appears to be leveling off. To reduce this ratio, we do not have to run a budget surplus or even eliminate the deficit. All that is required is that the debt grow at a slower percentage rate than the economy does. . . .

Yes, we can aim to reduce the ratio of debt to GNP and lower successive budget deficits gradually. But we should not forget that our ultimate goal is to improve economic performance. The purpose of conducting fiscal and monetary policies is to promote and enhance, if possible, sustainable economic growth. We should not be manipulating the economy for the sake of fiscal performance.

a critical thinking activity

Recognizing Argumentation Techniques

People who feel strongly about an issue use many techniques to persuade others to agree with them. Some of these techniques appeal to the intellect, some to the emotions. Many of them distract the reader or listener from the real issues.

A few common examples of argumentation tactics are listed below. Most of them can be used either to advance an argument in an honest, reasonable way or to deceive or distract from the real issues. It is important for a critical reader to recognize these tactics in order to rationally evaluate an author's ideas.

a. *scare tactics*—the threat that if you don't do or don't believe this, something terrible will happen
b. *strawperson*—distorting or exaggerating an opponent's arguments to make one's own seem stronger
c. *bandwagon*—the idea that "everybody" does this or believes this
d. *slanters*—trying to persuade through inflammatory and exaggerated language instead of through reason
e. *personal attack*—criticizing an opponent personally instead of rationally debating his or her ideas
f. *categorical statements*—stating something in a way implying that there can be no argument

The following activity can help you sharpen your skills in recognizing argumentation techniques. Some of the statements on the next page are adapted from the viewpoints in this chapter. *Beside each one, mark the letter of the type of appeal being used. More than one type of tactic may be applicable. If you believe the statement is not any of the listed appeals, write N.*

1. Increasing government involvement in business will lead to the loss of freedom.

2. It is important for Americans, like the people of other nations, to increase their rate of personal savings.

3. If America's present racist education policies continue, poor children, especially blacks and Hispanics, will be doomed to third-rate educations, low employment, and poverty.

4. While some point to America's growing debt burden as a sign of concern, it is important to recognize that the nation's increasing GNP makes the debt inconsequential.

5. Anyone who believes that over the last decade America's rich and poor have not grown farther apart economically has a mushroom for a brain.

6. The solution to America's economic malaise appears to be in developing its high-tech, aerospace, missile, and computer industries.

7. America's savings rate has plummeted dangerously, from an average of 7.9 percent in the 1970s to a paltry 2.7 percent during the late 1980s.

8. Every other industrialized nation has a savings rate of nearly 10 percent; the United States needs to bring its rate up to keep its economy on a level with these other countries.

9. When a country fails to save, its citizens must ultimately pay the terrible price of stagnation or depression rather than prosperity.

10. We should stop fretting about the alleged dearth of U.S. saving, about the alleged threat to our future living standards, and about our alleged vulnerability to a withdrawal of foreign investment.

11. The national debt is growing at the staggering rate of half a million dollars a minute.

12. If America does not start to live within its means, it will find itself in the dismal position of such once-profligate nations as Mexico and Brazil.

13. It is clear that America's economy can be improved only by improving the lot of ordinary working Americans.

14. The unethical legislators who continue to raise taxes while increasing their own salaries should feel the wrath of the voters.

15. No one can deny that the nation's economy would be healthier if taxes were lower.

Periodical Bibliography

The following articles have been selected to supplement the diverse views presented in this chapter.

American Legion Magazine and Paul Craig Roberts	"How Washington Killed the Economy," *American Legion Magazine*, October 1991.
Robert F. Black et al.	"Heavy Lifting," *U.S. News & World Report*, May 6, 1991.
Katy Butler	"The Great Boomer Bust," *Mother Jones*, June 1989.
John P. Dessauer	"Debt Equals Disaster, or Does It?" *World Monitor*, December 1990.
Christopher Farrell	"Learning to Kick the Debt Habit," *Business Week*, March 12, 1990.
Anne B. Fisher	"Don't Be Afraid of the Big Bad Debt," *Fortune*, April 22, 1991.
Milton Friedman	"What Is the 'Right' Amount of Saving?" *National Review*, June 16, 1989.
Marc Levinson	"Living on the Edge," *Newsweek*, November 4, 1991.
Don Mitchell and Andrew F. Quinlan	"Too Little Savings?" *The World & I*, October 1990.
Christopher R. Morris	"Are Things as Bad as They Look?" *The New York Times Magazine*, January 27, 1991.
Janet Novack	"Rich Folks Can Save More than Poor Folks," *Forbes*, March 19, 1990.
Michael Novak	"Who's on the Bottom?" *Forbes*, October 15, 1990.
Jonathan Rauch	Is the Deficit Really So Bad?" *The Atlantic*, February 1989.
Larry Reibstein et al.	"That Sinking Feeling," *Newsweek*, November 4, 1991.
Herbert Stein	"Economic Leadership," *The American Enterprise*, January/February 1990.

How Serious Is the Budget Deficit?

ECONOMICS IN AMERICA

Chapter Preface

In September 1990, the president and Congress signed a bill designed to reduce America's enormous budget deficit. In spite of the 1990 deal, the budget deficit, the amount of money the U.S. government spends every year that exceeds its revenues, has continued to grow. America's inability to decrease the deficit has led to widespread disagreement over how serious it really is.

Part of the debate over the deficit's seriousness stems from the disparate ways the budget deficit can be calculated. In his 1991 book *Within Our Means*, Alfred L. Malabre Jr. argues that Congress and the government exclude many major expenditures from the budget deficit in order to meet ceilings imposed by the 1986 Gramm-Rudman-Hollings deficit-reduction bill and the 1990 budget agreement. According to Malabre and other experts, leaving out expenditures such as the costs of the war with Iraq and much of the savings and loan bailout obscures the dimensions of the budget crisis. These experts believe the deficit, which they calculate to be about $300 billion, damages America's economy primarily by forcing the government to borrow ever-increasing amounts of money to cover deficit spending. In this way, the government devours the pool of money available for lending to businesses. Without this money, businesses have trouble succeeding and expanding, and the economy, which relies on the strength of America's businesses, fails to thrive.

Other experts disagree both with the estimates of the size of the deficit and with its seriousness. For example, economist Lawrence Kudlow maintains that "the reality is that the deficit isn't nearly as bad as people think." Kudlow and Roula Khalaf of *Forbes* magazine calculate that most of the budget deficit is used to pay interest on the $3.5 trillion federal debt. They argue that these interest payments do not represent current expenditures and therefore should not be added to the deficit. The true deficit is about $45 billion, Kudlow and Khalaf maintain. This estimate makes the deficit appear far less threatening. The Brookings Institution's George Perry also argues that the deficit is less serious than some maintain. Perry thinks problems such as education, homelessness, and aid to the former Soviet Union require more governmental attention. Perry states, "All [these issues] deserve more attention than they have been getting during the past several years of unending budget crisis. Congress and the administration can now afford to put the budget deficit issue aside."

Both the size of the budget deficit and its seriousness remain controversial issues for America. The viewpoints in this chapter mirror the controversy that surrounds the budget deficit.

"More money will be spent on interest on the deficit than on the environment, health, or any of the other pressing needs."

The Budget Deficit Is a Serious Problem

Mortimer B. Zuckerman

Mortimer B. Zuckerman is the editor-in-chief of *U.S. News & World Report*, a weekly newsmagazine focusing on economic and governmental issues. In the following viewpoint, Zuckerman indicts the government's methods of predicting yearly budget deficits and charges that low, false predictions obscure the seriousness of the deficit problem. He concludes that the budget deficit must become a priority in order to stop America's economic decline.

As you read, consider the following questions:

1. According to the author, how does the government make the budget deficit appear smaller than it really is?
2. How does the budget deficit damage the economy, according to Zuckerman?
3. What conclusions does the author draw from comparing America's economy with those of Europe and Japan?

Mortimer B. Zuckerman, "Deja Voodoo All Over Again," *U.S. News & World Report*, October 9, 1989. Copyright © 1989 by U.S. News & World Report. Reprinted with permission.

You *can* fool all of the people all of the time. That is clearly what they believe in Washington. They got away with fiscal deceit in the last administration and now they are cynically casual about it. How could a conservative President like Ronald Reagan triple the national debt and transform America from the world's largest creditor nation to the largest debtor? When *U.S. News & World Report* asked him, he said, "Don't believe the statistics." The answer was right, but not in the way Reagan meant. The statistics were wrong not because they overstated the debt but because they understated it; not because some bureaucrat was manipulating figures to embarrass the administration but because the administration was manipulating them to mislead the public.

Forecasting Deficits

The current director of the Office of Management and Budget is Richard Darman. He has a lot of skill with figures and no apparent scruples when it comes to playing with them—a lethal combination. His office is charged with forecasting federal deficits to the best of its professional abilities, and it is on these forecasts that the Gramm-Rudman law is activated to ensure that we get progressively reduced deficits. Under Darman, these forecasts are political, not professional. The figures are twisted to produce the smallest possible deficit forecast, thus escaping activation of Gramm-Rudman. Assumptions of growth and interest rates bear no relation to reality. Predictions on the rate at which appropriations will be spent are adjusted at will. Government pay dates that fall at the end of the fiscal year are shunted back and forth so that they fall in whatever fiscal year suits Darman's willing suspension of Gramm-Rudman reality. Expenses such as the savings and loan bailout are put "off budget," even though their funding comes from the federal treasury. More than $100 billion a year is being expropriated from surplus trust funds intended for other purposes.

The trickery does not end there. Even so, the financial finagling shows up in the actual deficits. Since 1986 the target has been overshot by an average of no less than $25 billion. When you read the President's lips, what he has been saying through his budget director is that the U.S. budget will remain a fraud, but a kinder, gentler fraud.

Outrageous Deficits

Does it matter? It is an outrage. Whether you are a Democrat or a Republican, a conservative or a liberal, you must find it shocking that more money will be spent on interest on the deficit than on the environment, health, or any of the other pressing needs. Since 1980, interest costs have increased over

$100 billion, to $180 billion. If you add interest the government owes for borrowing from the trust funds, the real interest figure for 1990 is about $265 billion, and in 1992 will climb to about $300 billion—roughly what America now spends on defense. Interest buys nothing but the right to continue the borrowing game.

Jeff Danziger for *The Christian Science Monitor*. Reprinted with permission.

How can anyone, least of all self-proclaimed fiscal conservatives, tolerate such a travesty? Tolerate? They revel in it. We now have a proposed cut in the tax on capital gains that may bring a short-term revenue gain, $3.3 billion in 1990, as people rush to sell assets, but which the Joint Committee on Taxation says will add $24.4 billion to the deficit over five years. If the argument is that we need lower taxes to stimulate growth, how is it that we are still growing more slowly and investing less than the prosperous nations of Western Europe and Japan even though we average a combined U.S. federal, state and local tax rate of 28 percent and they average 40 percent? The real reason we fall behind is that the deficit uses up savings and forces up the cost of capital. This deters investment and curbs growth and productivity gains. Reducing the deficit is not a matter of arcane bookkeeping. It would free up capital, lower interest rates and stimulate an investment boom.

Bush administration officials put forth new ideas for schools, for drugs, for space exploration, for the environment. Then, in the small print, you find they do not have the money. Being a successful President means more than being kind and gentle, more than reaching out to people in both parties. Popularity must have a purpose.

"The deficit is under adequate control."

The Budget Deficit Is Not a Serious Problem

George L. Perry

In the following viewpoint, George L. Perry maintains that the federal budget deficit is less serious than the debates in Congress have led the public to believe. Perry, a senior fellow in the Brookings Economic Studies program, contends that current government taxation and spending policies will eventually eliminate the deficit. The Brookings Institution is a research and education organization that studies issues of economics, government, and foreign policy. Perry directs the Brookings Panel on Economic Activity.

As you read, consider the following questions:

1. Why does Perry believe that the deficit will decline?
2. According to Perry, how has partisan political debate affected deficit reduction policies, and how could this debate continue to affect the deficit?
3. According to the author, what other national problems should take the place of pointless debate over the deficit?

George L. Perry, "Back to Budget Basics," *The Brookings Review*, Winter 1990/1991. Reprinted with permission of The Brookings Institution.

It is time to put aside the debate over the budget deficit that has preoccupied Congress and the administration for so long. There is only so much time and energy available to expend on economic and social legislation. The consensus needed to legislate in our political system can take only a limited amount of strain, and fighting over how to reduce deficits has tested that limit. Even though we are not headed for the budget surplus that many economists would like, the deficit is under adequate control for now, and other important economic and social matters demand the attention of legislators.

Controlled Deficits

The idea that deficits are under control deserves a little explaining. After all, the deficit will be a record $300-plus billion. But the current deficit is not the issue. It will be large both because economic activity is weakening, automatically cutting revenues and raising transfer payments, and because the deficit reduction agreement contained only small budget savings at the start. Steadily declining deficits in subsequent years lead to a projected surplus by 1995.

Although this longer-run path is what matters, it is fair to ask why anyone should believe it will happen. Past deficit projections under Gramm-Rudman-Hollings have never been met or even approached. But those projections specified only a wish list of deficits, with no spending or tax programs to achieve them. The new agreement specifies realistic and enforceable expenditure ceilings. Within broad expenditure categories, spending more on some program requires either spending less on another or adding new revenue. This leaves room for budget mischief, but not too much.

The official deficit projections still make unduly favorable economic assumptions and include a surplus after 1993 for the thrift bailout. After adjusting for these, the projected 1995 deficit at high employment is 1 percent to 1 1/2 percent of GNP. That may not be optimal fiscal policy. But it is a high-employment deficit only slightly larger than in the 1960s and 1970s, and well below the average of the 1980s.

A Broad-Based Tax System

Reopening the deficit debate would run a serious risk of being counterproductive if Democrats and Republicans started horse-trading over tax changes. You do not have to believe in the supply-side tooth fairy to prefer a tax system with a broader base, lower rates, and no loopholes to its opposite. Yet any attempt by the Democrats to raise more income tax revenues from upper income groups will renew the Republicans' drive to cut the tax rate on capital gains. There are plenty of arguments to be made on all sides of the capital gains issue. But what cannot be disputed is that a capital gains preference will open a new tax shelter industry that was largely closed by the 1986 tax reform. If tax shelters again become important to private decisions, a lot of investment funds will go not where they are most productive but where they are most sheltered from taxes. Such misdirection of funds would undo many billions of dollars of deficit reduction in its effect on growth and productivity.

Deficit Scare Tactics

As to the scare tactic that the deficit and the growing debt are stealing from future generations—that is simply rhetoric. The amount government spends, not those government receipts labeled taxes, is the real burden imposed on the public. If the national income is four trillion dollars, and the federal government spends a trillion dollars, that leaves three trillion dollars for state and local governments, institutions and private individuals to spend or invest as they wish, whether the government finances its spending by explicit taxes or by borrowing. As to the so-called debt burden we are piling up, the federal debt is a smaller fraction of the national income today than in any year from the end of World War II to 1960. Where were the doom-and-gloomers then? Certainly not among the Congressional big spenders.

The size of the budget deficit has been exaggerated as "monstrous," "gigantic," "obscene." As a percentage of the national income, the deficit is not out of line with levels frequently reached in the past.

Milton Friedman, *Reader's Digest*, March 1989.

Even more important, reopening the budget deficit would push other important issues off the political agenda. We need to find ways to contain the price and total cost of health care to slow consumer price inflation and the growing demands of medical care on the federal budget. At the same time, we should look hard for ways to reduce the risk for the 30-odd million Americans now without medical insurance. The financial crisis of the thrift industry is extending to other financial institutions that made bad real estate loans. The government needs to review its place in insuring and regulating such institutions as it considers overhaul of the banking system. Eastern Europe and the Soviet Union need our help in moving to democratic market economies. At home the problems of crime, drugs, and homelessness and the needs for better education and infrastructure all vie for our lawmakers' attention.

Some of these issues will cost additional money, others may save. But all deserve more attention than they have been getting during the past several years of unending budget crises. Congress and the administration can now afford to put the budget deficit issue aside, and they should.

"I advocate a policy . . . to gradually reduce the federal budget deficit."

Reducing the Budget Deficit Should Be a Priority

Tom Weisskopf

Tom Weisskopf teaches economics at the University of Michigan. He is also the author of *The Capitalist System* and *Beyond the Wasteland*. In the following viewpoint, Weisskopf maintains that the federal budget deficit must be reduced if America's economy is to continue to expand. He believes that by cutting unnecessary and inefficient programs from the budget, Congress will free funds that can be spent on much-needed, effective programs. Such programs could energize the economy, he concludes.

As you read, consider the following questions:

1. Why does Weisskopf advocate reducing interest rates as part of his deficit-reduction plan?
2. What deficit-reduction programs does the author propose? How do these programs differ from the others he discusses in the viewpoint?
3. What government policies does Weisskopf favor that would benefit from a stronger economy?

Tom Weisskopf, "Taking On the Deficit," *Dollars & Sense*, June 1989. Reprinted with permission. *Dollars & Sense* is a progressive monthly economics magazine. First-year subscriptions are available for $14.95 from the office at One Summer St., Somerville, MA 02143.

The new electronic billboard in New York's Times Square doesn't flash the time or the temperature. It reports the size of the U.S. national debt, which is now approaching $3 trillion.

It's a sign of the times. Concerns about the size of the federal government's budget deficit dominate current debates about U.S. economic policy. . . .

Phony Proposals for Economic Austerity

Perhaps the biggest worriers are the bankers, corporate executives, and other pillars of the U.S. economic establishment, who periodically beat the drums for "economic austerity." Because these austerity advocates use the size of the deficit as a club with which to beat back progressive social and economic initiatives, many leftists have reflexively opposed deficit-cutting proposals, adopting a "what, me worry?" position.

Dollars & Sense, for example, called the deficit-reduction debate a "red herring" in a 1987 article, going on to state a common left response to the deficit: "Much more important than the size of the deficit is whether government resources are being used to serve people's needs. . . ." If they are, the argument goes, then further deficit spending is justifiable as a means to finance needed public programs.

Many progressive economists—from liberal Keynesians such as Robert Eisner of Northwestern University to socialists such as David Kotz of the University of Massachusetts—view efforts to reduce the federal deficit as counter-productive. They advocate instead expansionary policies, including a looser monetary policy as well as increased government spending, as a way of simultaneously financing needed public expenditures, promoting private investment, and pushing the economy closer to full employment.

I think such views are mistaken. While the austerity advocates' political agenda must be opposed at every turn, their economic analysis is, unfortunately, correct in identifying some of the adverse consequences of further deficit financing. Specifically, given the current state of the U.S. economy, expansionary policies will not reduce unemployment, and faster monetary growth will not spur more private investment unless they are accompanied by deficit reduction. That is why I advocate a policy similar to that of the Jesse Jackson '88 campaign, which combined a call for increased government spending on key social and economic programs with a plan to gradually reduce the federal budget deficit.

We can all agree that the linchpin of any progressive strategy for revitalization of the U.S. economy is greatly increased public expenditures on activities neglected or cut back by the Reagan administration—both productivity-enhancing activities like education, civilian research, and transportation, and programs that meet people's real needs like child care, housing, health services and environmental protection. The key issue that divides alternative progressive polices is how best to finance sorely needed increases in public spending.

Earlier Deficit Reduction

It would, of course, have been better to start cutting the deficit several years ago when the economy was growing much more rapidly. The increase in capital formation and the reduction in interest rates that would have followed an earlier deficit reduction would have given us higher productivity and a stronger economy today. But we cannot turn back the clock. We can only hope that common sense will prevail before time runs out.

Martin Feldstein, *The Wall Street Journal*, September 5, 1990.

Instead of an expansion policy that relies on more deficit financing, I advocate a "reallocation" policy, insisting that new programs be financed by new taxes or spending cuts. This can be achieved by reversing Reagan administration policies, increasing taxes on the rich and reducing military spending.

The fundamental problem with further deficit spending is that it is inflationary, pushing up prices and interest rates instead of employment and output. Those who advocate expansionary deficit spending ignore several realities about the current U.S. economy.

Most important, the U.S. economy still relies on private enterprise for most of its production and investment. In the short run, any strategy for revitalizing the economy must include a means of stimulating private sector investment and research and development. This is not to deny that increasing public investment is absolutely critical; it is simply to recognize that most economic activity in our society is under private rather than public control. Economic policy-makers are therefore obliged to create a climate in which private businesses will find it profitable to channel their resources into productive investment rather than into leveraged buyouts, and to do so here in the United States rather than abroad.

Many factors contribute to the general "investment climate" for private businesses: overall economic stability, expectations of market growth, and recent profit performance. But among the most important are long-term nominal interest rates. The higher these rates are, the more it costs to finance investments in plant and equipment.

Some economists argue that the adverse effects of high nominal interest rates are neutralized if the rate of inflation is also high, since then the real cost of borrowing (and the real relative attractiveness of financial investments) is correspondingly lower. But lowering real interest rates by allowing inflation to rise does not encourage more productive private investment, because high inflation itself leads to heightened uncertainty and economic instability.

It follows that a strategy for economic revitalization must include a way to bring down nominal long-term interest rates. Many economists believe that the federal government can reduce interest rates simply by increasing the money supply. But if such monetary expansion leads to price inflation, it will at most bring down short-term interest rates. Long-term interest rates are very sensitive to expectations about future inflation, since long-term lenders take into account the extent to which they expect the value of loan repayments to be reduced by inflation. So it will be impossible for the monetary authorities to get long-term interest rates down unless they can convince lenders they can hold down the rate of inflation.

The Limits of Expansion

One of the most unpleasant realities about the contemporary U.S. economy is that inflationary pressures are generated at levels of economic activity well below what it takes to provide true full employment. It is difficult to estimate the level to which the official civilian unemployment rate would have to fall so that no one is involuntarily unemployed or obliged to take a part-time rather than a full-time job. We can be sure, however, that it is well below the official unemployment rates in the United States during the past two decades. A good guess is that the U.S. economy would attain true full employment at an official unemployment rate between 2% and 3%.

If we could reach the full employment target simply by stimulating the economy through more expansionary fiscal and/or monetary policies, then such policies would clearly make sense. Unfortunately, however, the evidence suggests that serious inflationary pressures begin to arise even as the official unemployment rate drops toward its current rate of about 5%. This means that expansionary policies yield less and less of a reduction in unemployment and more and more of an increase in inflation once the 5% level of unemployment is reached. It is therefore impossible to reach true full employment without either very high inflation or strong price controls—neither of which the U.S. economy could sustain for very long.

The problem is partly structural in nature. As the unemployment rate falls to 5% or below, product shortages begin to develop in key sectors of the economy and in certain regions of the country, and labor markets tighten for certain occupations. As a result, some prices and wages begin to rise even while excess supplies and unemployed workers remain in other sectors of the economy.

But the problem is also rooted in the distributional conflict characteristic of capitalism. As product and labor markets begin to tighten, more and more capitalists and workers gain the political and economic power to push up prices and wages in an inflationary spiral that reflects the struggle over how the economic pie is to be shared.

Unemployment and Capitalism

The fact that serious inflationary pressures arise at rates of unemployment well above true full employment is a terrible indictment of U.S. economic institutions. To a certain extent, this is inherent in any capitalist economy, but the problem can be alleviated by more activist government and business policies. Sweden and Japan, for example, do a much better job than the United States of educating, training and retraining workers, generating jobs when and where workers are looking for them, and promoting consensus about the distribution of income.

It would certainly make sense to promote the kind of restructuring of U.S. economic institutions that would make lower levels of unemployment attainable without inflationary pressures, but even if there were a strong public commitment to such an effort, this would take a good deal of time. In the meantime, the pursuit of expansionary economic policies when the official unemployment rate is close to 5% serves mainly to increase inflation, not to raise output or reduce unemployment. Distasteful as it is for progressives to accept, the only way to restrain inflation in the present U.S. economy is to limit the expansionary thrust of economic policy and leave unemployment well above its potential minimum.

Aggravating the perils of an expansionary fiscal and monetary policy is its effect on the U.S. trade deficit, which—like the budget deficit—has reached unprecedented heights in recent years. Expansion worsens the trade deficit in two ways. It increases U.S. consumers' purchasing power, which leads to more imports (as U.S. consumers purchase more foreign goods) and fewer exports (as U.S. consumers purchase more U.S. goods that could otherwise have been exported). And it increases domestic inflation, raising the prices of U.S. goods relative to foreign goods and thereby also encouraging more imports and fewer exports.

To offset the increase in the trade deficit, U.S. government policy-makers would then have two choices: either let the value of the dollar fall to promote exports and discourage imports, or try to attract more capital from abroad. Both of these alternatives would have undesirable consequences. A falling dollar would fuel inflationary pressures, as foreign goods became more expensive, and the resulting inflationary expectations would push up long-term interest rates. The alternative of attracting foreign capital would require tighter monetary policy and higher interest rates. Either way, interest rates would rise, and this would discourage private investment and curtail the growth of output and employment.

Options for the Left

These sobering realities about the U.S. economy severely constrain the policy options open to progressives as well as conservatives. The only way to increase public spending without reducing private investment is to finance it in a way that does not add to the expansionary stimulus already built in to the U.S. federal budget. Indeed, lowering interest rates may well require *reducing* expansionary fiscal stimulus below current levels, which are already causing inflation and interest rates to rise.

Face Up to the Deficit

The truth is that we have been playing games with the deficit over the last ten years. First we falsify the deficit's size; then we use mysterious accounting devices, rather than solid policies, to wish it away. Unless we face up to the deficit and deal with it honestly, it will grow to even more dangerous proportions.

Lee Hamilton, *Los Angeles Times*, May 10, 1990.

Monetary expansion is one essential component of a strategy involving reduced interest rates, but it must be complemented by greater fiscal restraint (lower government spending or higher taxes). This means financing new public spending in a way that allows the federal budget deficit to be reduced—in short, reallocation rather than expansion.

Up to now the need to reduce the U.S. budget deficit has been voiced mainly by the austerity advocates, who erroneously conclude that new social and economic policy initiatives simply cannot be afforded. The truth is that such initiatives can be afforded—as long as they are financed not by further borrowing, but by such alternative measures as reducing military spending and restoring taxes on the wealthy.

Now all of this may seem somewhat irrelevant—for progressives are obviously not going to be making economic policy decisions over the next few years. To lay out a progressive short-run economic strategy may nonetheless be a useful exercise. For one thing, it provides a solid basis for criticizing the economic policies likely to be pursued by the Bush administration and a compliant Congress. Further, it demonstrates the feasibility as well as the desirability of more progressive policies within a capitalist economy, and, by clarifying the limits of such policies, it also underscores some fundamental flaws in our capitalist economic system.

A Progressive Proposal

To do this convincingly, progressive economic policy proposals must be consistent and realistic. Rather than pretend that we can live happily with a huge budget deficit and expand our way out of economic trouble, progressives should help promote public understanding that deficit reduction can and should be accompanied by a drastic reordering of public spending priorities. The right has used the logic of deficit reduction as a weapon against any new public programs. The left can turn this weapon against useless forms of government spending and regressive tax breaks and in favor of the progressive social and economic initiatives that are so desperately needed after almost a decade of Reaganomic waste.

"The false crisis over the budget deficit prevents the nation from dealing with the real, deep-seated problems it faces. "

Reducing the Budget Deficit Should Not Be a Priority

Charles R. Morris

In the following viewpoint, Charles R. Morris argues that the budget deficit is not a serious problem for America's economy. The economy can continue to grow even if the deficit increases, he maintains. He further charges that calls for reducing the deficit mask an unwillingness to take on more serious problems in America's economy, such as decisions about allocating funds for the needy, the health care crisis, and the role of government in the economy. Morris is a contributor to the *New York Times* and the author of *Iron Destinies, Lost Opportunities*, a history of the arms race.

As you read, consider the following questions:

1. Why does Morris argue that the deficit is not a serious problem?
2. How should the government handle the budget deficit, according to the author?
3. According to Morris, how has the mythical budget deficit crisis replaced other crises in America?

Charles R. Morris, "Deficit Figuring Doesn't Add Up," *The New York Times*, February 12, 1989. Reprinted by permission of Russell & Volkening as agents for the author. Copyright © 1989 by Charles R. Morris.

Most economists, bankers, stockbrokers, editorial writers and Congressmen still believe that Federal budget deficits cause high inflation and high interest rates, sap savings and investment, are at the root of our trade deficit and have converted America into "the world's largest net debtor." But they are being reassured that, though all these bad consequences *do* follow deficits, they work so slowly as to be imperceptible. In other words, instead of a crisis, we have a mini-recession forever.

Deficit Pollyannas

Without doubt, a major quiver in the financial markets will send the deficit flags flying again. But for once, the deficit Pollyannas may have the stronger argument, if for different reasons than usually stated. Remarkably, there has never been strong evidence for the malevolent consequences of a Federal budget deficit: virtually all of the arguments in favor of urgent action on the current deficit are supported only by the most tenuous connections between theory and evidence, or are not supported at all, or are misleading or actually false. As David Hale, chief economist of Kemper Financial Services, who believes the deficit is important, freely concedes, the fundamental relations are "very murky . . . either very difficult to quantify or you can't quantify them at all."

The gap between the prevailing wisdom and the economic evidence is partly a matter of politics and partly just honest confusion. But more fundamentally, it points up basic flaws in our conventional understanding of how a modern economy works.

The standard model of a modern economy runs roughly as follows: A country's total output (its gross national product, or G.N.P.) is the sum of private consumption and investment and government spending. When the government increases its own spending beyond what it takes in as taxes—creating a budget deficit—it is putting more money into private hands. So total spending—and the G.N.P.—rise.

But the temporary stimulus to the G.N.P. comes at a cost. The increased borrowing by the government to pay its deficit will cause interest rates to rise, because the government action will have heightened competition among borrowers bidding for the available pool of capital. Alternatively, if the Federal Reserve increases the supply of money to accommodate the borrowing, the additional spending power will cause inflation to rise. Things get more complicated when international effects are taken into account, but, in general, the spur to consumption in the deficit country should cause a temporary spurt in imports, such as VCR's and autos, causing a deficit in trade.

How well does this conventional picture comport with reality? Do government deficits actually increase inflation and interest rates and reduce savings and investment? And what is the impact of deficits on America's trade balance and international financial standing? More fundamentally, how do we measure a deficit in the first place?

Defining the Deficit

The importance of a budget deficit depends crucially on the size of the economy. A $100 billion deficit will have five times the impact on a $1 trillion economy as on a $5 trillion economy, the current size of our own. Charting changes in budget deficits without reference to changes in the size of the economy is a gross misrepresentation; and the present deficits, in fact, become much less frightening when they are expressed as a percentage of the G.N.P.

Ensuring Prosperity

The really serious problem is not now the size of the government deficit but, as with most individuals or businesses, what the borrowing is being used to finance. If an individual borrows to finance gambling losses in Las Vegas that is clearly bad. If a family borrows to invest in a new home or the children's college education, most of us think that is good. And if business borrows to invest in productive new plant and equipment, not many of us would be critical.

It should be the same for government at all levels. It is past time for Mr. Bush and Congress to put behind foolish posturing over mismeasured deficits and to face up to our real needs. These are to assure a prosperous economy now and the real investment, public and private, on which our prosperity depends.

Robert Eisner, *The Wall Street Journal*, June 19, 1990.

The current policy debate also confuses Federal deficits with overall government deficits. State and local surpluses reduce private spending and retire debt just as Federal surpluses do. In recent years, in fact, state and local surpluses have been quite large, the recent problems in Massachusetts and New York notwithstanding.

The annual overall government deficits in the 1980's, expressed as a percentage of the G.N.P., have never reached the record level set in 1975, and the present deficit level is in a range seen rather frequently in the past, even in the conservative Eisenhower years. (Just as pacifistic Democrats make wars, fiscally upright Republicans have always run up the biggest deficits.)

Even more important is the changing nature of Federal spending. President Dwight D. Eisenhower's big deficits came from buying things like tanks or roads. But only about a third of the modern Federal budget actually is used to purchase goods and services. The remaining two-thirds are transfer payments of one form or another—including interest payments—and make no direct contribution to the G.N.P. Money is merely shuffled from one set of potential spenders to another. . . .

Inflation and Interest Rates

Assuming away the problem of how big the deficit really is, do budget deficits increase inflation and interest rates? The experience of the last 10 years provides an unequivocally negative answer. Interest rates and inflation fell as sharply as the Federal deficit rose. . . .

In fact, there is no evidence that over the last 40 years budget deficits have been associated with higher interest rates or inflation—if anything, the correlation runs in the opposite direction. Economists, like Paul Evans of Ohio State University, have conducted elaborate statistical analyses—controlling for lag effects, inflation, the experience in different countries—without finding any consistent effects from government deficits.

The United States Treasury Department conducted an exhaustive survey of the economic literature in 1984, and found "no systematic relationship between government budget deficits and interest rates. . . ." Some studies, to be sure, claimed to find some such effects; but there was always another drawing the opposite conclusion from the same data.

The budget deficit is frequently blamed for making American interest rates higher than in other countries—in the 1980's interest rates in this country have been higher than in, say, Japan or Germany. But American rates began to shoot up in the late 70's before the deficit rose, in reaction to the high, and extremely volatile, American inflation in the 70's, a time when German and Japanese prices were much more stable.

Tracking changes in American, Japanese and German rates shows no consistent pattern. For example, the gap between American and Japanese government bond rates more than doubled between 1980 and 1981, when the American budget deficit was actually falling. The gap then narrowed as the deficit peaked, and began to rise in 1988 as the deficit dropped. In all seven major industrial countries (including Canada, England, France and Italy) in the 1980's, in fact, inflation-adjusted interest rates almost always dropped as budget deficits rose, and vice versa. As Rudolph G. Penner, former director of the Congressional Budget Office, recently phrased it: "One would expect a positive relationship between the deficit and real interest rates. This relationship has been devilishly difficult to document statistically."

91

It is taken as a truism that government budget deficits reduce savings and investment: the spur to spending increases consumption, the logic goes, at the same time as government borrowing reduces total savings. The result is lower investment and, over the long term, a less-productive economy. The experience of the 1980's in the United States is consistent with that picture: both savings and net business investment have dropped as the deficits rose.

The Fuss over the Deficit

The anti-deficit people who kept crying wolf, and who are still crying wolf, have done themselves and the polity no favor. They have tried to turn the fiscal-policy debate into a one-sided argument, to the effect that anybody who cared about the country's economic health had only one rational choice: cut the budget deficit. In the end they have undermined their own position by claiming too much, and have left the country confused and adrift on the question of why we make such a fuss about deficit spending.

Jonathan Rauch, *The Atlantic*, February 1989.

But it is reasonable to ask whether it is generally true that budget deficits reduce total national savings. The surprising answer is that it is not. Robert J. Barro of Harvard University has tracked the interplay of savings and deficits in a number of countries, and the results are frequently—usually, Barro argues—the opposite of what one would expect. Canada and Italy have run very large budget deficits for the last decade, and both have seen very strong increases in private savings. In Israel, England and Denmark, private savings rose sharply to offset big government deficits in the early 1980's, then dropped sharply as their budgets moved into surplus, keeping overall national savings rates roughly constant. . . .

Why the Clamor?

The obvious question, then, is why all the clamor? There are a number of bad reasons and one or two good ones. Partisan political considerations, of course, rank high on the list; or as Carnegie Mellon's Professor Meltzer puts it: "Read my lips, eat my words." The deficit has been the major blot on the Republican economic record, and clearly puts President Bush on the defensive on his "no new taxes" pledge.

Irving Kristol, the editor of the *Public Interest*, points to the media bandwagon effect: "The media has been accustomed to organizing coverage around crises, and the deficit is about the only one on hand."

The deficits are also a powerful curb on the "Iron Triangle" of Washington special interests that resist spending cuts and create new spending needs:

• Congressmen, who don't score points with constituents by cutting spending. Without the deficit clamor, how could Congress sit still for $1 billion worth of military-base closings? The deficit provides the political air cover for a tax increase to ease the budget-cutting pressures.

• The financial community, which wants action on the deficit because markets move on gusts of emotion. If enough authorities insist there is a crisis, investors, in turn, may behave cautiously, as if there really was one.

• The economics profession, which is, as a whole, in an awkward position if there is no deficit crisis. It is one more confirmation of the deficiencies of the conventional wisdom, but there is no obvious new theory to replace the old one. Educating the political and journalistic elite in fundamental principles has been a long and painstaking process; jettisoning well-established rules is dangerous without new canons of equal clarity to take their place.

Frustration with the Government

The deficit has also become a kind of lightning rod, attracting all the pent-up frustrations of the public at the inability of a divided national executive and legislature to accomplish *anything* in the modern era of special-interest politics. A sensible farm policy, defense policy, entitlements policy, may all be beyond us, but surely the deficit is a problem of sufficient simplicity and starkness to deal with.

There is, finally, at least one good reason to worry about budget deficits: they are a form of moral hazard. The false crisis over the budget deficit prevents the nation from dealing with the real, deep-seated problems it faces, issues of resource allocation and intergenerational equity. What is the proper role of government in a modern mixed economy? What about the looming problem of caring for our aged? The Social Security trust fund is now running a surplus in the $100 billion range, accounting for much of the recent reduction in the Federal deficit. (Taxes are taxes, and one tax dollar closes a deficit as effectively as any other, regardless of its ultimate purpose.) The long-term question, however, is whether there will be enough of a surplus when the baby-boom generation turns 65.

It is unreasonable to expect fundamental problems such as these to be sensibly addressed in the present cloud of exaggeration and confusion. And they are far too complicated for decision making during a crisis. But there is, after all, no crisis—except for the inevitable crisis of credibility if we lean too long on the button for the siren marked "false alarm."

"Let's get serious about cutting the budget!"

Spending Cuts Will Reduce the Deficit

Rachel Flick

Rachel Flick contends that the federal budget deficit is a serious problem and should be reduced. In the following viewpoint, Flick proposes major cuts in government spending on a variety of domestic programs to reduce the budget deficit. Flick is a contributor to *Reader's Digest*, one of America's most popular periodicals.

As you read, consider the following questions:

1. What are some of the specific programs that Flick advocates reducing? Why does the author choose these?
2. Why does Flick oppose tax increases?
3. According to the author, how does political debate affect the budget deficit?

Rachel Flick, "Let's Get Serious About Cutting the Budget," *Reader's Digest*, September 1990. Copyright © 1990 by the Reader's Digest Association, Inc. Reprinted with permission.

The United States has two choices, says House Ways and Means Committee chairman Dan Rostenkowski (D., Ill.). We can either raise taxes or "hope the government wins the sweepstakes so we can pay our debts." Senate Republican whip Alan Simpson (Wyo.) offers up a whole panoply of potential new levies to combat the $169-billion deficit—"value-added taxes, additional user fees, taxes on booze and cigarettes . . . all sorts of things!" Even President Bush has yielded to the tax temptation.

Tax Increases Are Counterproductive

But Washington's Establishment has it wrong. "Raising taxes will not reduce the deficit," says Nobel Prize-winning economist Milton Friedman. "It will simply increase government spending." Further, high taxes hurt business growth. "Raising taxes would be counterproductive," says T. J. Rodgers, founder of one of America's fastest-growing high-tech companies. "The government just needs to stop spending so much money."

He's right. The way to reduce the deficit is to cut spending. There are plenty of ways to do it. Here are eight:

1. *Sell federal assets.* In 1986, one of America's biggest petroleum dealers made a bad deal. Oil was fetching $12.60 a barrel, but he had locked himself into contracts to sell for $4.90 per barrel. Losses amounted to $300,000 per day.

Nonetheless, the dealer is still in business. That's because he is Uncle Sam, and the oil he squandered was from the Naval Petroleum Reserves (NPRs) at Elk Hills, Calif., and Teapot Dome, Wyo.

Set aside early this century as emergency supplies for the Navy, the NPRs have long since been supplanted by the more accessible Strategic Petroleum Reserve. "For all practical purposes, the NPRs are not reserves and they have nothing to do with the Navy," admits a Congressional aide. "They're just a federal business." And as the 1986 fiasco made clear, the government does not belong in the oil business. Getting out could cut the deficit $2.5 billion.

The government also owns one-third of the nation's coal reserves, and leases the right to mine them. But it does not manage the reserves well. Fifty billion tons of coal are in just one holding, the Powder River Basin in Wyoming and Montana, but 80 percent is unleased. By selling this single reserve, we could reduce the deficit by $2 billion.

Six percent of the nation's electricity is generated by 127 federal dams, and then five Power Marketing Administrations (PMAs) sell it at bargain-basement rates. For instance, the Southeastern Power Administration supplies electricity for a ten-state area, including the district of House Appropriations Committee chairman Jamie Whitten (D., Miss.), at 1.78 cents per kwh [kilowatt hours]. The national wholesale average is 3.8 cents for private utility companies.

The PMAs are worth at least $10 billion. Yet only one—the smallest, in Alaska—has been marked for sale. In 1986, with Whitten helping to lead the charge, Congress barred the government from even studying the sale of others. Selling them, along with the NPRs and the Powder River Basin coal reserves, could produce $14.5 billion to reduce the deficit.

2. *Contract out federal services.* In 1981, the watchdog General Accounting Office found that the government could cut its custodial costs in half by letting outside contractors do the work. Nevertheless, 1400 custodians are still on the payroll of the General Services Administration (GSA), which manages government buildings. Why? In 1982, Congress forbade the GSA to "privatize" custodians—or guards, elevator operators and messengers. Altogether, 37 different statutes bar the contracting out of almost 70 percent of federal services to the private sector.

Congress requires the Defense Department to maintain its own security and firefighting personnel. The government may not even study the savings to be had from hiring private air-traffic controllers. Some civilian agencies keep their own planes for their senior officials' travel when it would be cheaper to buy commercial tickets. More amazing still, the National Park Service may not replace employees with volunteers, thus forcing Uncle Sam to pay for work he could get for free.

Cutting Federal Jobs

Across the vast federal government, the cost of protecting jobs big and small steeply mounts. The Office of Management and Budget says that by conducting privatization reviews of all qualifying federal jobs, the government could cut spending by up to $7.2 billion.

Total savings so far: $21.7 billion.

3. *Eliminate programs that produce more pork than beef.* From 1985 to 1988, as a ranking member and then chairman of the Senate Appropriations Committee, John Stennis (D., Miss.) forced the U.S. Economic Development Administration (EDA) to grant $16.5 million to the Institute for Technology Development. This institute was supposed to help Mississippi businesses apply new technologies. Its expenditures included $100,000 salaries for top executives, luxurious travel for senior staff and more than $135,000 in consulting fees for the Stennis aide who arranged the EDA financing and then went into business for himself.

Rep. Joel Hefley (R., Colo.) says that EDA exists "primarily for members of Congress to funnel money to their friends." Shutting it down would save $220 million.

Also ripe for the ax is the Small Business Administration

(SBA), which was set up primarily to guarantee loans and secure government contracts for deserving entrepreneurs. In 1989 the SBA secured loans or contracts for only 0.12 percent (22,000) of the nation's 19 million small businesses. And that tiny group has a poor record for repaying loans. Shutting down the agency would save $1.1 billion.

"The following documentary on the federal budget deficit has been made possible by a grant from the federal government."

© Harley Schwadron. Reprinted with permission.

Since 1964 the Urban Mass Transportation Administration (UMTA) has squandered billions on gold-plated transit systems. The author of a Transportation Department study of UMTA says, "There's often one single powerful Representative or Senator directing money toward each of these systems."
Miami's $1.5-billion Metrorail is a case in point. Dubbed

"Metrofail" by city wags, Metrorail owes its existence to Rep. William Lehman (D., Fla.), chairman of the House Appropriations Subcommittee on Transportation. A scant two percent of Dade County residents use Metrorail, so it loses over $25 million per year. Despite this failure, however, Lehman has earmarked $163 million to extend another equally underused system called the People Mover.

Nationwide, UMTA costs taxpayers $3.9 billion a year. Shutting it down along with the SBA and EDA would save $5.2 billion.

Total savings so far: $26.9 billion.

4. *Let the dinosaurs die.* The Export-Import Bank was established in 1934 to finance U.S. exports to the U.S.S.R. Now it makes loans at below market rates to foreign purchasers of U.S. goods—loans that default at an astounding rate: $4.5 billion of the $12 billion owed the bank is more than 90 days delinquent. Few of the firms Eximbank benefits—which include giants like Boeing, Bechtel, General Electric and Westinghouse—need to have the United States subsidizing their customers. Closing Eximbank would save $2 billion.

Obsolete Programs

Consider that Depression-era relic, the Rural Electrification Administration (REA). Its original job—to electrify U.S. farms—was accomplished long ago. Then the agency began supplying telephone service. Today, nearly all U.S. farmhouses have both electricity and phones.

How does the REA justify its existence? It subsidizes utility rates by lending almost $2 billion per year, half at five percent and less. The bulk of these loans go to 63 telephone and electrical cooperatives, including one in Aspen, Colo., playground of the super-rich. Closing the REA would save $1.2 billion.

U.S. taxpayers also sustain hundreds of obsolete military bases. For instance, the Army's Fort Ord, established in 1917 in the rolling hills of Monterey, Calif., costs $885 million a year to run. Yet because of its small size and proximity to civilian areas, the resident 7th light-infantry division must travel 80 miles to another base to conduct maneuvers and 100 miles to a National Guard outpost for live-ammunition drills.

Rep. Richard K. Armey (R., Texas) estimates that closing all unnecessary bases would cut spending $2 billion per year. Added to the savings from terminating Eximbank and the REA, that would yield $5.2 billion in dinosaur funds.

Total savings so far: $32.1 billion.

5. *Stop subsidizing agribusiness.* In 1989 corn was selling for $2.26 per bushel on the open market. However, under the farm price-support program, the government had promised American corn growers they would get $2.84 per bushel. Accordingly, tax-

payers paid each participating farmer 58 cents per bushel to make up the difference. The tab came to $3.5 billion.

That's not the only way the United States bolstered corn prices. To participate in the government program, each farmer agreed to take land out of production. Thus, in 1989, 10.8 million acres of farmland were not planted with corn. Less corn means higher prices worldwide.

Nonsensical Government Programs

Corn is only one of 14 commodities that taxpayers support as part of one of our costliest and most nonsensical programs. Not only do these price supports raise grocery bills by as much as $10 billion, but their drain on the U.S. Treasury will reach $11.7 billion. We should terminate all 14.

Savings now total $43.8 billion.

6. *End funding for research extravaganzas.* When the Superconducting Super Collider, a new proton smasher, was proposed in 1985, its cost was estimated at $5.9 billion. That figure has since risen to $8 billion, with the federal government paying three-quarters.

Will taxpayers get their money's worth? In 1988, Sigma Xi, a scientific honor society, asked its members which of nine projects would make the best use of federal funding. The proton smasher came in last, behind "other."

"Economic and technological spinoffs are unlikely in the extreme," James Krumhansl, former president of the American Physical Society, says of the project. Why then is it going forward? Politics: it will be one of the largest employment schemes that Congress can support.

Another program worth terminating is the permanent manned space station. In 1984, when President Reagan launched the project, its cost was estimated at $8 billion. Now NASA puts that figure at $30 billion.

"We've spent $4 billion so far," says Dr. Jerry Grey of the American Institute of Aeronautics and Astronautics, "and thanks to continuous Congressional demands, there isn't a nut or bolt to show for it." New hazards keep arising, requiring expensive solutions. Worst, with narrow exceptions, "its scientific uses are quite dubious," says Dr. James A. Van Allen, a celebrated space physicist.

Political Programs

Notwithstanding the station's problems, Congress continues to fund it. Political scientist Ronald D. Brunner and physicist Radford Byerly, Jr., explained why in a recent issue of the journal *Space Policy.* "This major new program," they wrote, "would move money and jobs to many Congressional constituencies." While the space program remains important, the space station was political from the word go.

Another federally funded science project—the massive $3-billion plan to decipher man's genetic makeup—has been sold politically as a source of new treatments for inherited diseases. However, only a small part of the comprehensive project has medical value.

Ending government support for gene-mapping, the manned space station and proton smasher would save $3 billion in one year.

Total savings so far: $46.8 billion.

Reducing Government Waste

Before a spendthrift Congress starts proposing another layer of taxes, it needs to do a lot more to reduce the waste, fraud, abuse and mismanagement that exists throughout the government. The truth is that over time a mere 10 percent reduction would virtually erase the deficit.

Donald Lambro, *Conservative Chronicle*, June 20, 1990.

---

7. *Economize in Congress.* Every month, the Defense Department receives about 50,000 phone and 9000 written inquiries from Capitol Hill. Someone has to respond to each request for information, so Defense employees spend a million hours a year working exclusively with Congress.

One thing Congress does in its oversight of the Pentagon is dictate equipment our military services can buy. In 1987, Armed Services chairman Les Aspin (D., Wis.) and committee member Rep. Marvin Leath (D., Texas) forced the Army to buy 3349 trucks it didn't want, at a cost of $500 million. The vehicles were made by the Oshkosh Truck Corp. in Wisconsin. The company has donated money to Leath's campaigns and paid him to speak at its plants. Says an Army spokesman diplomatically, "Congress has the final say on what we buy and what we don't."

Congressional Micromanagement

How do busy Congressmen find time for this expensive micromanagement? Since John F. Kennedy became President in 1961, the number of Congressional staff has soared from 5800 to 14,757, according to The Heritage Foundation. At the end of World War II, Congress's own annual budget was $54 million. Now it is $2.3 billion. To climb that high, it grew at more than six times the rate of inflation. Cut Congress's budget a mere ten percent and we would save $230 million, not counting our savings from the mischief a smaller staff couldn't start.

Total savings so far: $47 billion.

8. *Give the President a line-item veto.* When President Bush promised aid to the infant democracies of Panama and Nicaragua, Congress spied its opportunity. Knowing Bush could not veto the aid bill, they piled it high with wish-list spending. Included were $750,000 for a ferryboat for American Samoa, and funding for 40 Housing and Urban Development Department projects that HUD Secretary Jack Kemp had previously rejected, such as a performing-arts center in New Jersey.

The Panama-Nicaragua aid bill illustrates a hard truth. We won't control spending until the President has what 43 of the nation's 50 governors have—the line-item veto. Without authority to blue-pencil waste or proposals that do not merit federal funds, the President is hostage to the whims of 535 Senators and Representatives.

Benefits of a Line-Item Veto

Since Republicans have controlled the White House, and Democrats the Congress, the line-item veto has been seen as a partisan issue that benefits the GOP. In 1990, however, the Democratic-controlled Senate Judiciary Committee approved two versions of the line-item veto. "I was opposed when I first came to the Senate," Sen. Edward Kennedy (D., Mass.) acknowledged. "Now I think the line-item veto is necessary for accountability."

President Bush says he is eager to become accountable. Let's put him to the test. Economists say a chief executive armed with the line-item veto could save $18 billion. If President Bush found even half that much beyond the waste identified above, the deficit would fall by another $9 billion.

Total savings: $56 billion.

No government office is a total waste. Every one of the programs described in this article helps someone. However, none of them helps enough people to be worth what it costs. And all of them—plus many others—can be eliminated without harming the economy or the nation.

Cut the Budget

But Congress will continue its spending spree unless American taxpayers *demand* that needless expenditures be halted. If you are fed up with the squandering of your hard-earned tax dollars, send the message to your representatives in Congress: Let's get serious about cutting the budget!

"There is probably no more widespread myth about the U.S. budget system than the supposed need to raise taxes or cut spending."

Spending Cuts Are Unnecessary to Reduce the Deficit

Lawrence Lindsey

Lawrence Lindsey teaches economics at Harvard University in Cambridge, Massachusetts. He worked for the White House Office of Policy Development and served on President Reagan's Council of Economic Advisers. In the following viewpoint, Lindsey argues that the budget deficit will eventually be reduced as normal economic activity increases tax revenue. Rather than raising taxes or making drastic cuts in spending, Lindsey concludes that a simple freeze on spending would be enough to control the deficit.

As you read, consider the following questions:

1. Why does Lindsey reject arguments for raising taxes and cutting spending?
2. How does the author justify his claims that tax increases and budget cuts are unnecessary?
3. When and how does Lindsey expect the budget will be balanced, according to his proposals?

Excerpts from *The Growth Experiment* by Lawrence Lindsey. Copyright © 1990 by Lawrence Lindsey. Reprinted by permission of Basic Books, a division of HarperCollins Publishers.

Now for a short civics test. Answer "true" or "false." To balance the budget in the 1990s the Congress must either increase taxes or cut spending from current levels.

The right answer is "false." If you responded "true," however, I won't take off too many points. There is probably no more widespread myth about the U.S. budget system than the supposed need to raise taxes or cut spending.

Budget System Myths

Let's consider how the myth got started. We do have a budget deficit of some $160 billion. For the Congress to balance the budget in a single year, it would have to enact some $160 billion in combined tax increases or spending cuts. Since most of our budget is "uncontrollable," in that it is comprised of defense, Social Security, Medicare, and interest on the debt, cutting $160 billion is impossible. So the pundits say we need a major tax increase as well.

The fallacy in this analysis is that no responsible economist would suggest that the United States try to reduce its budget deficit by $160 billion in a single year. The result would almost inevitably be a very sharp recession, or even a depression, as the government desperately sucked spending power out of the economy. Most sensible people favor narrowing the gap by $30 to $40 billion per year, ridding ourselves of the deficit over four or five years. That requires neither raising taxes nor reducing spending below current real levels, for the current tax code will *automatically* provide $75 billion to $80 billion more in income tax revenue each year for as long as economic growth continues at its current rate. With an automatic $300 billion revenue increase already scheduled, we could increase spending by $140 billion (roughly enough to keep up with inflation) and still bring the deficit down to zero in just four years.

This viewpoint began with a trick question. The Congress does not need to raise taxes because taxes are going up anyway. There is no voodoo involved. Both the real growth in the economy and continued inflation effectively increase average tax rates and tax revenues over time. In the 1960s Keynesians called this effect a "fiscal drag," or a "fiscal dividend," depending on whether they were advocating more stimulus or arguing that such stimulus was largely self-financing. Table A summarizes this relationship for each of the major types of taxes the government collects, in each case showing the effect on tax revenue of a 1 percent increase in the economy's real output as well as a 1 percent inflation.

Start with the personal income tax. We are all aware of the phenomenon known as bracket creep by which inflation pushes us into higher tax brackets without our real income increasing.

ERTA's [Economic Recovery Tax Act] indexing provisions curbed this highly destructive practice. With indexing, if both your income and prices rise 1 percent, your tax payments—not your tax rate—will also rise 1 percent, and taxes will take the same percentage of your income as before. As a general rule, therefore, 1 percent inflation will cause personal income tax revenue to rise only 1 percent. But because not all parts of the income tax are fully indexed, tax revenues do rise slightly faster than inflation, or a bit more than 1 percent for every 1 percent rise in prices.

Taxes Rise as Income Rises

Of more importance is what happens when you get a real raise, not just an inflationary increase. Since indexing does not apply to changes in real income, you may be pushed into a higher tax bracket when your income rises. Even if your tax bracket does not change, your tax payments will go up because you will be paying on a bigger income. Moreover, your *average* tax rate will rise because a smaller percentage of your income will be protected by basic exemptions and deductions.

Table A

Tax Revenue and the Economy

Type of Tax	FY89 Revenue* Collections (in billions)	Percent Change in Revenue with	
		1% Real Growth	1% Inflation
Personal Income	$425	1.3-1.4%	1.0-1.1%
Corporate Income	107	1.4	1.4
Social Insurance	364	1.0	1.0
Other	80	0.4	0.0

*Estimates from the *Budget of the United States Government FY1990* for FY89.

Consider the case of a four-person family earning $30,000 in 1989. In 1989 the family is allowed a deduction of $2,000 for each person plus a standard deduction of $5,000, for a total of $13,000. The family's taxable income is then $17,000. The tax rate on *taxable* income up to $31,000 is 15 percent, so this family pays a tax of $2,550, which is 8.5 percent of its *total* income, or an average tax rate of 8.5 percent. Now assume the family's real income increases by 10 percent to $33,000. Its deductions are unchanged, so its taxable income rises to $20,000. The tax on $20,000, at the standard 15 percent rate, is $3,000. The family's tax payments rise 17.6 percent ($450 on top of $2,550) though the family's income went up only 10 percent. On average, every 1 percent rise in the family's income caused a 1.76 percent rise in its tax payments. The family's average tax rate rose from 8.5 percent to slightly more than 9 percent. This increase occurred even though the family remained in the same 15 percent tax bracket. A greater fraction of the family's income was taxed at the 15 percent rate while a smaller percentage was in the "zero" rate. Note that unlike bracket creep, in which inflation increases the rate applied to the same real income, this family is paying a higher average rate because it really is making more money. This is fundamental to any progressive tax code. The family is still better off.

On average, if everyone in the United States got a 10 percent raise, tax revenues would rise about 15 percent. Ordinarily this would imply that every 1 percent of real growth would produce about 1.5 percent extra revenue. But not all real economic growth can be attributed to salary increases for those currently working; about one-third is due to new workers joining the labor force. New workers add to tax revenues, but they do not produce the same average increase per point of economic growth that occurs when existing workers get higher wages. The actual average effect is thus about 1.3 to 1.4 percent extra tax revenue per point of economic growth.

Corporate income tax revenues also rise much faster than the economy, as long as the economy is expanding. Corporations pay a flat tax rate, and so are not subject to bracket creep. But corporate taxes are increased both by inflation and real growth because of the way that the tax system defines corporate profits.

Imagine the production process as a giant pipeline: Raw materials, labor, and capital enter one end and finished products come out the other. Corporate profits are the difference in value between what goes into the pipeline and what comes out, or the difference between costs and final sales. When the economy slows down, fewer finished products are purchased and items build up in the pipeline, a process known as inventory accumulation. Corporations thus incur the costs of producing the inventory without having any final sales, and corporate profits fall.

The Pipeline Effect

When, on the other hand, the economy speeds up, existing items in the pipeline, already largely paid for, are ready to move. Final sales increase faster than input costs, and corporate profits rise quickly.

This "pipeline effect" is most dramatic at turning points in the economy. When the economy turns up or down, corporate profits can easily change as much as 3 to 5 percent for every 1 percent change in the economy. As business expansion continues, the ratio drops to about 1.4 points of corporate profit for every 1 point of economic growth. As business expansion persists, rising demand for products can only be met by new investment: The pipeline itself must be expanded in order to accommodate the greater flow of products. This is where the tax system plays a part. Suppose a business invests in expanding the capacity of its pipeline by 10 percent. We might expect sales, profits, and costs, including capital costs, to rise together in proportion and the capital costs of a 10 percent bigger pipeline to be also 10 percent higher. But the tax system does not allow corporations to deduct the capital costs of the bigger pipeline right away; these added costs must be depreciated over many years. Because the costs of the expansion cannot be fully counted, profits appear to rise much more quickly than economic activity expands. Thus corporate profits, and therefore corporate taxes, increase more than point for point with economic activity during periods of real economic growth.

Inflation has a similar effect. Again, consider the goods moving through the pipeline. During periods of inflation, the value of the inventory in the pipeline rises with the general price level. The corporation does not really gain, because the cost of replacing the materials at the beginning of the pipeline also rises. But the tax system views the rising value of inventory as a source of corporate profit. This is particularly true for corporations which use the first in-first out (FIFO) method of accounting, under which the cost of products is based on the original cost of the materials that went into them, not their replacement or current costs. The last in-first out method (LIFO) uses replacement or current costs. A surprising number of firms use FIFO rather than LIFO, even though it overstates their corporate profits and therefore their corporate taxes.

Corporate Taxes

The tax system also fails to take into account the effect of inflation on the capital costs of the pipeline itself. When inflation is high, the depreciation allowances for the cost of the pipeline are far less than the cost of actually replacing the pipeline at inflated prices. The result, since corporations cannot fully deduct the true capital costs of production from their profits, is an artificial rise in both profits and taxes. All these factors combine to increase corporate tax payments about 1.4 percent for every 1 percent increase in the price level.

Social Security tax payments tend to rise point for point with both real economic activity and inflation because they are indexed to the price level and have a proportional rather than progressive rate structure. Unless social insurance tax rates change, these revenues will continue to grow almost exactly as fast as the economy.

Excise taxes, such as those on gasoline, alcohol, and cigarettes, included as "Other" in Table A, are generally levied on a "cents per unit" basis, and so are totally unresponsive to inflation. Sales of goods taxed in this way tend to increase more slowly than the expansion rate of the economy. As a result revenue from these sources does not rise as fast as overall economic activity. All together, however, tax revenues will grow significantly faster than the economy, and this rapid expansion will balance the federal budget if we are at all sensible about spending. The only question is how fast we can expect the economy to grow.

Table B

| | Revenue | | | Difference | |
Year	3.2%	2.7%	Spending*	3.2%	2.7%
1989	$976	$976	1137	–$161	–$161
1994	1425	1386	1382	+43	+4
1999	2100	1982	1752	+347	+230
2004	3115	2853	2142	+973	+711
2009	4649	4127	2880	+1769	+1246

*Data for 1989 from the FY1990 Budget. It shows $971 billion in program spending and $167 billion in interest. Under this scenario the program spending grows with inflation until 1994 and at inflation plus 2 percent thereafter. Interest payments are calculated at 7.6 percent of the outstanding debt and are then added to program spending to get total spending.

Long-term economic projections are chancy, but let us consider two possibilities. The long-term growth of the U.S. economy since the end of World War II, averaging out recessions and expansions, has been 3.2 percent per year. Though there is no reason to expect that we will do better in the future, there is also no reason to expect worse. We might reasonably project an average growth of 3.2 percent over the next twenty years. If we limit our base to more recent years, say from 1981, the peak of the last business cycle, through 1986, which includes the deepest recession we have experienced since the Great Depression, we get an average growth in the economy of only 2.7 percent per year. Projecting that figure forward would produce what we might call the bearish long-term forecast. Table B shows what would happen to revenues with these rates of growth over the next twenty years, assuming inflation continues at the average rate of the past several years, or about 4 percent. In both cases, revenues grow quickly over time, though an increase of just 0.5 percent in average real growth adds $530 billion per year by the twentieth year. This is an important indication of just how sensitive the U.S. budget is to continued economic growth.

To reduce the deficit we do not need to cut spending. But we must show some self-control. After all, the Congress could spend every penny collected in revenue and then some. To illustrate the long-term budget needs of the country, the "spending" column in Table B employs a five-year "flexible freeze" such as President Bush championed during his campaign. The flexible freeze limits spending growth to the level of inflation for five years, then allows real program growth of 2 percent per year. Thus program spending rises at a 4.0 percent annual rate through 1994 and at a 6.1 percent annual rate thereafter. We assume the interest rate on the national debt, which cannot be frozen, will be about 7.6 percent annually.

The Results of Spending Cuts

Table B shows that a tax increase is completely unnecessary. If spending is limited to the growth of inflation until 1994, we will have either a balanced budget (with slow growth) or a $40 billion surplus (with average growth). After 1994, a large surplus arises and begins to grow even though spending is allowed to grow faster than inflation. By 2004 we will be showing annual surpluses of roughly $800 billion and will have paid off the existing national debt.

Of course, this will not happen. Given such enormous revenues, the Congress will try to increase spending. Assuming the freeze holds until 1994, both spending and taxes will be 19.5 percent of GNP in that year. Over the next fifteen years, taxes would automatically grow to between 22.3 and 22.9 percent of GNP. The Congress could drastically increase the size of government and the government's share of the economy if it appropriated all of the extra tax revenue for that purpose.

Instead, the country should insist on a series of tax cuts in the latter part of the 1990s. The $300 billion surpluses forecast for 1999 would easily finance a 15 percent reduction in tax rates across the board. If the entire surplus were applied to reducing the income tax rates in the current code, the bottom rate could be reduced from 15 percent to 10 percent and the top rate lowered from 28 percent to 20 percent. . . .

All of this may seem magical given the headlines about the government's current fiscal crisis. Yet these calculations do not assume any behavioral changes on the part of the public, or any sharp drop in interest rates, or any unusual rate of economic growth. The only magic involved is the magic of normal economic growth compounded year after year, coupled with permanent restraint on the growth of government spending.

Understanding Words in Context

Readers occasionally come across words they do not recognize. And frequently, because they do not know a word or words, they will not fully understand the passage being read. Obviously, the reader can look up an unfamiliar word in a dictionary. By carefully examining the word in the context in which it is used, however, the word's meaning can often be determined. A careful reader may find clues to the meaning of the word in surrounding words, ideas, and attitudes.

Below are statements based on the viewpoints in this chapter. In each excerpt, one of the words is printed in italics. Try to determine the meaning of each word by reading the excerpt. Under each excerpt you will find four definitions for the italicized word. Choose the one that is closest to your understanding of the word.

Finally, use a dictionary to see how well you have understood the words in context. It will be helpful to discuss with others the clues that helped you decide on each word's meaning.

1. Wyoming senator Alan Simpson offers up a whole *PANOPLY* of creative ways to combat the $169-billion deficit—"value-added taxes, additional user fees, taxes on booze and cigarettes . . . all sorts of things!"

   PANOPLY means:

a) board game	c) impressive array
b) organization	d) unrelated group

2. The Export-Import Bank makes loans at below market rates to foreign purchasers of U.S. goods—loans that default at an astounding rate: $4.5 billion of the $12 billion owed the bank is more than ninety days *DELINQUENT.*

   DELINQUENT means:

a) old	c) interest-free
b) overdue	d) absent

3. The Rural Electrification Administration *SUBSIDIZES* utility rates by lending almost $2 billion per year to telephone and electrical cooperatives.

   SUBSIDIZES means:

   a) financially supports   c) regularly reduces
   b) quickly invents   d) interferes with

4. If you are fed up with the *SQUANDERING* of your hard-earned tax dollars, send the message to your representatives in Congress: Let's get serious about cutting the budget!

   SQUANDERING means:

   a) hoarding away   c) wasting
   b) taxing   d) undervaluing

5. Many unnecessary economic problems can be *ALLEVIATED* by more activist government and business policies.

   ALLEVIATED means:

   a) worsened   c) rearranged
   b) lessened   d) destroyed

6. Virtually all of the arguments in favor of urgent action on the current deficit are supported only by the most *TENUOUS* connections between theory and evidence, or are not supported at all.

   TENUOUS means:

   a) flattering   c) ordered
   b) intense   d) flimsy

7. Just as *PACIFISTIC* Democrats make wars, fiscally conservative Republicans have always run up the biggest deficits.

   PACIFISTIC means:

   a) historical   c) peaceable
   b) aggressive   d) wasteful

Periodical Bibliography

The following articles have been selected to supplement the diverse views presented in this chapter.

Nancy Amadei	"Federal Budget Squeeze: Sidelining Human Needs," *Commonweal*, April 19, 1991.
Business Week	"How Do We Measure the Deficit? Let Us Count the Ways," February 18, 1991.
Eleanor Clift and Ann McDaniel	"After You! We Insist!" *Newsweek*, May 21, 1990.
Robert Eisner	"That (Non-) Problem, the Budget Deficit," *The Wall Street Journal*, June 19, 1990.
Bill Frenzel	"They Never Tear the Cuff Links Off Congressmen Who Say No," *The Brookings Review*, Summer 1991. Available from The Brookings Institution, 1775 Massachusetts Ave. NW, Washington, DC 20036.
Joseph C. Goulden	"Smoke Screens Around the Budget Crisis," *The World & I*, January 1991.
David Hage	"Budget Ties That Bind," *U.S. News & World Report*, September 9, 1991.
John B. Judis	"One Thousand More Points of Rhetoric," *In These Times*, February 7-13, 1990.
Rhoula Khalaf	"Lies, Damned Lies, and the Budget Deficit," *Forbes*, December 9, 1991.
Robert Kuttner	"The Fudge Factor," *The New Republic*, June 19, 1989.
Dwight R. Lee and Cynthia D. Lee	"Politics, Economics, and the Destructiveness of Deficits," *The Freeman*, January 1991. Available from The Foundation for Economic Education, Irvington-on-Hudson, NY 10533.
John Miller	"Washington's Magic Act," *Dollars & Sense*, January/February 1990.
John Miller and James Goodno	"Much Ado About Nothing," *Dollars & Sense*, December 1990.
George J. Mitchell	"Federal Deficit," *Vital Speeches of the Day*, October 15, 1990.
Stephen Moore	"All Pain, No Gain," *National Review*, September 9, 1991.
The New Republic	"Beating the System," November 5, 1990.
The New Republic	"Bring Back Big Spending," March 27, 1989.
Rob Norton	"Should You Worry About the Deficit?" *Fortune*, October 7, 1991.
The Progressive	"Budget Burlesque," December 1990.
Louis S. Richman	"Report Card on Bushonomics," *Fortune*, November 4, 1991.

What Kind of Taxation Is Most Appropriate?

ECONOMICS IN AMERICA

Chapter Preface

United States Supreme Court Justice Oliver Wendell Holmes stated in 1904 that "taxes are what we pay for civilized society." Throughout the twentieth century, Americans have indeed used taxes to pay for such diverse services as good roads, public education, medical research, and welfare, and most Americans benefit from some of these services. While few Americans would argue that taxes are completely unnecessary, many question the fairness of America's system of taxation.

Critics of the federal government's tax policies argue that the middle class is paying more than its share of taxes while the wealthy are not contributing enough. These critics cite statistics from the Internal Revenue Service showing that those who earn less than $100,000 annually provide the federal government with 64 percent of its revenue from income taxes, while those making more than $100,000 provide only 36 percent. Frank Riessman, editor-in-chief of *Social Policy*, a progressive journal of opinion, asserts that this situation is unfair. Riessman and others want to increase taxes for the wealthy. He states:

> The wealth tax has the potential of uniting the poor, the working and the middle classes of all colors and persuasions. By reducing the enormous concentration of wealth, a wealth tax would embody a powerful American tradition consistent with an egalitarian society.

Others, such as syndicated columnist and social commentator William F. Buckley Jr., argue that the wealthy are already paying a disproportionate amount of their income in taxes. Buckley predicts that taxing the wealthy even more "will ultimately result in diminished tax revenues for the government," because they will search for tax shelters and other untaxed investments to protect themselves from the increases.

While critics such as Riessman and Buckley propose changes to the tax system, others, such as Rob Norton, writer for the weekly financial periodical *Fortune*, maintain that America's tax system *is* fair. Norton states, "The U.S. tax code is in better shape than critics either on the left or right let on." Norton argues that Americans pay much lower taxes for a higher standard of living than citizens of other world powers, including France, Germany, and Japan.

Whether the U.S. government taxes its citizens fairly has been an issue since the nation's founding. The authors in this chapter debate the merits of our current system.

"It's time to stop sacrificing the economic well-being of the vast majority of Americans and our children's future in order to underwrite the conspicuous consumption of the very rich."

Taxing the Wealthy Would Benefit America's Economy

Robert S. McIntyre

Robert S. McIntyre is the director of Citizens for Tax Justice, an organization in Washington, D.C., that lobbies in favor of the middle class and poor. In the following viewpoint, McIntyre contends that current taxes unfairly burden the middle class. As a solution, he proposes tax reform to increase taxes on the wealthy to provide increased revenue for the government.

As you read, consider the following questions:

1. How does the author characterize the middle-class tax burden?
2. What does McIntyre believe are the benefits of taxing the wealthy at a higher rate?
3. How does the author refute the argument that taxing the wealthy at lower rates improves America's economy?

Adapted from *Inequality and the Federal Budget Deficit* by Robert S. McIntyre. Reprinted with permission of the author and Citizens for Tax Justice.

More and more of our nation's wealth has been dissipated, as we have borrowed against tomorrow to pay for current spending. Less and less of that spending has gone into government programs that benefit average families or into the investments we need—both private and public—to improve our standard of living and to secure our children's future.

At the outset of the 1980s, our government undertook a reckless experiment in what was called "supply-side economics." It might better have been labelled "Borrow and Squander." In the past decade, federal borrowing averaged 4.2 percent of the gross national product, by far the highest sustained level outside of wartime in our nation's history. As a result, we have saddled ourselves and our children with an additional $2 trillion in debt, a large share of which is owed to foreign investors.

The radical build-up of government debt in the Reagan-Bush era is a sharp break from the past. Although budgets have rarely been completely balanced, every post-World War II administration until President Reagan's succeeded in reducing the national debt as a share of the gross national product. (By the end of the 1970s, the debt had dropped to only a quarter of GNP.) But we now face a national debt that exceeds half the GNP—a level unseen since the mid-1950s, when we were still paying off the cost of World War II. (In fact, counting the growing portion of the debt that is owed to the Social Security trust funds, the debt is now approaching a staggering two-thirds of the GNP.)

Redistributing Wealth

Coinciding with the growth in the deficit has been a sharp redistribution of income in favor of the wealthy. Indeed, this growth in inequality—and the strident, often self-righteous unwillingness of those who enjoy new-found riches to pay taxes on their enormous gains—underlies most of the government's deficit problem. . . .

We need to revitalize the American tradition of fairness. The truth is that stemming the tide of inequality is the only fair way, and probably the only politically conceivable way, to reduce the deficit and begin to recover from the irresponsible borrowing binge of the past decade. . . .

To understand that insufficient revenues are at the heart of our deficit dilemma is an important first step in moving toward a solution to that problem. But it is equally critical to recognize *whose* taxes we are talking about. Again, the data are very clear.

Study after study has concluded that despite all the rhetoric about allegedly "across-the-board" tax cuts under President Reagan, taxes have *not* been reduced for most Americans over the past decade and a half. The most thorough analysis comes from the nonpartisan Congressional Budget Office. In a May

1991 report issued by the House Ways and Means Committee, CBO looked at the entire range of federal taxes, including personal and corporate income, social insurance and excise taxes.

- The data show that all but the very richest and the very poorest American families now pay a *higher* share of their incomes in overall federal taxes than they did prior to the so-called "supply-side tax cuts" enacted in 1978 and 1981!

After rising sharply in the first half of the 1980s, taxes on low-income families recently were cut back to slightly below their pre-Reagan level. Except for this overdue relief for the poor, only the best-off 5 percent of the population has enjoyed a reduction in taxes since 1977, with most of the tax cuts concentrated on the richest 1 percent. . . .

In 1977, the wealthiest 1 percent of the population took in 8.7 percent of total pretax income. In 1992, 14.6 percent of total income will be concentrated on this elite group. The *average* pretax income of the richest 1 percent has zoomed from $314,500 each in 1977 (in 1992 dollars) to $675,900 each in 1992—a 115 percent jump. Over the same period, the share of total income going to the bottom four-fifths of all families fell from 53.6 percent to only 47.4 percent.

Changes in After Tax Income

The government's policy of cutting taxes on the rich even as their incomes skyrocketed has made the shift in inflation-adjusted *after-tax* incomes especially striking. For middle- and lower-income families in the first three-fifths of the income scale, after-tax incomes actually declined since 1977. The after-tax incomes of families in the fourth 20 percent grew by only 1 percent over 15 years. *But the after-tax income of the richest 1 percent of the population jumped by a staggering 136 percent!*

What does a 30 percent tax cut for the wealthiest 1 percent of the population add up to? Almost $84 billion in 1992. If instead of showering tax cuts on the rich, Congress had simply kept the tax system as progressive as it was prior to the "supply-side" tax changes of 1978 and 1981 (by adjusting the 1977 system for inflation), then:

- Three-quarters of all families—all but the poorest fifth and the richest 5 percent—would pay lower federal taxes than they do now, and
- The Treasury would collect almost $76 billion more annually in total taxes.

It's hard to imagine raising taxes on three out of four families yet ending up with $76 billion less in 1992 federal revenues, but that is exactly what the tax policies of the past decade and a half succeeded in doing.

Of course, the tax reduction for the very rich was not a one-shot, one-year event. Tax cuts for the wealthy have been a growing cost to the Treasury over the past 15 years, and those tax cuts were paid for with borrowed money.

As we have already seen, the federal government did not have to increase its borrowing rate in the 1980s to pay for additional spending on programs and services. On the contrary, while some kinds of spending—most notably defense—did go up substantially, the overall cost of non-Social Security programs (excluding interest and deposit insurance) actually declined as a share of the GNP from 1980 to 1990.

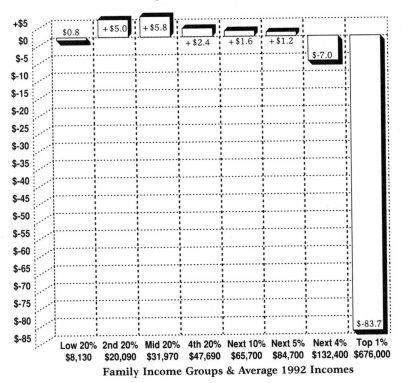

Tax Changes Since 1977 in Billions of Dollars

Actual 1992 Taxes Compared to 1992 Taxes at '77 Rates Adjusted for Inflation

Source: Citizens for Tax Justice, 1991.

But the government did have to borrow—heavily—to pay for the corporate and upper-income tax cuts that it enacted. In fact, if everything else had been the same except for those tax cuts, then government borrowing over the past 15 years would have been more than a *trillion* dollars lower than it actually was.

What does adding more than a trillion dollars to the national debt mean to the annual budget deficit? It means a huge increase in yearly interest payments. In fact, the interest due on the debt built up to pay for previous years' tax cuts for the very wealthy will be $81 billion in 1992.

Thus, the total 1992 cost of the supply-side tax reductions for the richest million families—adding up the $84 billion tax cut that they will enjoy in 1992 and the $81 billion in interest the government must pay on the debt incurred due to the rich's tax cuts in previous years—comes to a staggering *$164 billion!*

Now, from fiscal 1977-78 to fiscal 1992-93, the federal deficit will have almost doubled as a share of the gross national product—from 2.8 percent of the GNP to 5.1 percent of the GNP. That's an increase of $143 billion in fiscal 1992-93.

So the deficit is up by $143 billion, while tax cuts for the wealthy cost $164 billion. Coincidence? Hardly. In fact, the growing cost of tax cuts for the rich closely parallels the growth in the deficit over the entire past decade. In other words, *the tax cuts for the richest 1 percent can explain the entire increase in the size of the federal budget deficit. . . .*

The Rich Really *Are* Rich

We know what lies at the heart of our fiscal and social deficit problems: insufficient revenues—more precisely, the sharp decline in both the corporate income tax and personal income taxes on the richest Americans. And when it comes to revenues, our options are stark:

- We can continue in the spirit of fairness and reform reflected in the 1986 Tax Reform Act, which began to stem the flood of tax breaks to the very rich.
- Or we can search for new ways to raise taxes on middle- and low-income families, who continue to suffer from the tax-shift policies of the past.

The late 1970s and early 1980s showed us that showering tax breaks on the wealthy is not good economic policy. The supply-side promise that tax cuts for the rich (and tax hikes for everyone else) would boost savings and investment was proved false. . . .

Tax Increases

In 1990, Congress resisted the efforts of the Bush administration to raise taxes sharply on middle- and low-income families and to cut taxes even further on the rich. Instead, the deficit reduction act took back another small portion of the wealthy's tax cut, and reduced taxes on the poorest families back to their pre-supply-side level. 1990's act was far from perfect, but on balance it was a positive step forward. Much more remains to be accomplished, however, if we are to restore the level of tax fairness and progressivity that existed prior to the failed supply-side experiment. . . .

The solution to the long-term deficit problem should *not* focus on providing average Americans with an even lower level of public services and public investment. Rather it should be directed at the true cause of the deficit: the huge tax cuts granted to the very richest people.

To be sure, the choices will not be easy. Throughout the 1980s, many analysts warned that the excesses of overborrowing would have to be paid for eventually, but these warnings were largely ignored. Now, however, the time of reckoning is upon us.

Let us then compare the two available approaches on taxes. The regressive strategy, promoted by lobbyists for corporations and the wealthy, would augment the supply-side tax shift by moving to much heavier reliance on sales and excise taxes. A much better choice for most Americans is the progressive alternative. It would move to reverse the tax shift and continue in the spirit of reform, by closing income tax loopholes and raising tax rates on the wealthy.

There are those who recommend big increases in federal excise taxes or adoption of a new European-style national sales tax as the solution to the government's revenue problem. They argue that we need tax policies that will discourage consumption. Of course. That is the whole point of reducing the budget deficit—to shift our priorities more toward investment and less toward current spending. But virtually all tax increases, and many kinds of budget cuts for that matter, will have that effect.

The real issue is: *whose* consumption should be reduced?

Do we want to make it a bit more difficult for wealthy people to buy their second Mercedes-Benz, or do we want to put Plymouths and Chevrolets out of reach for many ordinary American families? Do we want to make it even harder for first-time homebuyers to achieve their dreams, or do we want to put a crimp in the style of people who buy 50,000-square-foot mansions?

The hard truth is that those who push for sales and excise taxes want to curb spending by poor and middle-income families. Those who push for progressive tax changes want to curb consumption by the wealthy. When all is said and done, that is the choice that our nation faces. . . .

The Progressive Alternative

Reversing the supply-side tax shift is not only the fairest way to address the deficit, it's also the most effective. We should keep in mind that, on the bottom line, every 1 percent levy on the incomes of the best-off 10 percent of Americans will add more than $17 billion to government revenues. In contrast, every 1 percent of income painfully extracted from the poorest fifth of all families adds only $1.7 billion a year to tax revenues. If the government is going to ask the American people to make sacrifices to reduce the deficit, it must go where the money is.

Taxing the Rich

During the 1990s, politicians increasing taxes will have to go where the money is—and the upward economic redistribution policies of the Reagan years have drawn a new bull's eye on upper-bracket America.

Kevin Phillips, *Los Angeles Times*, June 24, 1990.

The focus of a fair tax-based deficit-reduction strategy should be to continue in the spirit of income tax reform, by closing unwarranted loopholes that remain in the law and by establishing tax rates sufficient both to pay for the cost of government and to stem the rise in inequality in our country. Three principles should apply:

Principle 1: Take Back Tax Giveaways to the Richest 1 Percent

Since 1977, supply-side tax cuts for the richest million families in our nation have added more than a trillion dollars to the national debt. In 1992 alone, the cost of those tax cuts will exceed $160 billion. The wealthiest people have enjoyed a decade and a half of tax cuts, part of which they invested to make themselves even richer. It's only fair to ask more from those whose after-tax incomes have more than doubled in the past fifteen years.

Principle 2: Protect Middle- and Low-Income Families

After-tax incomes for middle- and low-income families have been stagnant or declining since the late 1970s. Why should people who didn't benefit from the Borrow and Squander eighties foot the deficit bill?

Principle 3: Plug Tax Loopholes

Despite several tax reform acts since 1981, business and investment tax breaks are expected to cost the Treasury $291 billion in corporate taxes and $285 billion in personal income taxes from fiscal 1992 to fiscal 1996. By shutting down remaining tax shelters and loopholes and by increasing the top personal and corporate tax rates, we can promote fairness and achieve real efficiency gains for the economy—while raising the revenues we need to cut the deficit and pay for needed government programs.

Some of the revenue-raising tax reforms that should be adopted include repealing capital gains loopholes, curbing excessive depreciation write-offs, getting multinational corporations to pay their fair share of taxes, ending the tax subsidy for leveraged buyouts and strengthening the Alternative Minimum

Tax on corporations and high-income people.

Income tax rates also should be on the agenda. In 1990, Congress supposedly corrected the notorious backward bend (or "bubble") in the personal tax rate schedule. Previously, the top tax rate rose to 33 percent when the income of a family of four exceeded about $100,000, and then dropped back to 28 percent above $250,000. But in fact, the backward bend remains in the law. Indeed, instead of a "bubble" in the rates, we now have multiple "bubbles" that vary depending on the type of income.

The marginal tax rate on wages, for example, now goes as high as 37 percent before dropping to 32 percent at the top of the income scale. The tax rate on interest and dividends reaches 34 percent for some taxpayers, but falls to 32 percent for the highest earners. Even the capital gains rate faces a "bubble." It hits 31.1 percent for families of four with total incomes between $150,000 and $290,000, before dropping to 28.8 percent for the very richest people (who have most of the capital gains). Asking truly rich people and corporations to pay a higher marginal tax rate than the near rich—say 40 percent—would raise more than $40 billion a year.

Closing loopholes and taxing corporations and the wealthy at higher rates can raise the revenues we need to pay for government, and at the same time reduce economic distortions that sap productivity and long-term growth. Instead of adding to the burdens of ordinary American families, the progressive approach would address the deficit by reversing tax cuts previously granted to the very richest people—those who can most afford to pay. . . .

Ensuring Tax Fairness

The federal deficit did *not* arise due to huge tax cuts for middle-class families and the poor. Far from it—as we have seen, most American families are paying higher federal taxes today than they did 15 years ago. These hard-pressed families, who by and large have watched their wages and incomes stagnate, are not the problem. The budget should not be balanced on their backs.

The ballooning of the federal deficit can be traced, essentially in total, to huge tax breaks granted to the most wealthy Americans over the past decade and a half. These people have watched their incomes and wealth grow by leaps and bounds, even as the nation that defends them, protects them and makes their way of life possible becomes poorer and more indebted by the minute. These are the folks to whom the bill should be sent.

The stakes are high: it's time to stop sacrificing the economic well-being of the vast majority of Americans and our children's future in order to underwrite the conspicuous consumption of the very rich.

> "Shifting the tax burden to upper income
> individuals does nothing to help the truly needy
> in society."

Taxing the Wealthy Would Harm America's Economy

Roy Cordato

In the following viewpoint, Roy Cordato maintains that tax increases for America's wealthiest citizens would decrease consumer spending and decrease the amount of capital available for investment. If taxed more, the wealthy would spend less to save money, Cordato maintains. The wealthy would also borrow less, leaving banks with less capital to invest. As a result, Cordato concludes, tax increases would reduce economic activity and weaken the economy, negating any benefits the middle and lower classes would derive from their decreased tax burden. Cordato is an adjunct faculty member at the Johns Hopkins University in Baltimore, Maryland and an economist for the Institute for Research on the Economics of Taxation (IRET), a Washington, D.C.-based organization that develops and promotes tax policies designed to strengthen the free-market system.

As you read, consider the following questions:

1. According to the author, how would increased taxes for the wealthy affect the middle and lower classes?
2. Why does the author oppose all tax increases?
3. How should America's tax system be reformed, according to Cordato?

Roy Cordato, "The Mirage of Tax Fairness." Reprinted with permission from a *Byline* published March 8, 1991 by the Institute for Research on the Economics of Taxation (IRET) based in Washington, D.C.

During the 1980s debates on tax policy dealt primarily with keeping the tax system from discouraging economic growth. Taxation, it was argued, should not excessively discourage work effort, business activity, saving, etc. This brought about the 1981 tax cuts, the reforms in capital cost recovery (subsequently repealed), and the rate reductions found in the 1986 Tax Reform Act. Implicit in this policy focus is a recognition that wealth creating activities, no matter who undertakes them, always benefit society as a whole and not just those whose income is immediately enhanced.

Fairness Issues

Unfortunately this lesson appears to have been forgotten in recent years. The primary focus of tax policy debates has shifted from concerns about economic growth and prosperity to concerns about "tax fairness" and the relative progressivity of the tax system. Few seem to recognize that all Americans, rich and poor, are likely to be made worse off as the tax system becomes more progressive. The opposition to capital gains tax cuts, the higher taxes on "luxury items," and the higher tax rates on top individual income earners are examples of a "soak-the-rich" mentality that is influencing members of both political parties. The resulting tax changes are detrimental to the economic well being of all citizens. They are also at odds with fairness and justice.

Partly responsible for this tax policy orientation is a wrongheaded view of how the economy works and how wealth is created and distributed. From this view, the economy is similar to a pie whose size, in all dimensions, is fixed. Therefore, one person's slice can be made bigger only by making another person's slice smaller. The fact that in an economy like ours people get ahead by producing and making the pie bigger goes unrecognized. Instead, many policy makers seem to believe that wealthy people get that way only by making others worse off. From this perspective, it is not only acceptable but morally righteous and fair to penalize higher-income Americans through the tax system.

Even within the context of a fixed-pie view of the economy, shifting the tax burden to upper income individuals does nothing to help the truly needy in society—those, who by the very fact of their poverty, are not part of the taxpaying public. Even if a progressive tax system worked as its proponents envision, it would simply be a way of making some taxpayers better off at the expense of other taxpayers. When it is realized that the cost of progressive taxation is a less productive economy, it becomes clear that a soak-the-rich tax policy makes it less likely that the well being of the truly impoverished will be improved at all.

Adam Smith's famous invisible hand is true in reverse. In a free economy, policies that discourage people from pursuing their interests will also harm society as a whole. As an example, take the 10% excise tax on "luxury items." Included in the list of newly taxed items are all leisure boats selling for more than $50,000. At first glance, this may appear to be a soak-the-rich tax policy, and certainly it was touted as such. But take a close look and a different picture appears. This tax discourages the purchase of expensive boats such as yachts, cabin cruisers, etc. The burden of the tax, however, is borne, in large part, by participants in the boat industry. These boats are not built by the rich. The burden of the tax is on all of the non-rich people who make up the industry. Job opportunities in boat building plants, in showrooms, at boat launch sites, etc. are reduced. In the attempt to increase the tax load on the wealthy, an even greater number of non-wealthy members of society are likely to end up worse off. In fact, rich boat purchasers can avoid the tax simply by not buying the boats, but the non-wealthy who work in the industry face no such option in avoiding their hardship.

THE POLITICS OF "FAIRNESS"

WHAT THE GOVERNMENT GETS FROM THE RICH PEOPLE:

WHAT THE POOR PEOPLE GET FROM THE RICH PEOPLE!

Chuck Asay by permission of the *Colorado Springs Gazette-Telegraph*.

As a second example, consider the increase in the top statutory income tax rate. Once again, superficially it appears that high income individuals will bear the burden of this tax change. But once we look past the strictly superficial, another side of the story is revealed.

All income taxation penalizes productive, income generating activity relative to other activities whose rewards are not subject to tax. It also discourages saving and investment relative to consumption. The higher tax rate, the more aggravated these effects become.

The upper income persons whose taxes are hiked are likely to do less in the form of income generating activity. Beyond this, their response to the disincentives of higher taxes have adverse effects on others and will not be confined to those who have to pay the higher tax rates. Few if any of these higher income persons work in isolation. Their efforts are joined with those of others in productive activity. They can succeed in advancing their own economic well being only if their activities result in the production of more goods and services, the discovery of innovative technologies, the marketing of new enterprises, or other growth-generating activities. Where these activities are discouraged by higher taxes, no matter who is targeted, poor and rich alike bear the cost of the forgone output, new and better products, and more efficient production.

Problems with Higher Taxes

Higher tax rates also discourage saving and elevate market interest rates. This raises the cost of capital and, therefore, reduces the amount of capital available for economic growth. The result is lower levels of productivity and fewer jobs. Higher interest rates do not discriminate between the wealthy corporation and the family making $25,000 a year trying to buy their first home. Whether they recognize it or not, everyone pays the price of higher taxes on the well-to-do. In an integrated market economy, it is impossible even to separate out the effects of taxation according to income. Both rich and poor are harmed by all taxation, regardless of who is directly targeted by a particular tax.

Those moralists who advocate soak-the-rich policies are seldom persuaded by economic analysis. The notion that the rich should pay for government, regardless of the benefits they receive, is viewed as a simple case of fairness. Soak-the-rich tax policies, however, are insupportable even from this perspective. Any tax is a penalty on some activity. Since, in a market economy, wealth is a manifestation of successful productive activity, taxes targeted specifically at the wealthy penalize such success. In a society where laws, including the tax code, are supposed to be consistent with individual liberty and equal treatment under the law, such penalties are not only morally unjustifiable but blatantly unfair. Contrary to what many politicians seem to believe, wealth that is obtained through voluntary activities in the market place, does not reduce the well being of others, but enhances it. The acquisition of such wealth is not a moral evil, but a sign of virtue. The pursuit of higher incomes and the productive activity that it inspires should be encouraged by the tax system. To do otherwise is to treat all taxpayers unfairly.

A Fair Solution

During the budget debates of 1990 the focus was on whether the rich should be made to bear the cost of deficit reduction. As it has turned out, there has been no deficit reductions and all new taxes are going to support greater government spending. The real issue with regard to reducing the deficit is whether this goal can be accomplished by any form of tax increase. The consistent pattern has been that the government spends all the revenues that it collects, and then some. The focus of current budget and tax policy debates should not be on who pays the bill but how big that bill should be. Fundamental questions concerning the relationship between the size of government and the economic well being of society need to be addressed, particularly during this time of recession. Concern for a prosperous economy suggests that the cost of deficit reduction should not be borne by the wealth producers in society, i.e., all taxpayers, at all. Taxes, regardless of what groups are directly targeted, cause the economic pie to shrink and all income groups are injured. Reductions in government spending, on the other hand, transfer resources from the public sector to more efficient uses in the private sector. The economic pie grows and everyone is made better off. This is truly the "fair solution."

"The capital gains tax cut truly is fair because of what it will do for the poor—indeed, for everyone in the country."

The Capital Gains Tax Should Be Cut

Jack Kemp

A capital gain is income from the sale of a personally owned asset that has increased in value. This income is taxed through the capital gains tax. In the following viewpoint, Jack Kemp argues that cutting the capital gains tax would benefit America's economy. Such a tax cut would encourage Americans to spend and invest their money, which would benefit business, help create more jobs, and help relieve poverty. Kemp is a former member of the House of Representatives from New York. He was appointed secretary of housing and urban development in 1989 by George Bush.

As you read, consider the following questions:

1. What does the author predict would happen if the capital gains tax is not cut?
2. According to Kemp, why would cutting the capital gains tax be fair to both the rich and poor?
3. Why would the federal government's revenues increase as a result of the capital gains tax cut, according to the author?

Jack Kemp, "Cutting Capital Gains Taxes." Reprinted from *USA Today* magazine, May 1991. Copyright © 1991 by the Society for the Advancement of Education. Reprinted with permission.

As the world hurtles toward democratic freedom, it's ironic that some here in our own country want to move in the opposite direction. Senators Bill Bradley (D.-N.J.) and George Mitchell (D.-Maine) say that their proudest moment was defeating the President's capital gains tax reductions. Congressmen Richard Gephardt (D.-Mo.) and Dan Rostenkowski (D.-Ill.) want to raise taxes on millionaires to "soak the rich" and massively redistribute income.

Democrats seem to be more concerned that some people are getting rich in America than that poor people are falling deeper into poverty as a result of their anti-growth policies. Pres. Bush believes in a different course when he calls for a lower capital gains tax for the nation and its elimination in pockets of poverty we would designate as Enterprise Zones.

Some claim that Democrats will beat Republicans mercilessly with the dreaded "fairness" argument. I say bring it on. As Abraham Lincoln taught us, fairness does not tear down the rich, it forges stronger links between individual human effort and reward; it does not quarrel about dividing old wealth, it concentrates on creating new wealth; it doesn't recognize limits to growth and life as a static, zero-sum condition, it expands opportunities for all people of any color, condition, or background to reach their God-given potential.

Take the Democrats' notion of fairness as equality of result and match it against the Republican principle of equality of opportunity. I have no doubt that Republicans overwhelmingly will be elected today just as Lincoln's party won virtually every election from 1860 to 1932 by drawing a clear dividing line over fairness—rightly understood!

A Fair Tax Cut

The capital gains tax cut truly is fair because of what it will do for the poor—indeed, for everyone in the country. Contrary to the Democrats' claims, cutting the capital gains tax is an overwhelming incentive for small businessmen, especially in our inner cities and among minority entrepreneurs.

Between 1977 and 1982, when the Steiger Amendment reduced the capital gains tax from 49% to 28%, the number of black-owned businesses exploded by nearly 50%—one of the largest gains on record. We need to at least double the number of minority-owned businesses in the next few years. However, it can't be done under the current high capital gains tax rate.

Capital gains taxes could reach 75% or more for long-term assets purchased during the inflation of the 1970s. This is the highest capital gains tax in American history. Faced with a 75% effective bite, most people will not sell their assets, thereby locking up capital in *status quo* companies and current investments.

No one needs new capital more than minorities, who own a tiny portion of Americans' total assets. Cutting capital gains would help free up existing money to fund high-risk enterprises, which create most of the new jobs and business opportunities for poor and minority Americans.

Capital Gains Cuts Benefit All

For most of American history, a low or nonexistent capital gains tax opened opportunity for millions of immigrants to join the mainstream of society. Tragically, just as legal and racial barriers have come down, another wall—the high capital gains tax rate—could condemn today's minorities and poor to yet another chapter of denied opportunity and economic despair. Cutting capital gains is today's pressing civil rights issue.

Chuck Asay by permission of the *Colorado Springs Gazette-Telegraph.*

The Democratic leadership rejects this tax rate reduction because they say it would help the rich and lose revenue. That's not surprising. The Democrat-dominated Congressional committees who control the revenue "black box" always tell us that our tax reductions are costly and unfair and their own special interest programs and budget gimmicks are equitable and beneficial to the Treasury.

Yet, static revenue estimates repeatedly have been proven

false. The truth is that the capital gains tax is largely a voluntary tax for the wealthy. They can avoid paying it simply by not selling their assets. By lowering the capital gains tax, upper-income earners will be more willing to sell their assets and realize their accumulated gains. The government, in turn, will collect far more taxes from the wealthy and lift the tax burden proportionately from the poor and working Americans.

If revenue gurus fully took account of this "unlocking effect," the government would gain revenue from cutting the tax in the short run and upper-income earners would contribute more to the U.S. Treasury. Unlocking of assets is only a one-time phenomenon, the critics counter, and, in the long run, revenues would fall.

The dynamic consequences of cutting capital gains taxes go beyond short-term unlocking. There is also a boost to asset values and a permanent lift to the economy by reducing people's preferences for consumption and increasing their demand for stocks and bonds, farms, factories, real estate, and other investments.

Savings and loan bailout costs also would be reduced, because cutting capital gains taxes would raise the value of the government's real estate holdings. By helping the real estate and financial industries, a reduction in the capital gains tax would aid those economic regions and coastal areas experiencing severe economic difficulties. Astonishingly, the Congressional revenue estimators in the Joint Committee on Taxation don't take these dynamic consequences into account—not the higher assets values, reduced budget outlays for the S&L bailout, stronger tax collections from Federal income or payroll taxes, higher stock prices or real estate values, not even, except in the tiniest, most understated way, the unlocking of trillions of dollars in unrealized capital gains.

Lower Revenues

No wonder the Joint Committee on Taxation calls the capital gains tax a revenue loser. Others, not so tunnel-visioned, assert just the opposite—that it raises revenue. Fiscal Associates, a Washington economics firm, estimates that cutting capital gains would generate anywhere between $25,000,000,000 and $65,000,000,000 over four years. Even economist Allen Sinai—never a strong proponent of tax cuts—has concluded that reducing the capital gains tax would raise Federal revenue approximately $30-40,000,000,000 by 1995.

Our economic future must not be determined by those who told us that the Reagan/Bush tax cuts of the 1980s were a giveaway to the rich and should not have been passed—the same people who lost the debate when Jimmy Carter lost the White House. Because Pres. Reagan and then-Vice Pres. Bush had the courage to tell the zero-sum thinkers to go back to their computers, tax rates were cut; the 1980s economy boomed; inflation came down; and—despite the naysayers—the higher-income earners pulled out of tax loopholes, tax shelters, and tax-exempt bonds and put their money into new taxable investments.

As a result, the rich shouldered a higher portion of the total income tax load; the poor and middle class less. According to recent IRS [Internal Revenue Service] statistics, between 1981 and 1987, the tax burden on the top one percent of taxpayers shot up by nearly 40%; the top five percent paid a 23% greater share; and the top 10% saw their share jump by over 15%. Meanwhile, the lower half's income tax burden fell by about 19%.

Creating Revenue

Every single time that we have cut the capital gains tax rate, revenues have gone up, jobs have increased, and the economy has soared. Now that ought to be good enough to convince those people on Capitol Hill. . . .

I hope that Congress gets on with it and passes our capital gains tax reduction. This is not going to be a drain on the treasury. It will create more jobs and in fact will create more revenue for the federal government.

Dan Quayle, *Human Events*, September 14, 1991.

Many middle- and lower-income families had their total tax bill go up because the payroll tax rose. We can and should remedy that payroll tax hike and also give the economy the stimulus it needs by cutting capital gains. Sinai estimates this would increase GNP [gross national product] by almost three percent, or more than $150,000,000,000; create 2,500,000 new jobs; and boost business capital spending by 1.3%.

Minorities and the poor have the most to lose from the liberal left's anti-growth campaign. The poor most need the jobs, higher incomes, and business opportunities that the capital gains cut would help generate. However, it's not they alone who would benefit.

The states experiencing the greatest budget difficulties and electoral discontent are those which passed major new tax increases. Massachusetts, New York, and New Jersey are obvious and dramatic demonstrations that popular tax revolt is alive and well. As soon as he was elected, New Jersey Gov. Jim Florio carried out a "tax the rich" agenda which created a backlash that nearly cost Sen. Bradley his re-election. So many states have raised taxes recently that a national recession may have resulted as much from state as Federal policy developments.

It's no coincidence that the fiscal condition of many states began to deteriorate steadily after the 1986 law that raised Federal
capital gains taxes. In the 1980s, states enjoyed cumulative surpluses of $10-30,000,000,000. Today, two-thirds of states are in
the red. New York and California, which had large surpluses in
1986, are both facing billion-dollar budget deficits in the 1991
fiscal year.

Ways and Means Chairman Rostenkowski has warned governors and mayors not to expect any additional help from the Federal government in balancing their budgets. "You can't get something from us that we haven't got," he was quoted as saying.

Well, there *is* such a thing as a free lunch! We need a Bush/
Quayle tax cut that will do for the state economies in the 1990s
what the Reagan/Bush tax cuts did in the 1980s. If the capital
gains tax is reduced, not only would the Federal government
gain greater revenues, but states and localities also would reap
revenue windfalls, since the new asset sales pass through state
and local "tax gates" as well as Federal ones. One economic
group with a good track record estimates states would enjoy between a $15,000,000,000 and $40,000,000,000 windfall.

This is not an accountants' squabble. There is a struggle going
on for the heart and soul of the Republican Party, and it can be
stated simply: Is it going to be the party of economic growth, expanding opportunity, entrepreneurial capitalism, and free-market solutions to poverty? Or will it be the *status quo* party that
regards all wealth as fixed, static, and immutable?

Economic Expansion

The 1980s were not built on credit cards, but on record pri-
vate-sector investment in plant, equipment, jobs, and new businesses. Pres. Reagan's policies of tax reduction, sound money,
and less regulation generated the strongest peacetime expansion
on record, created more than 21,000,000 new jobs, launched
over 4,000,000 new businesses, and generated record increases
in real after-tax income for all sectors of our society. While the
nation's gross national product grew by 26.3% between 1983
and 1989, Federal tax revenues expanded by 35.7%, twice as
fast as they did in the 1970s.

The Republican Party's legacy of economic expansion is not
the only thing under attack. Empowerment ideas to fight
poverty are being challenged as new and untried. They are no
more untried than Lincoln's Homestead Act was. There really is
no such thing as the "New Paradigm." There is only the tried-
and-true paradigm of democratic capitalism—the principles of
private property, free markets, and individual incentive on
which America was built.

"A capital-gains tax break would so overwhelmingly benefit the wealthy that it would make the Reagan tax cuts . . . seem progressive by comparison."

The Capital Gains Tax Should Not Be Cut

John Miller

Capital gains, the amount earned from the sale of an asset that has increased in value, are taxed by the government at a higher rate. Cutting the capital gains tax would only provide another tax break for the wealthy, since they are the ones with the assets to sell, according to John Miller in the following viewpoint. Miller argues that such a cut would necessitate a tax increase for the middle-class to compensate for the lost revenue. He concludes that cutting the capital gains tax would be unfair and ineffective. Miller is a member of the Dollars & Sense collective that publishes the monthly socialist journal, *Dollars & Sense*.

As you read, consider the following questions:

1. Instead of cutting the capital gains tax, what does the author propose to do?
2. According to Miller, how would the capital gains tax cut affect America's economy?
3. How does Miller think revenue from capital gains taxes should be used?

John Miller, "Helping the Rich Help Themselves," *Dollars & Sense*, June 1989. Reprinted with permission. *Dollars & Sense* is a progressive monthly economics magazine. First-year subscriptions are available for $14.95 from the office at One Summer St., Somerville, MA 02143.

Only in a supply-side world would a President propose a tax cut in order to increase government revenues. And only in trickle-down America would this President herald the cut as "tax reform" when 64% of the benefits are targeted to the richest 0.7% of taxpayers, while the bottom 60% of taxpayers would receive less than 3% of the largess. Yet this is precisely what George Bush is proposing with his capital-gains tax cut plan.

Defining Capital Gains

A capital gain is income from the sale of a personally owned asset—be it stocks, bonds, real estate, gold, or old paintings—that has gone up in value. Under current laws, effective since the Tax Reform Act of 1986, capital gains are taxed at the same rate as other income. But the Bush administration wants to exempt almost half of some categories of capital gains from taxation, claiming this will spur trading in financial assets, which in turn will lead to growth in tax revenues. Not only that, the Bush team argues that the tax break will trigger more long-term investment, helping to revitalize the economy.

There are a few things wrong here. Most evidence indicates that reducing taxes on capital gains will decrease tax receipts, not boost them. In addition, the tax cut is unlikely to have much effect on long-term investment—and particularly on the productive investments needed to rebuild the U.S. economy. That leaves one reason for the tax cut: to give the rich a bonus. A capital-gains tax break would so overwhelmingly benefit the wealthy that it would make the Reagan tax cuts of the early 1980s seem progressive by comparison.

The Bush administration is right that the capital-gains tax needs reform. But true reform would go in the opposite direction—closing old loopholes, not opening new ones.

The Unkindest Cut of All

Here's how the Bush proposal works. The proposal effectively cuts the capital-gains tax rate from 28% to 15%. Forty-five percent of profits from the sale of most assets held for three years or longer would be excluded from taxation. This means that a wealthy taxpayer with capital gains would pay a 28% tax on only the remaining 55% of the income from their long-term capital gains, or the equivalent of a 15.4% tax rate. Actually, the rate would be "capped" at 15%—the same rate currently charged on the taxable income of the poorest families. In a feeble gesture toward curbing speculation, the tax break would not exempt capital gains on real estate and art objects, nor gains on assets held for less than three years.

Setting a lower effective tax rate for capital gains than for other income is not a new idea: capital gains were taxed at bargain rates continuously from 1921 to 1986. But the 1986 Tax Reform Act marked a significant departure. In return for dramatically lower personal income tax rates, the Reagan administration agreed to tax capital gains as ordinary income. As Vice President, Bush promised Congress that broadening the tax base to include all capital-gains income would provide the necessary revenues to offset the revenues lost from lowering tax rates on the wealthy.

Now, as President, Bush wants to keep the new lower personal income taxes for the rich and to reinstitute the preferential treatment of capital gains. The combination of the two would leave the tax on capital gains at its lowest level since 1942. At the same time, Bush asks us to believe that he can now increase revenues by reversing the very measures he argued earlier were necessary to maintain tax revenues.

Supply-Side Magic

The supply-side rationale behind Bush's revenue claim is simple, if fanciful. The supply-siders claim that if capital-gains taxes are cut, property owners will suddenly begin to sell previously hoarded assets. They point out that currently, there is only one way to beat the capital-gains tax: hold onto your assets until you die. When inheritors sell the property, they only pay taxes on capital gains that accrue after the date of inheritance. So, the argument goes, with gains taxes so high, substantial numbers of wealthy individuals have decided to hold onto their property for life—or at least until the tax rate drops. If the capital-gains tax was lowered, many of them would sell the property to realize the capital gains.

In theory, property owners' increased willingness to cash in on capital gains could boost the total amount of taxable capital gains enough to offset the decreased tax rate. Bush administration projections hold that Treasury revenues would rise by nearly $5 billion in the next year (as capital gains increase 120%) and continue to grow for the following two fiscal years.

But in 1980, when presidential candidate Ronald Reagan made similar claims about the effects of cutting income taxes, George Bush denounced them as "voodoo economics." And today, almost no one outside the Oval Office agrees with the Bush administration's projections. If asset owners don't sell more, the annual loss to the Treasury from the tax cut would be $17 billion—increasing the projected deficit by almost one-fifth—and few tax experts believe that they'll sell enough to wipe out this loss.

For instance, two major non-partisan institutions of Congress examined the effects of the proposed changes in the capital-gains tax. The Congressional Budget Office estimated that the Bush scheme could lose from $4 billion to $8 billion a year. The Joint Congressional Committee on Taxation projected that while the proposal would raise revenues the first year, it would lose

$13.3 billion over five years.

The history of capital-gains taxation offers confirmation that asset-owners' responsiveness to tax changes is not strong enough to justify Bush's optimistic revenue claims. After Jimmy Carter and a Democratic Congress lowered capital-gains taxes in 1978, stock sales rose in 1979, only to decline in 1980. And since 1986, when capital-gains taxes rose from 20% to 28%, capital gains have not decreased, but rather increased by more than 15% in nominal terms.

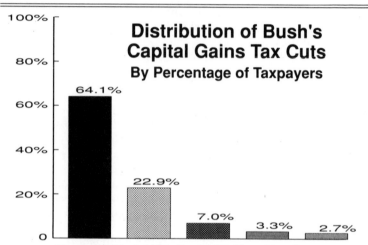

Distribution of Bush's Capital Gains Tax Cuts
By Percentage of Taxpayers

Source: Citizens for Tax Justice.

The Bush administration asserts that in addition to enhancing government revenues, a tax break on capital gains would revive long-term investment in the 1990s—this time by affecting how the wealthy act as buyers. Lower taxes on capital gains would increase investors' rate of return, encouraging more investment and contributing to higher growth rates in the decade ahead. Because the tax cut applies only to gains on property held for three years or more, it allegedly would lengthen the planning horizon of investors. And with lower capital-gains taxes, owners of stocks supposedly would become more active traders, supplying capital to new, more productive uses.

But many in the business world find these arguments almost as far-fetched as the supply-side revenue claim—and progressives have even less reason to accept them. *Business Week* editorialized, "The issue is how to guide [the money of large institutional investors] into long-term investment. . . . It won't be easy, but tinkering with the capital-gains rate is like pouring buckets of water on a burning house." Other business interests have expressed alarm that cutting the capital-gains tax rate would lead to investment guided by tax avoidance, rather than by market conditions.

Instead of taxing capital gains at a lower rate than ordinary income, *Business Week*, the *Los Angeles Times*, and others have argued that investment can better be stimulated by adjusting capital gains for inflation before taxing them. They contend that inflation has discouraged long-term investment by forcing investors to pay taxes not only on profits but also on capital gains generated by inflation. With inflation indexing, investors would pay taxes only on their "real" capital gains, not on inflation.

Effects of Capital-Gains Taxes

From a progressive viewpoint, both the Bush plan and the inflation-indexing alternative fall short as ways of encouraging productive investment. For one thing, both proposals overstate the influence of capital-gains taxation on new investment. These tax-cutting proposals seek to spark new investment by making new stock issues more attractive to investors. But the vast majority of stock sales affected by capital-gains taxes are not new issues but resales of existing stock, which generate no new investment. Furthermore, stock issues finance only a small fraction of new investment. In the 1970s and 1980s less than 10% of the money corporations raised from outside sources has come from selling stock. Even *Business Week* concludes that "the real problem in venture capital" is not that potential investors are deterred by the high tax rate on gains, but rather that there is "too much money chasing too few opportunities."

Since tax changes have limited effects on the volume of investment, the important question is whether they help to redirect the investment. Cutting capital-gains taxes across the board does nothing to direct capital to productive uses—such as plant, equipment, infrastructure, or education. But cutting capital-gains taxes selectively could affect the character of investment. By denying the capital-gains exemption to income from the sale of non-productive property, the capital-gains tax could discourage financial speculation and direct investment toward more productive uses.

While cutting capital-gains taxes is unlikely to increase government revenues or do much for investment, it will certainly succeed in redistributing income—to the rich. Capital gains go almost entirely to the wealthy. The wealthiest 5% of all taxpayers receive 85% of capital gains; the richest .7% of taxpayers receive 70% of capital gains. Five of every six taxpayers with incomes of more than $1 million a year have capital-gains income, but fewer than one in every 20 taxpayers earning $10,000 or less have it.

Thus, cutting capital-gains taxes amounts to what Robert McIntyre, Director of Citizens for Tax Justice (CTJ), calls a "bonanza for the wealthy." CTJ estimates that about two-thirds of the benefits of the Bush cut would go to the richest 685,000 people in the nation, or less than 1% of taxpayers. These taxpayers, all with incomes over $200,000, would receive an average tax cut of about $25,000. For the 80% of families earning less than $60,000 a year the average tax savings from the Bush plan would be only $20.

The one-sided distributional effect of cutting capital-gains tax is reinforced in the Bush proposal by the fact it does not apply to the sale of homes, which qualified for the capital-gains exemption prior to 1986. As a sop for the less fortunate, the Bush proposal would allow families with taxable income of less than $20,000 to sell their homes tax free.

The Nation's Future

A capital gains tax cut hurts rather than improves the Nation's future, because the resulting revenue loss forces the Government to borrow and use up far more private savings than can be stimulated by the tax cut. This leaves the Nation further short and further behind our historic savings rate, our needs for the future and our international competitors. It is time to reject the delusion that more revenues can be raised by cutting taxes.

Leon Panetta, September 28, 1989.

A more progressive tax policy would stiffen taxes on capital gains, not cut them. . . .

Even some investors and economic theorists support such policies. Fifty years ago, John Maynard Keynes, the economist whose theories underpin much of modern economic policy, favored "a substantial securities transfer tax" to mitigate "the predominance of speculation over enterprise in the United States." On Wall Street today, Warren Buffet, the head of Berkshire Hathaway and arguably the most successful securities investor in America, favors "a confiscatory 100% tax on short-term capital gains"—taxing away all short-term gains to remove the incentive for speculation.

Increasing short-term capital-gains taxes has also found support in state and local governments. Since 1973, Vermont has imposed a short-term capital-gains tax on land sales in an attempt to slow the pace of development. Rhode Island also recently considered taxing short-term capital gains on real estate in order to curb housing speculation.

Both the Rhode Island bill, defeated by fierce opposition from the real-estate lobby, and the Vermont law contain several features that could be adopted in a progressive national capital-gains tax:

• To favor long-term investment, impose higher taxes on short-term capital gains, not lower taxes on long-term gains as Bush proposes.

• Define the short term in several different gradations subject to different tax rates, including near-confiscatory rates for the shortest term and most likely speculative investment. The Rhode Island tax proposal defined the short term to be 5 years and imposed tax rates ranging from 80% for six-month investments to 15% for investments held the full five years. The Vermont law has a similar feature and also mandates a tax rate that increases with the amount of profit, similar to the income tax.

• Specify the type of investment subject to the short-term capital-gains tax, directing the flow of investment away from speculative activity. The Rhode Island bill applied only to non-owner-occupied housing, exempting owner-occupied residences from the short-term gains tax.

• Use the revenues from the short-term capital-gains tax to fund domestic spending or non-speculative public investment. In the Rhode Island bill, tax revenues were to go to a neighborhood preservation fund.

Progressive Tax Policies

Unlike the Bush proposal, these progressive alternatives would promote equality, raise revenues, and strengthen the economy. The burden of a beefed-up capital-gains tax would fall chiefly on those with incomes above $200,000, the same people who benefited most from the Reagan tax cuts. Furthermore, such a tax could be the first step toward a more explicit and progressive industrial policy, cooling speculation and directing investment into needed areas. Selective tax rates could guide resources into more socially worthwhile investments, such as education. Finally, the revenues raised from the capital-gains tax would provide funds to restore the cuts in domestic spending, or to reduce the budget deficit, or even to fund investment in publicly-owned industry. Instead of Bush's thinly disguised giveaway to the wealthy, we could have a capital-gains tax policy that would actually do us all some good.

"Tax rates can be cut further during the 1990s, and dramatically. To stop now and rest on our laurels would be to disregard the fundamental lessons of the 1980s."

America's Economic Future Depends on Lower Taxes

Lawrence Lindsey

The following viewpoint is excerpted from Lawrence Lindsey's book, *The Growth Experiment*. In it, Lindsey discusses the legacies of the Reagan Administration's economic policies, including the astonishing economic growth that resulted from Reagan's tax reform policies. Lindsey argues that policies such as reducing the capital gains tax and applying a flat tax rate will provide a basis for solid economic growth into the twenty-first century. A Harvard University economist and author, Lindsey worked for the White House Office of Policy Development and served on Reagan's Council of Economic Advisers.

As you read, consider the following questions:

1. How would tax reform and reduction affect government spending on social programs, according to the author?
2. What effect does Lindsey believe his proposed reforms would have on the middle class?
3. According to Lindsey, how will tax reform complement the tax reductions he proposes?

Excerpts from *The Growth Experiment* by Lawrence Lindsey. Copyright © 1990 by Lawrence Lindsey. Reprinted by permission of Basic Books, a division of HarperCollins Publishers.

Why do we need another round of tax reform? During the 1980s, we had a new tax bill almost every year. Hasn't there been enough tinkering? Things are going pretty well with inflation down and the economy up. Why not leave well enough alone?

We need another round of reform because with all we have learned we can do better, and so can our competitors around the world. The experiments of the 1980s have taught us a set of lessons about what works. Those lessons were hard learned and a lot of political blood has been spilled in their behalf. It would be wrong to waste them. No country yet has taken all the lessons of the 1980s to their logical conclusions, reaping their full benefits. We can and should. We've earned it.

No More Soaking the Rich

Punitive taxation is dead, in theory. Only a few vestigial redistributionists cling rhetorically to the notion that we should soak the rich. Yet the United States still imposes punitive tax rates. Because the government continues to tax the illusory profits of inflation, which remains at 3-6 percent, the effective tax rate on real interest income is well over 50 percent. It approaches 100 percent for taxpayers who keep their money in traditional savings accounts.

We still levy a hefty marriage penalty tax, in the thousands of dollars, on two-income families. The effective tax rate on a welfare mother seeking to join the labor force and establish a decent life for herself and her children often exceeds 100 percent. Entrepreneurs, and the people who back them in risky ventures also face punitive tax rates. The government will share richly in their success, but not their failure. Punitive tax rates are still levied on those Americans who do the most to help our economy work harder and work smarter.

Ordinary taxpayers face tax rates that are still too high, although lower than they were a decade ago. Middle-class families earning roughly $50,000 face marginal tax rates of roughly 40 percent: 28 percent federal, 7.5 percent for Social Security, and 5 percent for state taxes. For most of history a 40 percent rate on the middle class would have been considered an unconscionable tyranny.

The 28 percent federal rate alone is a hefty burden. Consider that 28 percent means that 11.2 hours in a taxpayer's 40 hour work week, all day Monday plus Tuesday until lunch, are devoted to work for the federal government. For someone who goes to work just out of college, at age twenty-two, and retires at age sixty-five, it means working purely for the federal government for a bit over twelve years, say from age twenty-two to age thirty-four or from age fifty-three to age sixty-five. It means that to buy a $15,000 car a taxpayer must earn $20,800. To pay $750 rent one must earn $1,040. All this just to cover federal income tax.

If it were impossible for us to do better and still raise enough revenue to pay for the legitimate functions of government, we would have an excuse for these burdensome and damaging levies. But tax rates can be cut further during the 1990s, and dramatically. To stop now and rest on our laurels would be to disregard the fundamental lessons of the 1980s.

LURIE'S BU$INE$$ WORLD

Lurie, © 1990 Cartoonews, Inc. Reprinted with permission.

We have learned that well-designed savings plans can help increase national saving. The IRA program of the early 1980s was a tremendous success in promoting long-term savings. Sharply restricting it, as we did after 1986, was a serious mistake. The program should rather be broadened and made more efficient, so that all Americans can take part. The true revenue consequences of such a plan are much lower than the apparent upfront revenue costs.

We have learned that the 28 percent capital gains tax rate is too high. It loses revenue, hampers entrepreneurship, and blunts national competitiveness. It is punitive in the true sense of the word, kept high out of envy and demagoguery, and it punishes everyone: the taxpayer, the government, and the economy.

We have learned that ever increased spending on government social programs has had very little effect, and that private philanthropy might do a better job. The tax system offers a way of increasing private social spending by much more than $1 for every $1 forgone in tax revenue. The charitable deduction can be an efficient means of providing funds to the most efficient providers of public services.

We have learned that any tax increase will collect less revenue than it purports to, because it distorts individual behavior and reduces economic activity. Conversely, we have learned that almost any tax cut will reduce revenue by less than static-revenue assumptions suggest. Equally important, we have learned that other nations have learned the same lessons. They are applying those lessons to streamlining their economies to make themselves more competitive during the 1990s.

It would be a shame not to benefit from our education. The risks of applying our knowledge are extremely low: We are not gambling with new ideas as we were in the eighties. The risks of standing pat are much greater. We risk squandering all that we have learned, even as our competitors take advantage of our experience. By applying the lessons of the 1980s in another round of tax reform, further reducing rates, increasing incentives, and ending tax distortions that reduce efficiency and waste resources, we can keep our role as the leader of the world economy.

Tax Reductions

To see how much further we can go in reducing tax rates and tax distortions, consider the following tax reform package. Though we will not play out all the calculations here (they would fill a small book), it happens to produce as much revenue with roughly the same distribution of tax payments as the current income tax even without a behavioral response by taxpayers. The one important exception is that this suggested reform substantially reduces the tax burden on low- and moderate-income families with children. The new tax code would:

• Levy a single flat tax rate of 19 percent on all taxable income (including capital gains), substantially increasing the rewards of work, saving, and investment.

• Raise the basic zero-tax threshold much higher than current law:

$12,000 for married couples

$6,000 for single individuals

PLUS: a $5,000 exemption for each dependent under age three; a $3,000 exemption for each dependent over age three.

AND: a substantially liberalized child care credit. These increased exemptions and credits will ease the presently onerous tax burdens on families with children. Besides broadening options for families, better child care should provide long-term benefits to the economy.

• Give low- and moderate-income taxpayers effective use of homeowner and other deductions now effectively available only to upper-income taxpayers.

• Index all interest and capital gains income for inflation, restraining the government from taxing illusory profits and encouraging entrepreneurship and investment.

• Allow all taxpayers a deduction for charitable contributions, with a double deduction for contributions over 5 percent of income, establishing a new social standard—the half-tithe—for all Americans to strive for.

• Establish an Individual Savings Account program with deductible contributions of up to $5,000 for each worker in the family, raising the national savings rate, helping finance business investment, and helping Americans provide for retirement, education, and health expenses.

More Tax Reduction Needed

The Reagan boom of the 1980s was the greatest economic expansion this country has ever had. Eight straight years of economic growth. Inflation down. Interest rates down. Almost 20 million new jobs created. The driving force behind this unprecedented economic growth was the reduction of personal income tax rates. The top marginal rate was 70 percent when Reagan was elected in 1980; when he left office it was 28 percent. There is still room for more reductions. . . .

Our immediate economic policy goal should be to reduce personal income taxes by 5 percent. We can "pay" for that nice healthy cut—without increasing the deficit—with a slightly more than 2 percent reduction in federal spending. With the exception of interest, virtually no spending is "uncontrollable." What Congress has wrought, Congress can change. We need to tackle federal spending and taxes with the same ferocity, skill, and determination that we used on Saddam Hussein.

Martin Anderson, *Policy Review*, Spring 1991.

So far we have been reducing tax obligations. For the most part these reductions will be net revenue losers, though in practice there would be some revenue feedbacks from the demand, supply, and pecuniary effects of rate reductions. We have ignored such effects here because the positive revenue effects of cutting the top rate from 33 to 19 would be very small compared to the positive effects of cutting the top rate from 70 to 50 or even from 50 to 33. We would pay for these reductions by a series of changes that recover the lost revenue while eliminating burdensome inefficiencies in the old tax code, reducing the excess burden of achieving our revenue goals. These additional changes would:

• Establish a cash flow corporate income tax. Allow immediate expensing of all new business investment in a cash flow business income tax, offset this with an elimination of the interest deduction, restoring powerful and balanced incentives for genuinely productive new business investment without subsidizing marginal or even wasteful investments.

• Expand the tax base to include all forms of labor compensation, including fringe benefits. This single change will bring in enough revenue to offset nearly two-thirds of the losses above, yet the net burden on workers will be minimal because of the dramatic reduction in tax rates. Moreover, as this change prompts labor contracts to offer more cash and fewer benefits workers will benefit from the efficiency of being paid in cash and shopping for their own benefits. The cost of some benefits should drop as providers are exposed to stiffer, tax-neutral competition for workers' dollars.

• Place limits on the deductibility of certain items, such as state taxes, limiting use to taxpayers in need and ending abuse by upper-income taxpayers.

• Limit the homeownership deduction to $10,000 of real interest payments and property taxes for a married couple and $5,000 for a single taxpayer, ending tax subsidies for mansions and reducing housing inflation.

• Eliminate the standard deduction, superfluous under this plan because of the vast increase in personal and dependent exemptions and because all taxpayers will have full access to itemized deductions. . . .

Tax Reform

The complexities introduced in Form 2000 have a twofold purpose: reducing tax rates and curbing inefficient tax shelters that waste precious resources of labor and capital as well as losing revenue. The two go hand in hand. The evidence from the early 1980s shows that simply reducing the tax rate lures income and capital out of hiding, and may actually enhance tax revenue. But this happens most dramatically when rates are cut from very high levels. At the current 33 or 28 percent rates, a lot of money has already come out of the closet. A reduction to 19 percent will not coax out much more or produce big revenue feedbacks. So in addition to reducing rates we must explicitly limit or even abolish some tax shelters in order to get both enough revenue and greater efficiency for the economy. Form 2000 does just that: It trades off lower rates for limits on tax shelters.

The first big trade-off is that we sharply reduce the effective tax rate on capital income, but make it nearly impossible for taxpayers who receive net capital income to avoid paying taxes. As previously noted, the effective tax rates on capital income are far higher than the statutory 28 or 33 percent maximum rates, because the tax code taxes nominal capital income, not real capital income. Form 2000 both cuts the rate to 19 percent and limits taxation to real interest and real capital gains income. In return, the personal exemptions and most personal deductions are limited to earned income and transfer income. Taxpayers with net capital income must therefore pay taxes. In effect, we encourage investors and entrepreneurs, who generally come from the ranks of the well-off, to do their best for themselves and the economy, but deny their capital income tax benefits designed for working people. . . .

Reduced Taxes, Reduced Spending

I have long favored cutting federal taxes at any time in any way and in any manner whenever the opportunity strikes. This applies to fiscal year 1991, fiscal year 1992, and fiscal year X. The reason is that the real problem for the nation is not the deficit but excessive governmental spending. Government spends whatever the tax system will raise plus the largest level of deficits that the nation will tolerate. Cutting federal taxes is the only effective way of cutting government spending.

Milton Friedman, *Policy Review*, Spring 1991.

The worldwide move to more or less free markets has just begun. Tax reform, and particularly tax rate reduction, has been integral to that liberating process—probably the most important part of it. It too will continue worldwide. As with any revolution in technique, however, the easiest gains come first. The tremendous reduction in the top marginal tax rate in the United States, from 70 percent at the start of the decade to 33 percent at the decade's close has exploited most of the potential for improving incentives by rate cuts alone. Nor can there be much more revenue feedback from rate cuts alone. Except for some specific taxes, such as capital gains, the American tax system is today clearly on the correct side of the revenue maximization curve.

The Kennedy tax cuts, which reduced the top rate from 91 percent to 70 percent, were universally hailed as a success and Reagan's reductions, while not as universally acclaimed, were clearly successful. But there are no further improvements to be had by taking a meat axe to the existing rate structure. Future tax reform will require more skill and more attention to detail. We have gained the skill and learned the details. What we need now is the political courage and perseverance to create a tax system that liberates economic energy, not enervating envy; a tax system that puts people before political pandering; a tax system that will keep America great in the 1990s and beyond.

"We can survive the next 50 years despite the drag of these rising budgets and these terrible taxes."

America's Economic Future Does Not Depend on Lower Taxes

Herbert Stein

Herbert Stein is a senior fellow at the American Enterprise Institute for Public Policy, a Washington, D.C. think tank that studies a wide variety of economic and public policy issues. Stein has served as a member of President Reagan's Economic Policy Advisory Board and as the editor of *The American Enterprise*, the bimonthly journal published by the American Enterprise Institute. In the following viewpoint, Stein argues that America's economy has grown dramatically during the twentieth century despite significant increases in both government spending and tax rates. Stein maintains that there is no economic crisis in the offing because as need for even greater government expenditures becomes apparent, taxes will increase to offset these needs.

As you read, consider the following questions:

1. How does the author support his claim that government spending and taxation do not hinder overall economic growth?
2. According to Stein, why must taxes and government spending increase?

Excerpted from *Tax Policy in the Twenty-First Century* by Herbert Stein, © 1988 by Philip Morris Companies Inc. Reprinted by permission of John Wiley & Sons, Inc.

Nobody is looking forward with great eagerness to being taxed in the 21st century. But as the need for revenues increases—and it will increase—obtaining them will be increasingly difficult, and that leaves the question of what's going to give. The common, if not quite universal, conclusion is that we are going to be living with increasingly unsatisfactory taxes.

Revenues Must Increase

I must explain what I mean by the increasing "need" for revenues. I think there is a general presumption that without radical changes of policy and attitudes, which most economists do not foresee, expenditures will rise relative to our national incomes. Three sources of this rise are foreseen.

First, there are the costs of the aging of the population—the pension costs and the health costs. Second, there are the growing interest burdens that we foresee, as the ratios of debts to national income and gross national product rise. Third, there is something commonly labeled egalitarianism, which more broadly means, I suppose, the general political pressures.

Almost no one, so far as I can see, wants this increase in spending. We speak of it with despair and disdain, as very nearly inevitable and totally unfortunate. Hardly any case is made for more spending on education and health and infrastructure in order to increase productivity. Almost no one speaks about the need to spend money to defend Western civilization, which is certainly an important consideration.

Some people foresee some change in attitudes towards government which would slow down this trend of expenditures. But the expectation of a change in attitudes seems to be a minority view. So is a position that foresees a rise in affluence by itself tending to reduce the demand for government services relative to our incomes.

Reducing the Deficit

The need for more revenues will result not only from the trend of rising expenditures but also from the need to reduce deficits. In many countries, deficits are big enough to raise the ratio of debt to GNP. As economists are fond of saying, this cannot go on forever. And as I have said—this is Stein's first law—if something cannot go on forever, it will stop. This does not mean that it cannot go on throughout the 21st century. But presumably at some point in the 21st century, there will be a desire or a need to reduce deficits, and that will require revenues to rise more than expenditures.

This brings me to the other side of the equation: the difficulty of raising revenues. Most people assume that raising revenue relative to the national income will require raising taxes. That is, we cannot raise revenues by cutting taxes. If this assumption were incorrect, if we could raise revenue by cutting taxes, the future would look much brighter and easier. But few believe this is so.

To say that raising taxes is difficult can mean any of three things. First, that it is administratively difficult; second, that it has adverse economic consequences; and third, that it is politically unattractive.

Fair Taxes

While taxes should not be confiscatory, they at least should present the perception of fairness. Nevertheless, I am not overly troubled. Tax reform will be followed by revenue enhancement. Who can be so unpatriotic as to wish not to pay an additional percent or two to help reduce our Federal deficit—especially, in the name of progressivity, at the higher levels? It *will* happen. Read *my* lips.

Jeff A. Schnepper, *USA Today*, September 1989.

Several reasons are adduced for thinking that further tax increases will become increasingly difficult in all of these senses. First, there must be some law of increasing marginal costs. It hurts more to raise a 50 percent rate to 51 than to raise a 25 percent rate to 26, because the percent change in after-tax incomes is greater in the first case.

Second, international integration of business and international resource mobility increase the difficulty of raising taxes. From the standpoint of business, higher rates increase the damage from the double taxation and the inconsistencies that exist in a system in which businesses operate in more than one jurisdiction. From the standpoint of government, international competition limits the rates that can be charged.

Third, various structural changes domestically will make taxation more difficult. As our economies advance, an increased share of total income will come from capital, which is more difficult to tax than labor income, mainly because of measurement and timing problems. The increased flexibility of the financial organization of businesses enhances the ability to escape some kinds of taxes. . . .

New Kinds of Taxes

Some have suggested that we can reduce the costs of raising taxes, or reduce the adverse consequences, by several kinds of tax changes. The income taxes could be reformed by broadening their base. Reliance on income taxes, especially on the taxation of income from capital, could be reduced by more reliance on a broad-base consumption tax, or expenditure tax. A value-added tax has numerous proponents in the countries that do not already have it—the United States and Japan. International agreements could harmonize accounting standards and reduce the likelihood of double taxation and the influence of tax differences on the location of business. International coordination could reach agreement on tax levels and limit the erosion of revenue by international competition. And there could be more reliance on user charges and effluent fees.

A minority view presents some doubts about whether such reforms of the tax system would have any significant economic effect. What really counts, it is claimed, is the average rate of taxation, or even more, the level of total spending, which will not be reduced by tax reform.

There is even more doubt about the political feasibility of these reforms. This seems to be especially acute with respect to matters that require international agreement. Many people find it difficult to envision any substantial submergence of national sovereignty about taxes. Also, public opinion in Japan and the United States does not seem to be receptive to broader-based consumption taxes, such as the value-added tax, although the tax's proponents hope that opinion about them will change in time.

A provocative question that is occasionally raised is whether tax reform would be desirable if it could be achieved. The argument is that the "badness" of taxation and international competition both serve to limit the amount of taxation and, therefore, the growth of government, which is the real evil to be feared. But I suppose most economists have too much of a stake in preaching tax reform to be willing to entertain the notion that tax reform might be a bad thing.

The Prospect of More Taxes

But what is to be said about the gloomy predictions that we are going to live for a long time with more expenditures than we would like, financed by more and worse taxes than we would like?

I would make two observations. First, there has been little attempt to estimate how much difference this all makes. It would be important to know whether we are expressing an aesthetic preference for small budgets and neat tax systems, or whether the differences we are talking about matter seriously. In another connection, I have made a simple comparison of the performance of the United States economy in the 40 years since the end of World War II, which was a period of high budgets and high taxes, to the 40 years before 1929, which was a period of much lower taxes and budgets, relative to national incomes. I found, to my surprise, that in this period of high budgets and high taxes the economy has grown as rapidly in total GNP, per capita GNP, and productivity—in the usual measures of economic performance—as it did in the period of much smaller budgets and lower taxes. This suggests to me a certain warning against drawing weighty conclusions about the performance of the economy as government grows.

I would also refer to a study by Angus Maddison of Groningen University in The Netherlands, covering the growth experience of the United States, the Western European countries, and Japan over a fairly long period. Professor Maddison shows that in the 25 years or so after World War II growth was much higher in all of these areas than in the preceding 50 years or so, when governments had been smaller and taxes lower.

New and Necessary Taxes

There is no way to bring the Federal deficit down to an acceptable level without new taxes.

The politics of new taxes may be difficult, but the economics are easy. . . .

The days of lip reading and even mumbling about taxes are over. So why keep it a secret that we can raise taxes and economic performance at the same time?

Lawrence Summers, *The New York Times*, July 23, 1991.

Of course, since 1973 rates of growth have declined, and there has been a general deterioration of economic performance as it would ordinarily be measured. But in most cases—the United States is an exception—performance has been superior to what it was in the earlier days, when budgets were smaller and taxes lower.

Avoiding Europe's Problems

A good deal of attention has been paid to the very weak performances of European economies in the last 10 or 15 years, difficulties that are commonly associated with tax systems, budgets, and related variables. We should be aware, however, that this attribution is disputed, and we still know very little about what moves the big aggregates of our economies.

Growth washes out a lot of other problems, as a little experiment will show. Let us assume that per capita income before tax will rise by 1 1/2 percent per annum for 50 years, which would approximately double before-tax income. And let us suppose that during this period, taxes rise from 25 percent of before-tax income to 35 percent of before-tax income. We find that per capita income after tax still rises by 70 percent in that period. Apparently, we can survive the next 50 years despite the drag of these rising budgets and these terrible taxes. Except for the youngest among us that must be some comfort.

A second, more serious point is that even if these predicted trends have serious consequences, we should not feel hopeless about the possibility of changing the trend. Economists and a lot of other people these days seem to be in the grip of a very pessimistic view of public policy. This has something to do with public-choice theory. We are a bit obsessed with the notion that public policy is determined by pressure groups, politicians, and bureaucrats who, unlike us economists, are all very selfish, short-sighted, and unresponsive to considerations of the long-run national interest.

Impact of Crises on Policies

While this notion may often be accurate, there are critical points at which it seems not to have been correct. There are some cases in which talking, writing, thinking, and ideas have made some difference. It seems to me unquestionable that the Keynesian revolution in economic thinking made a difference. (Now many people are unhappy about the difference it made, but the important point is that it made a difference.) More recently, the revival of thinking and writing about the virtues of the free-market system has had an influence on policy in the United States and elsewhere.

In both of these cases, the influence of thinking on policy was certainly accentuated or facilitated by a present crisis. There was the crisis of the Great Depression. In the 1970s, there was a much smaller crisis, but nevertheless an acute concern, about inflation. The question is really whether we are capable of exercising any forethought about policy as applied to some date out there 50 years from now when we are not face to face with a crisis. Can we adapt our policies to concerns whose consequences will not be felt for quite a long time? That, of course, is a more difficult question, but I do not think you can be entirely negative about it, either.

We do see, at least in the United States and in many other countries, that we go on spending large amounts for national defense as security against some danger that is certainly not imminent and whose timing we cannot see but that we know we have to do something about now. The United States and many other countries have invested fairly large amounts in aid to foreign countries, where the benefits to us were remote in both time and proximity for a considerable period. In most countries, the increase of the ratio of debt to GNP (aside from war) is a fairly recent phenomenon. We do see in the political process a good deal of what we would call responsibility about that. So I do not think it would be appropriate or even permissible for us to accept as inevitable too many gloomy predictions.

Our need is to try to make these predictions as vivid and believable as possible, so that they will have some effect on policy. And I think we should regard the more worrisome thoughts as warnings, rather than predictions, of what is going to happen.

Distinguishing Between Fact and Opinion

This activity is designed to help develop the basic reading and thinking skill of distinguishing between fact and opinion. Consider the following statement as an example: "The tax on capital gains is 28 percent." This is a fact that could be checked by calling the Internal Revenue Service. But the statement "The capital gains tax should be reduced" is an opinion. Many people may favor increasing the tax to increase revenue and decrease the deficit.

When investigating controversial issues it is important that one be able to distinguish between statements of fact and statements of opinion. It is also important to recognize that not all statements of fact are true. They may appear to be true, but some are based on inaccurate or false information. For this activity, however, we are concerned with understanding the difference between those statements that appear to be factual and those that appear to be based primarily on opinion.

Most of the following statements are taken from the viewpoints in this chapter. Consider each statement carefully. *Mark O for any statement you believe is an opinion or interpretation of facts. Mark F for any statement you believe is a fact. Mark I for any statement you believe is impossible to judge.*

If you are doing this activity as a member of a class or group, compare your answers with those of other class or group members. Be able to defend your answers. You may discover that others come to different conclusions than you do. Listening to the reasons others present for their answers may give you valuable insights into distinguishing between fact and opinion.

> O = *opinion*
> F = *fact*
> I = *impossible to judge*

1. Income taxes for middle-class families rose during the 1980s.

2. America's national debt exceeds $2 trillion.

3. Between fiscal year 1977-78 and fiscal year 1992-93, the federal deficit will have almost doubled as a share of the gross national product.

4. Before Ronald Reagan became president in 1980, America's tax policies were much fairer, with the wealthy paying their share of the tax burden.

5. A national sales tax would solve the government's financial problems.

6. Increasing taxes for the wealthy would slow economic growth.

7. Although the tax burden is difficult for everyone, taxes are necessary because they are government's greatest source of revenue.

8. Between 1977 and 1982, the capital gains tax declined from 49 percent to 28 percent.

9. The capital gains tax should be cut because it unfairly penalizes the rich.

10. Abolishing the capital gains tax would unleash unparalleled economic growth.

11. Many representatives only want to cut the capital gains tax to benefit the wealthy.

12. Cutting the capital gains tax would reduce direct government revenue by $4 billion to $8 billion every year.

13. The wealthiest 5 percent of all taxpayers receive 85 percent of all capital gains.

14. The government should "soak the rich" by making them pay more taxes.

15. A middle-class family earning roughly $50,000 must pay a tax rate of nearly 40 percent.

16. U.S. income taxes are lower than those of any other Western country.

17. The top tax rate should be reduced to 19 percent.

18. At one time, the top tax rate was 91 percent.

19. Demands for government services will continue to rise and taxes will continue to rise to pay for the increased services.

20. Higher tax rates have not inhibited economic growth in the past and will not inhibit them in the future.

21. The U.S. needs tax revenue to pay for both domestic and foreign spending.

22. Taxes must be raised to pay for the government services we enjoy.

Periodical Bibliography

The following articles have been selected to supplement the diverse views presented in this chapter.

Bill Archer	"Who's the Fairest of Them All?" *Policy Review*, Summer 1991.
Ralph Kinney Bennett	"This Tax Hurts Us All," *Reader's Digest*, August 1990.
Dollars & Sense	"Soaking the Poor," July/August 1991.
Robert S. McIntyre	"Borrow 'N' Squander," *The New Republic*, September 30, 1991.
Daniel J. Mitchell	"Still a Raw Deal," *Reason*, October 1991.
Stephen Moore	"Dire States," *National Review*, July 29, 1991.
Stephen Moore	"License to Spend," *Reason*, October 1990.
Ralph Nader	"Rip-Off, Inc.," *Mother Jones*, June 1991.
James L. Payne	"The Real Case Against Taxes," *The Freeman*, May 1990.
Charles Peters	"Besieged and Beleaguered on $200,000," *The Washington Monthly*, May/June 1990.
Alan Reynolds	"Want More Money, Mr. Bush, Raise Taxes," *The Wall Street Journal*, July 5, 1990.
Frank Riessman	"Time for a Wealth Tax," *Social Policy*, Summer 1991.
Ed Rubenstein	"Decade of Greed?" *National Review*, December 30, 1990.
Herbert Stein	"Taxing Capital Gains," *Society*, March/April 1990.
C. Eugene Steuerle	"Tax Policy in the 1990s," *The American Enterprise*, May/June 1990.
Lawrence H. Summers	"A Tax Package with Social Benefits," *The New York Times*, July 23, 1990.
Ann Withorn	"Taxation for the General Good," *The Nation*, April 23, 1990.

How Can America's Banking System Be Strengthened?

Chapter Preface

In the mid- and late-1980s, thousands of American savings and loan associations became insolvent. Although a federal insurance program covered a small portion of the losses, millions of private and corporate customers could have lost vast sums of money. To avoid the panic certain to follow widespread losses, Congress voted to bail out the S&Ls by using tax revenues to pay for their losses. According to the *Los Angeles Times*, taxpayers may end up paying $500 billion over the next thirty years in this effort.

By the early 1990s, many feared a similar crisis could affect banks. More than twelve hundred banks failed in the 1980s, the vast majority in the final years of the decade. By the early 1990s, another thousand or so were on the brink of failure, according to the Federal Deposit Insurance Corporation (FDIC), the federal agency that insures banks. One reason was that for decades many banks had unwisely loaned vast amounts of money to unstable countries. Another was that banks have lost business to other financial institutions that have assumed many kinds of banking transactions. Money market investment firms offer customers a way to obtain higher rates of return for their money than traditional savings accounts do. Credit card companies offer more economical terms to customers and were thus able to take over the banks' lucrative card operations. Corporate-owned finance companies offer lower rates of interest on loans, leaving many banks struggling to compete for customers. Taxpayers wondered if once again they would be forced to bail out America's financial institutions.

In early 1991, at what appeared to be the height of the banking crisis, the Bush administration presented a major proposal to Congress, suggesting ways to save the banking system. This proposal included recommendations to expand bank powers and allow their entry into investment ventures forbidden since the Great Depression, reform the federal deposit insurance program, and change the ways banks are regulated. This controversial proposal was the first of dozens from both the public and private sectors to be considered by Congress. Pundits from Capitol Hill and Harvard Business School as well as people in the street argued about what would save America's banking system—and indeed, whether it *should* be saved. Some argued that America's banks were no longer needed while others said the system would save itself after a period of instability.

While they may disagree about what to do to strengthen banks, most people agree that the condition of the banking system is less than ideal. The authors of the following viewpoints debate ways to strengthen it.

"Segregating core banking would improve the economics of the [banking] business."

Establish a Core-Bank System

Lowell L. Bryan

Lowell L. Bryan, a director of McKinsey & Company, is the author of *Bankrupt: Restoring the Health and Profitability of Our Banking System* and *Breaking Up the Bank: Rethinking an Industry Under Siege.* Bryan's opinion, expressed in the following viewpoint, is that the American banking industry must be restructured to include both federally insured, tightly regulated banks, called core banks, and uninsured, less-regulated money market investment institutions and finance companies. Core banks would be America's basic financial institutions, dealing in conservative savings and loan transactions and offering no risk of loss to their customers. Money market institutions and finance companies would handle riskier transactions with their customers' full knowledge. This kind of restructuring is the only way, Bryan believes, that both stability and profitability can be restored to the American banking system.

As you read, consider the following questions:

1. Why does the author recommend changing the American banking structure to incorporate both tightly regulated core banks and uninsured investment and finance organizations?
2. List three ways banks would be different than they are now if the U.S. instituted Bryan's system.
3. In Bryan's system, where would a person's savings be safer? Where would they have the greatest opportunity to increase?

Reprinted by permission of *Harvard Business Review.* An excerpt from "A Blueprint for Financial Reconstruction" by Lowell L. Bryan, May/June 1991. Copyright © 1991 by the President and Fellows of Harvard College; all rights reserved.

America's banking crisis presents choices both perilous and promising. Perilous, because the failure to act intelligently will lead to the most serious economic collapse since the Great Depression. As much as 25% of the U.S. banking system—representing assets of more than $750 billion—has begun to post such massive loan losses that it must focus on collecting loans rather than making them. Healthy banks, shaken by their competitors' plight (and worried about more intense scrutiny from bank examiners), are losing confidence in their ability to make sound loans. This credit crunch has the potential to turn a mild recession into a downward economic spiral that feeds on itself.

Stopping the Downward Spiral

The immediate challenge is to stop the downward spiral while there is still time. The broader challenge, and the promise, is to create a new banking industry without artificial boundaries, without wasteful duplication of effort, and with only as much regulation as is needed to create an orderly financial system. It would be an industry in which banks that add value thrive and those that don't perish. It would also be an industry that could earn reasonable economic returns—a prerequisite to restoring the franchise value of banks. . . .

The outlines for the new banking system would go something like this:

Only "core banks" would have government insurance. These banks would experience dramatic consolidation. Core banks take deposits through savings accounts, checking accounts, and money market accounts. They finance home mortgages, market credit cards, lend to small businesses to finance accounts receivable, and provide other traditional banking services. After a restructuring, the core banking industry (that is, the amount of deposits covered by federal insurance) would be at least $1 trillion smaller than it is today, a reduction in scale of 25%. It would also be decidedly more profitable. The United States would have 10 to 15 highly skilled, multiregional core banks, each with $100 billion to $200 billion of deposits and annual profits of $1 billion to $2 billion. These banks would be headquartered in cities like Columbus, Ohio; Charlotte, North Carolina; Detroit, Michigan; and San Francisco, California. Essentially, they would represent the consolidation of the 125 largest bank holding companies with combined deposits of $2 trillion. This consolidation would not significantly affect the thousands of small, profitable local banks with deep roots (and thus real competitive advantage) in their communities.

Money center banks would be restructured. All banks would have to separate their "core banking" activities from their other businesses since the government safety net would be limited to core

160

functions. . . .

Industrial companies would own banks. . . .

Washington would play a limited but focused regulatory role. Ultimately, the FDIC, the primary agency for banking oversight and insurance, would be privatized. For traditional core banks, Washington oversight would become much more strict. There would be floating ceilings on the interest rates banks could offer insured depositors, pegged to rates on Treasury bills. Washington would also limit the terms and conditions of the loans core banks could extend. Banks would compete freely on service, efficiency, and innovation, but competition on the terms and availability of credit would be tightly constrained.

On the other hand, Washington would no longer guarantee or monitor credit activities outside the core bank—sovereign lending to the Third World, financing LBOs [leveraged buyouts], underwriting commercial real estate. Investors (rather than bank examiners) would evaluate the profitability and soundness of high-risk banking activities and demand returns commensurate with the risk. This is, of course, precisely how "supervision" takes place at American Express, Fidelity Investments, GE Capital, or GMAC—giant financial institutions outside the government safety net and thus untouched by federal examiners. These "unsupervised" institutions today represent the soundest segment of the U.S. financial system. . . .

Successful Core Banking

The U.S. banking system already is moving in [the core banking] direction. Banc One in Ohio became one of the most successful banking organizations in the United States by pursuing a "core banking" strategy. Bank of America essentially used the strategy to return from its brush with death in the mid-1980s. More recently, large banks like Wells Fargo and Chemical Bank have announced fundamental shifts in their banking strategies from commercial real estate, LBO, and other high-risk corporate lending to making loans to consumers and smaller businesses.

Robert E. Liton, *Harvard Business Review*, July/August 1991.

The credit disaster of the 1980s underscores the essential dilemma of banking reform: how to protect small depositors and the payments system without creating massive credit distortions or interfering with business innovation and healthy economic forces. The essence of the solution is to rewrite the social contract between banks and government based on lessons from history, yet to still embrace the new forces of economics and technology that will continue to reshape banking through the 1990s.

What might the new social contract involve?. . .

Core Banks. The primary customers for core banks would be individuals, community businesses, and midsize companies—a large market. Excluding loans on commercial real estate, these customers already represent more than 90% of all loans made by nonmoney center banks. Core banks would accept deposits in savings accounts, checking accounts, money market accounts, and so on. They would lend to individuals for home mortgage debt, home equity loans, credit cards, installment loans, and auto loans. They would lend to businesses for accounts receivable financing, equipment leasing, commercial mortgages, unsecured lines of credit. They would offer trust and custody services for retail and wholesale clients. In short, they would perform activities that have been the traditional province of banks for more than a century.

The point of creating core banks is to return to those activities that have proven over time to be relatively safe and *where banks have a demonstrated advantage over nonbanks.* Many pundits have looked at the range of financial innovations in the 1980s, especially securitization, and pronounced banks "obsolete." This is nonsense. There are real limits to what categories of assets can be securitized, and there remains a huge base of depositors willing to pay for safety. Indeed, core banking is the *only* segment of the industry that makes money today. Once the system is reformed to eliminate the excesses of the 1980s, the economics of core banking will become even more attractive.

New Regulations Needed

But creating safe core banks requires imposing strict controls over what they can do. Many bankers won't like many of the rules needed to make core banking work. Over the long term, however, these rules will control the distortions that have led to self-destructive practices and make it possible for banks to earn reasonable profits again. Some of the most important regulations are:

1. Peg the interest rates that core banks can pay on insured deposits to floating rates on Treasury securities. The goal here is to ensure that core banks can't offer depositors overly generous returns for the risks they are incurring. Washington would create a "floating" interest rate ceiling that reflected rates paid by the U.S. Treasury on securities of equivalent maturity. For example, if the six-month Treasury rate was 7.5%, the maximum interest rate a core bank could pay on a six-month insured CD [certificate of deposit] would be 7.5%. Because the rate would float, the ceiling would not create the same competitive problems for banks that fixed-rate ceilings created before deregulation. Banks would be free to compete for deposits through terms and conditions, convenience, service, and price-up to the floating Treasury

ceiling. This would not dramatically undermine bank competition; today more than 70% of all branch-based deposits pay below the equivalent Treasury rate. The ceiling would prevent weak banks from abusing deposit insurance and forcing strong banks to match their reckless pricing.

2. Limit the size of loans core banks can make. The goal here is to ensure that large core banks have reasonably diversified loan portfolios. Most banks, regardless of size, are allowed to lend up to 10% of their equity to a single borrower. This rule already keeps small banks from making imprudent commitments. But in a big bank, 10% of equity can represent a sizable risk. So core banks would face a sliding scale—the bigger the bank, the smaller the maximum percentage of equity it can lend to a single borrower. Banks with capital between $10 million and $100 million could lend only 5% of their equity above the first $10 million to a single borrower. Banks with more than $100 million in equity could lend only 2% of their capital above the first $100 million. These kinds of limits would essentially force core banks to make most of their loans to individuals, small businesses, and midsize companies.

Real-Estate Limitations

3. Permit real-estate lending to local developers but with strict regulation of terms and conditions. Given the atrocious record in commercial real estate today, it's reasonable to ask whether core banks should be allowed to make any such loans in the future. But there are pragmatic reasons for permitting them to do so. Who but the local bank can finance a midsize company's warehouse or a small medical office building? Still, even these local credits must be strictly regulated. The prudent standards that prevailed historically should be reinstated. For example, regulators could require that developers provide 30% of the equity in a project, that the building be 90% preleased (for construction loans), and that committed leases provide at least 100% coverage of principal and interest payments.

Money Market Investment Banks. The money market investment bank would serve corporations, financial institutions, and governments with a broad array of commercial banking and investment banking products. It would trade securities, derivatives, and currencies. It would buy, sell, underwrite, and distribute corporate debt and equity. It would make loans that could be traded on secondary markets. But unlike the core bank, which is funded with insured deposits, the money market investment bank would be funded with interbank deposits, uninsured CDs and other wholesale funds. . . . Money center banks also engage in many activities that would be classified as money market investment banking. But these activities are thoroughly entwined with businesses associated with insured deposits, a legacy of the bundled model of the 1930s. Under the new system, they would have to be separated from the core bank and could not take advantage of the federal safety net.

In the Global Market

Money market investment banks would represent the United States in the global capital markets. As a country, the United States needs no more than a handful of them to maintain economic sovereignty. But each bank in this handful would need unquestioned financial strength. Spreads in global capital markets are so thin that they leave no room for institutions with *any* perceived risk. Since, under this proposal, money market investment banks would not be insured, their principal sources of strength would be their earnings stream, the quality of their assets, and their capital base. For that reason, the creation of money market investment banks would spark such a sharp consolidation in trading and underwriting that only the strongest would survive.

Forcing Banks to Health

Core banking would force banks to become healthy and strong precisely because it would steer them to the markets to raise funds for their newer and riskier investments.

Charles E. Schumer, *The New York Times*, July 11, 1991.

As for government oversight, these institutions would be subject to regulation by the SEC [Securities and Exchange Commission]. Washington would also need to protect against a precipitate default by a giant money market investment bank that would bring down the entire financial system. But this can be achieved *without* insuring liabilities and without overly burdensome regulations. First, Washington would be prepared to extend a liquidity line of credit during times of crisis (such as the 1987 stock market crash). If the liquidity line were used, the government could secure its loans by taking preemptive collateral. Moreover, Washington would require that money market investment banks mark to the market on a daily basis the vast majority of their assets. (Marking to the market most assets is quite feasible, since, by definition, virtually all assets on a money market investment bank's balance sheet have current market values.) With mark-to-market accounting, institutional safety and soundness become transparent. As long as marketable assets exceed liabilities, an institution can be liquidated without losses to any constituency other than shareholders.

Finance Companies. Finance companies would provide credit

and other "banking" services that are too risky to be included in the core bank: big corporate loans of the sort made by money center banks and the regionals, financing for highly leveraged transactions and commercial real estate, large lease transactions for capital equipment and aircraft. As with the money market investment banks, these and other risky activities would be conducted by separately capitalized companies that do not draw on insured deposits.

Unlike commercial banks today, whose risky loans come under the supervision of Washington bank examiners, finance companies would be completely unregulated other than having to comply with SEC disclosure requirements, as do all public companies. Rating agencies and accounting firms—not bank examiners—would be responsible for assessing the quality of the assets. There would be no safety net beneath these institutions. They would need sufficient equity capital (probably as much as 15% of their assets) to convince the market to provide them with funding. They would need sophisticated credit skills to stay out of trouble. But if they did stumble, they would be allowed to go bankrupt. The only role for regulators would be to protect affiliated core banks or money market investment banks from being brought down by the troubles of the finance company.

This blueprint liberates the economic forces that are reshaping banks. The securitization process would proceed to its natural limits without the constraints imposed by Glass-Steagall [a law mandating the separation of commercial and investment banking]. Disaggregation would be enhanced by breaking up bundled commercial banks into three new categories whose economic and business logic is different. Consolidation would accelerate. Core banks could combine with other core banks. Money market investment banks, with roots in either the traditional "commercial banking" sector or the "securities" industry, would combine with other money market investment banks. And the artificial separation between banking and commerce would disappear. Industrial companies would own core banks, money market investment banks, and finance companies.

Safety of Core Banks

The blueprint also raises two obvious questions: How safe and how profitable would core banks be? It is difficult to identify a commercial bank of any size that got into serious trouble by lending to individuals, small businesses, and midsize companies. As for profitability, core banks would certainly be more profitable than today's commercial banks, since the evidence is clear that commercial banks have been making uneconomic loans.

Indeed, the banking stars of the 1980s were the "super-regional" bank holding companies such as Banc One, Barnett Banks, Core States, First Wachovia, NBD (the old National Bank of Detroit), National City (Cleveland), NCNB, PNC (the old Pittsburgh National Bank), Sun Trust, and Wells Fargo. These super-regionals are the big exception to many of the damaging trends described earlier. They have grown in size and profitability and have kept credit losses to a minimum by making the traditional core banking model work better than their high-flying competitors did. As a result, they have remained profitable enough to avoid exccessive credit or interest rate risk.

Moreover, segregating core banking would improve the economics of the business. Imposing flexible interest rate controls would certainly shrink the industry. Some $600 billion of price-sensitive deposits would leave banks and $400 billion of deposits would leave thrifts. But these controls would increase returns on the deposits that remain because they eliminate overbidding by weak competitors. And depositors would still be willing to pay a premium for safety.

"The [core] bank concept is a reactionary and an ill-thought-through response to a serious problem."

A Core-Bank System Will Not Work

Bert Ely

Bert Ely is a financial consultant and president of Ely & Company, Inc., a financial consulting firm in Alexandria, Virginia. In the following viewpoint, he attacks proposals for a new banking system centering around core banks, which he calls narrow banks because of their limited functions—primarily conservative savings and loan transactions. Such a plan, he says, addresses the pain Americans are feeling because of losses sustained during the thousands of failures of savings and loan associations and banks during the late 1980s and early 1990s, but it does not deal with the causes of the failures. Consequently, such a plan is doomed to fail, Ely says.

As you read, consider the following questions:

1. Why does Ely believe removing all risk from banks is a foolish idea?
2. According to the author's interpretation of the way things are, would customers of failed, uninsured, high-risk institutions, such as money market investment companies, be likely to lose their money? On what precedents does Ely base his judgment?
3. List three drawbacks Ely sees in a system based on insured narrow banks and other, uninsured financial institutions.

Bert Ely, "The Narrow Bank: A Flawed Response to the Failings of Federal Deposit Insurance," *Regulation*, Spring 1991. Reprinted with permission of the Cato Institute.

The bankruptcy of the Federal Savings and Loan Insurance Corporation (FSLIC) will cost American taxpayers some $200 billion in present-value terms. There is now growing concern that the Bank Insurance Fund, which protects depositors in commercial and savings banks, may also need a taxpayer bailout. Narrow banking proposals are a response to the increasing burden federal deposit insurance is placing on taxpayers. Narrow banking is seen by its advocates as the best hope, perhaps the only hope, for reducing future taxpayer losses in federal deposit insurance programs. . . .

A Definition of Narrow Banking

Narrow banking, as envisioned by its advocates, would create a set of low-risk banks that would constitute the payment system for the American economy. These banks would accept checkable deposits and savings accounts (in the form of passbook savings or certificates of deposit) from individuals, businesses, and governments. Narrow banks would then invest these deposits in low-risk financial assets, such as U.S. government securities or high-grade, privately issued debt, such as commercial paper. Narrow banks' investments would generally be of short- and medium-term maturity to match the maturity of their deposits. All funds transfers, whether in the form of checks or by electronic funds transfers, would flow through narrow banks.

Because narrow banks' assets would be of low risk, the probability of their insolvency would be substantially reduced. Thus, narrow bank advocates argue, federal taxpayers, acting through the federal government, could afford to insure deposits in narrow banks.

Unfortunately, the narrow bank concept is based on a faulty analysis of the causes of the FSLIC fiasco and the emerging problems of the Bank Insurance Fund. Advocates of narrow banking reason that bank and S&L [savings and loan institutions] insolvencies occur because the assets of these institutions lose value. These insolvencies are widespread for two reasons. First, managers of some banks and thrifts take excessive risk with federally insured deposits relative to the amount of equity capital invested in these institutions. Second, government regulators are unable to restrain excessive risk-taking by bank and S&L managers or to force depository owners to invest sufficient equity capital in these high-risk institutions. The answer to these problems, according to narrow bank advocates, is to regulate the problem out of existence. By prohibiting managers of federally insured institutions from making risky investments, narrow bank advocates seek to make the regulators' job more manageable and thus to protect taxpayers.

But the narrow bank solution addresses the consequences of the problem, not the causes. Like any solution that focuses solely on consequences, narrow banking would itself create other difficulties. The narrow bank solution does not come to grips with *why* federally insured banks and S&Ls invest in assets that lose value. Why do some bank managers take on excessive risk? And why are bank regulators unable to prevent excessive risk-taking when it occurs?

Core Banks Offer No Solution

Is it really a solution to further divide the banking industry into core banks, money market investment banks, and finance companies? Wasn't the collapse of the S&L industry evidence that the government's creation of special-purpose financing bodies tailored to a particular market environment—without the ability to respond to changes in that market—will fail? The Bryan proposal is another one of those imaginative responses to a contemporary problem that does not take into account that today's economy may have only the slightest resemblance to tomorrow's.

Bryan says that core banks would accept savings accounts, checking accounts, and money market accounts, and they would make loans to local businesses through accounts-receivable financing, equipment leasing, commercial mortgages, and the like. In other words, core banks would borrow short and lend long but by definition would not have access to the liquid money markets in which they could match their assets and liabilities. One of the most persuasive diagnoses of the thrift industry's failure was that its very essence was a mismatched portfolio, so its collapse was only a matter of time. We can expect the same outcome with core banks.

Peter J. Wallison, *Harvard Business Review,* July/August 1991.

The economic incentives faced by bank and thrift owners and managers lie at the root of the excessive risk-taking apparent among depository institutions. Unfortunately, the traditional regulatory view of the world does not attempt to understand or accommodate economic incentives; instead, regulation attempts to force economic actors to behave in a way contrary to their economic incentives. The narrow banking approach is very much in this tradition, relying as it does on regulatory prohibitions to correct an undesirable behavior. It is only by shaking off the shackles of a regulatory world view that we can fully appreciate the role of economic incentives and understand why bank insolvencies have become so costly for taxpayers.

Although formal government deposit insurance schemes vary

from country to country, in reality every industrialized country has a too-big-to-fail policy that effectively protects most bank deposits, and *all* deposits in large banks, against any loss of principal, interest, or liquidity. Only in limited cases involving small depository institutions are a relative handful of explicitly unprotected depositors forced to suffer a loss. . . .

Bank deposits receive such universal government protection because they represent what I have termed "hazardous liabilities." Bank liabilities represent a hazard because these deposits, many of which are payable on demand, are used to fund less liquid bank loans and investments.

Market-driven economies cannot function without hazardous liabilities such as bank deposits and money market mutual funds. No sophisticated marketplace can operate unless buyers have access to readily withdrawable financial assets with which to purchase goods and services or to pay their debts. Likewise, a major function of the financial intermediation process carried out by banks is "maturity transformation." That is, banks traditionally stand between borrowers who seek debt that can be repaid over a relatively long period and savers and bank creditors who prefer to have access to their funds on short notice. Thus, the payment instruments we must have are generally invested in assets of longer average maturity. . . .

Side Effect: Shrinking Deposits

The narrow bank concept seeks to reduce maturity transformation within federally insured banks by forcing them to invest in short-term liquid securities. It also seeks to reduce the credit risk associated with these assets. A side effect of the strict asset limitations faced by narrow banks would be to shrink substantially the amount of explicitly insured deposits, perhaps by as much as half, or $2 trillion. But the demand on the part of businesses and individuals to hold financial assets with the characteristics of hazardous liabilities and to seek debt contracts with longer terms will not go away just because the scope of permissible assets for insured banks was narrowed. Thus, mandated narrow banking would shift that demand to uninsured institutions that would exhibit the same risk characteristics now seen in banks and thrifts.

Thus, narrow banking does not solve the problem. It merely shifts it to another set of institutions. Indeed, the problem might be made worse because regulators, especially the central bank, would then face greater ambiguity in dealing with uninsured failing institutions funded by hazardous liabilities. Letting such an uninsured institution fail would raise concerns about the solvency of comparable uninsured institutions. Depositors would find it prudent to run from uninsured institutions into government-insured banks and thus would aggravate the economic waste and systemic instability that deposit insurance was designed to prevent.

High Costs

The price of [a core-banking] system is the closure of 13,000 banks and 3,000-plus thrifts as well as the real cost of handing the core banks regional monopolies on lending and deposit-taking in their districts.

Carliss Y. Baldwin, *Harvard Business Review*, July/August 1991

The pragmatic political response in this situation would be to extend the taxpayer safety net to uninsured institutions to stabilize them. Surely that would be the response if a major run developed tomorrow on money market mutual funds. The Federal Reserve's discount window would fly open, and billions of dollars would be lent to these funds to stabilize them. Fed loans would be used to fully protect departing money market mutual fund depositors from loss. But such a move in a narrow banking world would defeat a key goal of the narrow bank concept—to shrink the scope of the taxpayer safety net. By effectively encouraging funds to flow out of insured narrow banks and into uninsured bank-like institutions, narrow banking would expand a free-rider problem that already exists, that is, the implicit government protection of explicitly uninsured institutions such as money market mutual funds. The free-rider expansion sparked by narrow banking would worsen, not lessen, taxpayer risk in maintaining financial stability. . . .

Other Problems with the Narrow Bank Concept

The narrow bank concept suffers from several other shortcomings. I shall discuss three of the most important of these.

Exempting the Small Bank. Proponents of narrow banking generally recognize the impracticality of applying this concept to smaller banks. Therefore, they usually propose a small bank exemption. Burnham, for example, suggests that banks with assets under $100 million be fully exempted from narrow bank requirements and that banks in the $100 million to $500 million range receive a partial exemption. If we assume that all banks within a multibank holding company would be combined for the purpose of determining the exemption, only 7 percent of all bank and S&L assets were held by institutions with less than $100 million in assets as of September 30, 1990. Another 12 percent of all bank assets were held by institutions falling into the $100 million to $500 million size range. Thus, the narrow bank concept would apply fully to more than four-fifths of the assets owned by American-domiciled banking institutions.

The small bank exemption would prompt the formation of many small banks, especially in urban areas. Although electronic technology increasingly favors smaller organizations, many larger banking organizations are viable competitors in larger urban areas where substantial economies of scale can be captured by acquiring a significant market share. For the most part, the full cost savings arising from these economies of scale are only available in larger metropolitan areas to banks and thrifts with more than $500 million in assets. Thus, the narrow bank concept would promote additional fragmentation of American banking and would thus increase financial instability within the economy and add to the inefficiency of the banking industry.

Reducing the Number of Banking Offices. Today there are approximately 87,000 banking offices (including branches) in the United States operated by commercial and savings banks and S&Ls. (This count does not include credit unions.) Imposing narrow banking would force federally insured banks and thrifts to reduce the size of their operations and to sharply restrict the range of their loans and investments. As a result, the net interest margin earned by these institutions would decline. Fee income earned by banks and thrifts on their lending activities would also be reduced. Consequently, the income earned by banks and thrifts could easily fall by approximately the same proportion as the asset downsizing required by narrow bank legislation.

Fewer Places to Bank

If bank and thrift assets shrank by one-third in a world of narrow banking, then conceivably the number of banking offices would also shrink by one-third, or by almost 30,000. Many observers believe there is an excessive number of bank and thrift branches in the United States. But are there twice as many as there need to be? That is doubtful. Therefore, a shift to narrow banking, even with the small bank exemption, could significantly impair the access of many consumers and businesses to banking services.

The reduction in the number of banking offices could be alleviated somewhat if the insured and uninsured subsidiaries of bank holding companies were allowed to share branch offices. Under such an arrangement, the fixed costs associated with operating a branch could be spread across a larger business base. This structure would be less efficient than today's integrated banking activities, however, because of the firewalls that would have to be built to isolate the narrow bank from its less regulated affiliate.

Alternatively, massive closures of branch offices might simply be forbidden. Such a reaction is consistent with the growing attitude that federally insured banks and thrifts should be regulated as if they were public utilities. Restricting branch closings would increase the operating expenses of narrow banks, however, and higher operating expenses would further depress the interest rates paid to depositors, which in turn would drive even more deposits into accounts in uninsured institutions. Such a flight to uninsured institutions would only heighten the risk of financial instability.

Severing Credit-Granting from Deposit-Taking. Advances in electronic technology have increasingly acted to integrate the production and delivery of financial services, as is evidenced by growing conflicts between various financial regulators. The narrow bank concept moves in precisely the opposite direction by severing, except in small banks, the two classic bank functions: credit-granting and deposit-taking or payment services. In fact, many business banking relationships and an increasing number of personal banking relationships tie these activities together in a single product, within a checking account with overdraft privileges, for example, or in two linked accounts.

Narrow banking, carried to its logical extreme, would bar these types of relationships by forcing credit-granting into an organization legally distinct from a deposit-taking, payment services bank. This is simply an extension of the philosophy underlying the Glass-Steagall Act of 1933, which forced the unnecessary separation of investment from commercial banking. The separation envisioned by narrow banking's advocates would increase further the operating expenses of American banks and thrifts.

Conclusion

The narrow bank concept is a reactionary and an ill-thought-through response to a serious problem—the growing inability of banking regulators to control bank insolvency losses. By dealing with the consequences rather than the causes of the problem, however, narrow banking advocates have crafted a solution that would both increase financial instability within the American economy and decrease the efficiency of the banking business.

Only in America is the narrow bank concept being seriously entertained. Perhaps other industrialized nations understand that there must be a better way to shield taxpayers from the costs of protecting bank depositors from bank insolvency losses. The lack of interest elsewhere in narrow banking is perhaps the most cogent evidence against the narrow bank concept.

"*Deposit insurance has made sound financial institutions indistinguishable from insolvent ones in the public's mind.*"

Reduce Federal Deposit Insurance

Thomas M. Garrott

In the following viewpoint, Thomas M. Garrott argues that federal deposit insurance, the government program that insures all bank deposits up to $100,000, has outlived its usefulness. It costs American taxpayers more than it benefits them, he says, by encouraging unsound banking practices for which the public ends up paying. Garrott is president of National Commerce Bancorporation.

As you read, consider the following questions:

1. According to the author, how has federal deposit insurance encouraged unsound banking practices?
2. How does the author respond to the argument that deposit insurance protects the small saver?
3. What banking reforms does Garrott recommend instead of maintaining or increasing present federal deposit insurance?

Thomas M. Garrott, "Deposit Insurance: How Much Can We Afford?" *Regulation*, Winter 1991. Reprinted with permission of the Cato Institute.

In recent months across an ever-widening spectrum of our society, the calls for deposit insurance reform have begun to grow louder. As president of a Tennessee bank holding company, let me add my voice.

Deposit insurance was created by Congress in the 1930s to deter any future runs on banks such as the ones that occurred during the Great Depression. Originally, deposits were insured up to $2,500. As recently as 1980, coverage was $40,000. Today, deposit insurance stands at $100,000, but with creative accounting and the government's tacit "too big to fail" policy, virtually all deposits are insured by the government—or rather, they are guaranteed by the taxpayer.

False Sense of Security

Deposit insurance has become an opiate that has dulled the American consumer's otherwise market-driven quest for quality bank products and services. Deposit insurance has made sound financial institutions indistinguishable from insolvent ones in the public's mind. Well-managed banks pay the same insurance rates as the most recklessly run banks. Both banker and depositor have become addicted to the false sense of security deposit insurance provides. The problem is analogous to drug use in that our society as a whole must eventually bear the economic burden of deposit insurance abuse.

Slowly, comprehension of the staggering cost of the thrift bailout is beginning to dawn on the American public. It is almost impossible to put $250 billion in perspective. If paid today, it would cost every man, woman, and child in the United States more than $1,000 each. But we chose instead to defer the cost to a later day. The government now proposes to finance this deposit insurance bailout with 30-year bonds. Interest expenses are projected to run the final cost closer to $500 billion. How, in good conscience, can we leave this shameful legacy to future generations of yet unborn taxpayers?

From such an expensive and painful experience as the S&L [savings and loan institutions] debacle, surely there must be some significant lessons to be learned. What led to the demise of an entire industry? Could it happen to our banking system? The causes most often cited are fraud, disintermediation, speculative lending practices, and inept regulatory supervision. In reality, however, these were merely viruses that found a receptive breeding ground in an industry already susceptible to infection as a result of unrestrained deposit insurance abuse. There were no incentives for either depositors or the owners of low-net-worth S&Ls to exercise caution or restraint. The incentives actually ran the other way. Millions of brokered deposits sought out the highest rates without regard for any safety and soundness considerations. The natural immunities of our free-market system had been destroyed. Bank owners were not playing with their own money.

By Mike Luckovich for the *Atlanta Constitution*. Reprinted with permission.

Nor is our commercial banking system immune to these problems. The most important difference is that while thrifts had about $900 billion in deposits, commercial banks have about $2.5 trillion. If the nation's banks are ever stricken to an extent similar to thrifts, the consequences could be truly catastrophic. Our entire payment system would be at risk.

Higher Coverage?

Incredibly, there is a vocal segment within the banking industry calling for even higher deposit insurance coverage—possibly unlimited protection. These bankers contend that the solution is not free-market discipline, where deposits flow to the safest and most efficiently run institutions, but ever-increasing government control, regulation, and guarantees. They contend that all banks should be reduced to the same common denominator. Deposits in Bank A would be as safe as those in Bank B, distinguished only by the rate of interest that one might pay as opposed to another. Interest rates are normally a function of risk—but not in this scenario. There would be no risk to anyone except the taxpayers. And conceivably, the sad history of the thrift industry might be repeated by an unwitting banking industry.

The time for deposit insurance reform is now. There is growing public sentiment as well as ever-increasing conviction within the banking community that the systemic disease that grows from excessive deposit insurance should not be allowed to threaten the viability of our nation's commercial banks. As with any addiction, withdrawal will be painful, and the inclination will be to postpone it. The remedies required will certainly have some unpleasant side effects. Taxpayers must be convinced that a reduction in deposit insurance is in their best interests. Bankers must accept the inevitable fact that some banks will fail. The strongest and best managed banks, not necessarily the largest, will flourish. Those that have existed on the artificial life support of government guarantees will either adapt to a new environment or wither. At a minimum, the prescribed regimen should include the following steps.

Not Real Insurance

What the government calls deposit insurance doesn't remotely resemble what we generally know as insurance. Real insurance coverage is based on risk, meaning the cost of coverage varies with an insurance company's analysis of the hit it will take if it has to pay out. For federal deposit insurance, however, banks pay a flat fee. Good and bad bankers alike pay the same price for insurance. When a bank goes down the tubes and the FDIC pays off, healthy banks foot the bill. Moreover, whatever statutory limits the government has placed on deposit insurance, in practice the program covers all losses, especially for institutions that are "too big to fail." So whatever the reforms in the new legislation, bankers can maximize risk-taking because they know they are playing with statutorily obligated funds from a third party. They can win, but they can't lose. If the banking industry crashes as dramatically as the thrift industry, a crash the FDIC won't be able to handle with the meager resources of healthy banks paying unfair insurance premiums, to whom is the government going to turn for the bailout?

The Washington Times, August 13, 1991.

• Reduce deposit insurance coverage from $100,000 to $50,000, or as an alternative, adopt a coinsurance feature beyond a minimum threshold. Give the public some incentive to put its money in well-managed institutions. Draw a distinction between insuring the savings of depositors and guaranteeing the capital of rate-sensitive investors.

• Abolish, once and for all, the tacit policy of "too big to fail."

Put money center banks on the same playing field as smaller banks. The cost of a "too large" bank failure could not be any greater than the risks we now face.

• Make insurance premiums paid by banks a function of risk. Reward well-run institutions. Penalize the reckless. Consider privatizing the insurance, with the FDIC as insurer of last resort.

• Give depositors a yardstick to measure their banks. Require regulators to publish annually a uniform rating of each bank.

Deposit insurance reform will require real political courage. It should not become a Republican or Democratic issue. Responsibility for the demise of the thrift industry rests on both sides of the aisle. Saving our banking industry from a similar fate will require a truly bipartisan effort. The standard of living we have all come to enjoy in this country depends on it.

4

"Deposit insurance was created for the purpose of stabilizing our economic system to the benefit of all Americans. It has succeeded."

Reducing Federal Deposit Insurance Would Endanger the Banking System

Fred Webber and Lawrence J. White

In the following two-part viewpoint, two writers express their belief in the importance of the FDIC (Federal Deposit Insurance Corporation), the federal agency that insures banks. They assert that this program protects the deposits of average Americans, thereby helping to maintain the stability of the nation's economy. The author of Part I is Fred Webber, president of the U.S. League of Savings Institutions. Part II is by Lawrence J. White, professor of economics at New York University's Stern School of Business.

As you read, consider the following questions:

1. According to the authors, who benefits most from federal deposit insurance?
2. List three FDIC reforms the authors say various experts have suggested. Why do the authors believe these reforms would be harmful?
3. In addition to maintaining or increasing federal deposit guarantees, what reforms in the banking system do the authors recommend?

Fred Webber, "The System Is Working," *The Washington Times*, September 19, 1990. Reprinted with permission. Lawrence J. White, "Remedy for Shaky Banks," *The Christian Science Monitor*, March 5, 1991. Reprinted with permission.

I

Federal deposit insurance has come to the front burner as a critical domestic issue during the savings-and-loan cleanup, with the specter looming of a follow-on wave of commercial bank failures.

Central to the understanding of this debate is what deposit insurance really is and who benefits from it.

Federal deposit insurance was not created for the purpose of insuring or "bailing out" bankrupt banks and savings and loans. When a bank or a savings-and-loan association fails, the institution is not bailed out. In fact, stockholders lose out. Owners and managers are kicked out. They walk away with nothing.

FDIC Benefits Individuals

The sole beneficiary of federal deposit insurance is the individual depositor whose savings are backed by the full faith and credit of the United States government to $100,000 per account.

Some theoreticians argue that in a free-market economy the government should not be in the business of protecting depositors; that depositors ought to fend for themselves and determine on their own the financial health of an institution before making a deposit.

That was the prevailing theory before 1929 and the subsequent Great Depression, when hundreds of banks failed. Individual and family savings—life savings in many cases—were wiped out virtually overnight.

Today, we see none of that sort of personal tragedy, and that is due entirely to federal deposit insurance. Massive and simultaneous runs on financial institutions are a thing of the past, and federal deposit insurance is the reason for it.

You've heard it before, but believe it: No one has ever lost a penny in an account insured by the federal government up to the $100,000 insurance limit established by federal law.

Change Would Cause Harm

What are some of the proposals for change?

One would reduce the level of insurance coverage from the current $100,000 to, say, $75,000 or $50,000. Either figure may seem like a lot to most people, but are they really?

Ask the widow who has sold the family home, collected on her husband's small insurance policy and, combining these proceeds with a retirement savings, needs a secure place for safekeeping those funds. Clearly, an individual approaching retirement years with $100,000 in the bank earning interest at the rate of $8,000 a year is not "rich."

Another proposal would limit the number of insured accounts

an individual could hold. Imagine the record-keeping requirements that would be imposed on institutions, and imagine the
restrictions on savings options that suddenly confront individuals.

Instilling Confidence

By instilling depositor confidence, deposit insurance deters
against widespread runs that can bring even healthy institutions
to collapse. . . .

Restricted coverage will put smaller institutions at a competitive
disadvantage and exacerbate the trend toward the demise of the
community bank.

Michelle Meir, *Nation's Cities Weekly*, March 4, 1991.

Others have suggested having the individual states or private
insurance companies write insurance on deposits. That was
tried before the federal system was created in the 1930s, and
two states—Ohio and Maryland—recently demonstrated convincingly that states can't handle runs, and depositors either
lose or have to wait years for their money.

Some advocates of privatizing deposit insurance would have
banks insure each other, collecting insurance premiums based
on risk.

But if a bank is going to insure its neighbor, that bank is going
to want access to the other bank's books. Does Macy's tell
Gimbels? This carries serious anti-trust implications.

Furthermore, some bankers have not been especially skilled at
assessing risk. Can you imagine how insufficiently low the premiums would have been when the major banks were confi-
dently making loans to the Third World in the firm belief they
would actually collect on those loans?

Too Big for Private Sector

It boils down to this: The business of insuring depositors is too
big for the private sector to handle. The best protection for the
federal government against losses through its insurance fund is
tough regulation and supervision of financial institutions, coupled with meaningful capital requirements.

Owners of banks and thrifts must have their own money in
the form of retained capital at risk, and in sufficient amounts to
provide an adequate firewall between the risks inherent in lending and the deposit insurance fund.

Deposit insurance was created for the purpose of stabilizing
our economic system to the benefit of all Americans. It has succeeded. Ask anyone who was around before the Great Depression.

II

Conventional wisdom holds that deposit insurance coverage by the Federal Deposit Insurance Corporation should be cut back. A report on reforming bank regulation and deposit insurance, released by the Treasury, advocates this position. Many in Congress seem ready to support it.

This conventional wisdom is misguided, but the idea has a great deal of surface appeal. After all, the public has suffered grievously because of the excesses of hundreds of imprudent savings and loan associations, and taxpayers may well have to bear additional costs in cleaning up hundreds of insolvent banks.

The public outlays are being used to honor federal insurance guarantees to depositors. With reduced coverage, the government's future exposure to losses would be lower. And depositors would be expected to be more cautious about where they place their funds, thereby exercising "market discipline" on wayward banks and further reducing the government's costs.

Would Reduced Coverage Work?

But would reduced coverage really work this way? I think not. First, if effective coverage *per account* were cut back, many people and companies would just break their deposits into smaller packets and spread them among more banks. There would be more telephone calls, more postage, more "deposit advisers," but little reduction in government exposure.

Second, suppose the insured deposit limit were changed to a fixed amount *per person* that applied system-wide across all banks. Would this limit apply during a person's entire lifetime? What about separate accounts for separate family members? Record keeping and enforcement could be a nightmare.

Third, can we really expect many depositors—even business depositors—to be knowledgeable enough about bank accounting and finances to exercise informed market discipline?

Most important, to the extent that a cutback in coverage is effective in exposing depositors to potential losses, those depositors will become more skittish, and we are likely to see many more runs on banks and greater instability in our financial system.

More widespread depositor runs would be an inevitable consequence of reduced coverage. The bank regulators already know this to be true. That is why they have consistently protected the large depositors in major banks and ignored the current $100,000 limitation on insurance for those depositors. But no one in Washington is prepared to acknowledge openly this connection between proposed reduced coverage and the bank runs that will surely follow.

Wouldn't the Federal Reserve, as a lender of last resort, damp down runs? Maybe. But if the Fed is prepared to lend to banks without receiving adequate collateral in return, it has become a *de facto* federal deposit insurer.

Incredible Proposal

Incredibly, some supposedly smart economists are now arguing that the banking system and the real economy would be better off without deposit insurance. In this view, rational consumers will differentiate between risky banks and more prudent ones. The riskier banks, appropriately, will pay higher interest rates. The more conservative banks will pay less.

Consumers with a taste for risk will keep their money at the fast-and-loose banks. Those more concerned about safety will settle for lower yields and safer banks. After all, these are financial transactions "between consenting adults"—so who needs the government?

First fact: Nobody has perfect foresight. . . .

There will always be bankers who speculate with other people's money, and there will always be innocent souls. . . .

But the solution is not to turn the whole economy into a casino. It's to throw out the deregulators and get serious about bank supervision.

Robert Kuttner, *Los Angeles Times*, January 9, 1991.

Wouldn't private deposit insurance fill the void? Not really. Even if private deposit insurers were to spring into existence (which is far from certain), depositors would soon want to know who would guarantee the private insurers' ability to honor their obligations—especially after the recent failure of private insurance in Rhode Island and earlier failures in Maryland and Ohio.

Don't Cut Back Coverage; Expand It

I believe a radical counterproposal is in order: Instead of cutting back on deposit insurance, the federal government should expand coverage to 100 percent of all deposits. We would thus put an end to the specter of bank runs, once and for all. We would also put an end to the disparate and arbitrary treatment of large depositors (including charities, churches, and nonprofit organizations), who have been covered in the failures of major banks such as Bank of New England but exposed to losses in the failures of smaller banks such as Harlem's Freedom National.

An important side benefit to complete coverage would be the

opening of bank supervisory and disciplinary proceedings to public scrutiny. Bank regulators (as well as the banks themselves) have resisted such transparency in the past, basing their secrecy on their fear of bank runs.

With the costs of the current cleanup already so high, can we afford the potential cleanup costs of broader deposit insurance coverage? Yes, because the numbers and costs of future insolvencies can be drastically reduced if expanded coverage is accompanied by a package of tough reforms in the safety-and-soundness regulation of banks (and of S&Ls and credit unions).

Add Tough Reforms

These regulations should include: (1) better accounting information to be provided to bank regulators, focused on current market values rather than on historical costs; (2) better net-worth (capital) standards, based on market value accounting information, so that owners of banks would have a larger stake in their enterprises and would be more concerned about protecting the insurance; (3) risk-based deposit insurance premiums to discourage risk-taking; and (4) stronger powers for bank regulators to intervene earlier in a shaky bank's downward slide.

To bring more market discipline to bear, the regulators should require banks to issue long-term subordinated debt—explicitly uninsured—to knowledgeable institutional holders, such as insurance companies, pension funds, and mutual funds.

Though this package may appear ambitious, consider the alternative: the Treasury's recipe for bank runs and financial instability. Can we really afford that?

"Lawmakers should . . . clear away perverse regulation and allow market forces . . . to encourage stability through diversification."

Allow Banks to Diversify

Ron Chernow and William G. Laffer III

Ron Chernow is the author of *The House of Morgan,* a best-selling book about the American financier J. Pierpont Morgan and his banking empire. William G. Laffer III is McKenna Fellow in Regulatory and Business Affairs at The Heritage Foundation, a Washington, D.C., think tank that focuses on economic and political issues. In the following viewpoint, the two authors assert that the American banking system can be strengthened by eliminating the regulations that have hampered it for decades and by allowing banks to diversify into new, more profitable enterprises. Chernow is the author of Part I, Laffer of Part II.

As you read, consider the following questions:

1. According to the authors, how have regulations like Glass-Steagall harmed the banking system?
2. How do the authors answer those who fear deregulation would lead to chaos and increased bank closings?
3. What consequences do the authors predict if banks are not allowed to compete in broader financial markets?

Ron Chernow, "Don't Punish the Banks, Liberate Them," *The Wall Street Journal,* September 24, 1991. Reprinted with permission of the Wall Street Journal © 1991 Dow Jones & Company, Inc. All rights reserved. William G. Laffer III, "How to Reform America's Banking System," The Heritage Foundation *Backgrounder,* February 26, 1991. Reprinted with permission.

I

We stand on the eve of this century's third great wave of financial reform, as giddy stock markets and merger fever once again yield to fear and retrenchment followed by reform and regulation. The bull market of the early 1900s and the rise of big trusts led to the 1912 Pujo hearings, spurring the Federal Reserve Act a year later. The 1933 Pecora hearings exposed Wall Street's Jazz Age excesses, speeding passage of the Glass-Steagall Act. Now the savings and loan crisis and the mounting toll of bad property, LBO [leveraged buyout], and Third World loans will force a fundamental revamping of the U.S. banking system.

Once again reform will come when cool heads are least likely to prevail and when the political power of the banks stands at its nadir. Many of today's banking problems, indeed, have roots in the sensational Pecora probe, which straddled FDR's [Franklin Delano Roosevelt] national bank holiday of March 1933. A disenchanted public wanted to slay the bankers rather than hear their problems. Not surprisingly, the reform that emerged had a strongly populist tinge, reducing the scope of banks' activities and fragmenting the banking system. The fragmented banks, epitomized by the S&Ls [savings and loan institutions], were unable to carry diversified portfolios or spread their risks over different businesses. This is a recipe for risk and failure.

Populist Indignation

As our own post-Crash recession looms, once again populist indignation will demand that the culprits be stripped of their powers, like children of their toys. But the next reform cycle must favor deregulation and consolidation of the banks, rather than further atomization—political passions to the contrary. The last crumbling remnants of Glass-Steagall (the 1933 act that separated commercial from investment banking) and the McFadden Act (the 1927 law that forbade interstate banking) must fall. By granting J.P. Morgan & Co. the power to trade and underwrite corporate stocks, the Federal Reserve Board took a momentous step in the right direction. Such a change will satisfy no public craving for revenge. Rather, it will seem as if brazen, self-serving bankers are being rewarded for their blunders just when they should submit to condign punishment.

Things were simpler in the New Deal. After the 1929 market crashed, Main Street surveyed the wreckage with *Schadenfreude*. The political outrage gathered force only when people began to trace their joblessness to Wall Street speculation. Wall Street financiers—yesterday's idols—were suddenly pilloried by a pugnacious new populist hero, Senate counsel Ferdinand Pecora.

In retrospect, the Glass-Steagall Act seems a historical *non sequitur*. It addressed glaring evils, such as the ability of commercial bankers to waylay depositors into risky securities investment. But it didn't curb speculation or repair the banking system's instability.

Glass-Steagall's architects wanted to insulate savings from speculation. Safe, humdrum commercial banking would be shielded from volatile investment banking. The result has been otherwise. For 20 years now, our commercial banks have courted disaster. The list of their lending fiascoes—shipping, real estate investment trusts, farmland, oil, Third World debt, leveraged loans, commercial property—is truly astounding. Unless we assume that all commercial bankers are dunces, we must suspect some deep, systemic flaw behind this flirtation with disaster.

Reducing Risk

To reduce risk even further, banks should be allowed to offer a wider variety of financial services. Currently, commercial banks are limited mainly to providing checking and savings accounts and making loans. But commercial banks should be allowed to engage in other lines of business, such as underwriting the sale of securities, providing brokerage services and mutual funds, and selling insurance to their depositors. This would enable them to be more competitive with other financial institutions by giving their customers the convenience of "one-stop shopping" for financial services. The additional diversification also would enable banks to achieve significant further reductions in their overall portfolio risk.

William G. Laffer III, "A Guide to Current Banking Reform Legislation," The Heritage Foundation *Issue Bulletin*, September 30, 1991.

By no coincidence, the tide of bad loans has risen with the defection of corporate clients to the capital markets and depositors to money-market funds. As corporations have bypassed banks to issue securities, commercial banks have been saddled with less creditworthy customers. In the 1920s, Latin debtors issued bonds. In the 1970s, they resorted to banks because bondholders would have balked at their sovereign junk. Bolstered by creditworthy clients, investment banks have seemed safer havens than commercial banks, subverting Glass-Steagall's intention.

Meanwhile, the geographically segmented banking system created by the McFadden Act turns regional downturns into full-blown banking catastrophes. Instead of large, diversified national banks, such as England, France, and Germany enjoy, the U.S. supports 13,000 localized banks. In the 1920s, many Southern and Western banks failed when oil and agriculture slumped. In the 1980s, the S&Ls eerily re-enacted this precedent. A bank's fortunes are now tied to Texas oil, Nebraska wheat or Boston real estate. When the regional economy falters, the bank fails; these bank failures then aggravate regional distress.

Resisting Downturns

National banks could resist local downturns through offsetting profits in prosperous regions. Banks that offered a fuller range of financial services than Glass-Steagall permits wouldn't be victimized by changes in the way companies finance their operations. They could simply shift emphasis along with their clients. With diversified portfolios, banks could more readily enforce prudential limits on the amount loaned to any single country, company, region or industry. And since banks increasingly package loans into securities, the distinction between commercial and investment banking has become meaningless.

A system of diversified, national banks would encounter the historic American antipathy toward concentrated financial power—the main reason for the splintered U.S. banking system—an antipathy aggravated by recession. Populist rage will boil over as property, Third World and LBO disasters dangerously drain the deposit insurance fund.

Some differences between the present and the 1930s do offer hope. This time, banking reform will occur against a backdrop of foreign competition. In the 1930s, American banks were global powers and could afford some shrinkage of their domestic market share. Today, the four biggest U.S. commercial banks scarcely make the world's top 50. Seven of the 10 largest banks are Japanese; two are French. It's hard to rail against concentrated financial power when America's giants are dwarves abroad.

Americans may also be shedding their sentimental faith in small-town banks. In the 1920s and 1930s, thousands of small-town banks foundered upon corruption or mismanagement, but political anger was directed against the New York banks, which had for the most part survived intact. (Franklin Roosevelt feared deposit insurance would prop up small-town, Republican banks.) The S&L crisis has again shown how fraud and cronyism can riddle small banks. Perhaps taxpayer disenchantment with the thrifts may create a new receptivity toward national banks. The growth of strong regional banks over the past decade—thanks to regional banking pacts—will buffer any raw power plays by New York banks.

Back in the days of Pierpont Morgan or Jacob Schiff, there

was some truth in the stereotype of the all-powerful banker. When capital was scarce, bankers lorded it over companies and investors. Now multinational corporations that issue debt and institutional investors that buy it have slashed the power of financial intermediaries. In the 1980s, companies circumvented banks, selling debt straight to institutional investors. Banks compete with clients. General Electric Financial Services, with $91 billion in assets, would rank fourth if listed as a commercial bank, nosing out J.P. Morgan & Co., GE 's traditional banker.

Old Laws Hinder Banks

Banks have been restricted in their service offerings and in their affiliations over the years to guard against coercion of customers, to prevent banks from gaining unfair competitive advantages, and to avoid excessive concentrations of economic power. Unintended consequences of these restrictions, however, have been that they have prevented banks from responding to changing market conditions, from offering their customers the advantages of new financial technologies.

If strong banks are needed by local communities, then local officials must be concerned if their banks are being weakend by 50-year-old laws that cause them to lose their best customers to competitors that can replace their checking accounts with case management accounts and replace their bank loans with commerical paper.

Similarly, local officials must be concerned if their banks are being prevented from raising needed capital by similar laws that prevented other corporations from investing in or owning banks.

Jake Garn, *Nation's Cities Weekly*, March 4, 1991.

The power of investment bankers has eroded too. This sounds strange in an age when yuppie bond traders and deal-makers earn astronomical salaries. But trading and deal-making are secondary functions of the financial system. They have grown important because of a crisis in the primary system: the provision of money for business, whether through commercial bank credit or issuing securities. And in this primary activity, fierce competition is shrinking margins. Wall Street's "creativity" in the 1980s was a desperate attempt by commercial and investment banks to find comparative advantage in a commodity business.

One advantage of deregulating commercial banks right now is that for the moment they cannot capitalize excessively on new opportunities. Hobbled by scant capital, poor credit ratings and low stock prices, they lack the means to expand rapidly. Best to let the tiger out of the cage when he's not hungry. The Federal Reserve should insure a gradual transformation of the system through friendly, well-capitalized mergers. The process has in fact already begun, as out-of-state banks buy up ailing thrifts.

Fearful Politicians

Politicians who understand the need for reform, but fear being tarred as buddies of the banks, may want to portray the repeal of Glass-Steagall as a populist assault on investment bankers— the fat cats of the 1980s. As commercial banks enter capital markets, they will intensify the pressures in a profitless under-writing scene. Nor need politicians fear that these guests at a bleak banquet will reap "obscene" profits. Nobody will be making much money from underwriting anytime soon.

Universal banks will make the current regulatory structure obsolete. A new federal regulatory structure based on function must be designed. In exchange for new powers, universal banks will have to accept stricter, broader supervision from banking authorities; as an additional safeguard, some form of risk-based deposit insurance would enforce discipline on the use of small depositors' money.

Reforms in banking regulation can make bank failures less likely, but they can never eliminate them. Nonetheless, a broader range of bank powers, joined with tougher supervision, seems preferable to the mix of narrow powers and lax supervision that has led to the frightening present impasse. The need to face unpleasant realities is urgent: More than a thousand commercial banks are already in trouble and the downturn has just begun.

II

America's system of banking and financial services institutions is in need of a fundamental overhaul. The spate of banking failures in recent years could mean insolvency for the Federal Deposit Insurance Corporation (FDIC), the federal agency that insures deposits held in most banks. The FDIC has been losing money since 1988 and could run short of reserves to cover claims. Congress then might feel compelled to prop up the FDIC—at a cost of hundreds of billions of dollars—to head off a banking collapse.

Yet the FDIC itself, by providing insurance for the same premium cost to depositors in prudent and reckless banks alike, has encouraged risky loan policies by banks and so has endangered the banking system. Moreover, various rules and statutes further jeopardize stability in the system by preventing banks from spreading business risks through diversification and by establishing branches in different states. What is needed, therefore, is a major reform of laws governing the commercial banking system, to remove those regulations and policies that weaken the system. . . .

Several federal statutes restrict the investments banks can make and the services they can offer. In particular, the Glass-Steagall Act of 1933 created an artificial legal distinction in the banking industry between commercial and investment banks. Investment banks can underwrite corporate equity, acting as the middleman between buyers and sellers of stock offerings. They also can finance corporate debt by handling bonds issued by a business, and offer consulting services to businesses. Commercial banks are prohibited by the Glass-Steagall Act from engaging in most of the activities performed by investment banks. They are restricted primarily to taking deposits and making loans to individuals and businesses. The Bank Holding Company Act further restricts bank activities, principally by limiting bank holding companies to those nonbanking activities that the Federal Reserve Board determines "to be so closely related to banking or managing or controlling banks as to be a proper incident thereto." Among other things, this prevents banks from offering mutual fund accounts and from selling insurance or real estate.

Banking Regulations

Defenders of this division in banking argue that allowing commercial banks to go into new types of activities would increase the risk inherent in their business and hence the banks' likelihood of failure. This in turn, it is said, would mean increased losses for the FDIC and the risk to taxpayers of a costly bailout. Just the opposite would be true.

The principal effect of these statutes is to prevent banks from diversifying along product and service lines, and thus the laws actually add to risk and instability. The restrictions also reduce healthy competition in both commercial and investment banking, and within the financial services, brokerage, and insurance industries. Another effect of these restrictions is to block large nonbank companies with an interest in financial services, such as Sears, Roebuck and Company, General Motors Acceptance Corporation (GMAC), and General Electric Credit Corporation, from acquiring and recapitalizing troubled banks.

Ending the artificial "wall of separation" between the two halves of the banking industry, and between banks and other financial companies, would provide enormous benefits to consumers. Americans would be able to obtain insurance, buy stocks, and take out a loan for any purpose from the same bank that handles their checking account. Furthermore, those same banks would be less likely to fail in difficult economic times because their business would be more diversified.

Some opponents of removing the restrictions on commercial bank activities argue that deposit insurance would, in effect, unfairly subsidize banks competing with brokerage firms, insurance companies, and other financial service firms. But if anything, the costs associated with mandatory deposit insurance premiums, reserve requirements, minimum capital standards, and other such restrictions that apply only to banks, actually would put most commercial banks at a price disadvantage.

Congress and the states should abolish all restrictions on bank investments, products, and services. . . .

Clearing Perverse Regulations

The federal regulatory structure poses enormous dangers to America's financial system. If current trends continue unchecked, the American banking industry could encounter the same fate as the savings and loan industry, with an even larger potential bailout cost for taxpayers. . . .

The Administration and Congress need to recognize that federal regulation of the banking industry is a problem that cannot be corrected by fine-tuning. Instead of trying to refine the regulatory structure and improve the behavior of the regulators, lawmakers should instead clear away perverse regulation and allow market forces to discourage reckless management by banks and to encourage stability through diversification.

"Regulators may do the banks a favor by keeping them out of the securities market. "

Do Not Allow Banks to Diversify

Herman Gold

Herman Gold is the pseudonym of a group of professional and academic authors. These authors argue that allowing banks to diversify—that is, to participate in gambling in investment markets and other financial endeavors forbidden to them since the Depression—will further destabilize the American banking system.

As you read, consider the following questions:

1. According to the authors, in what important way do banks differ from securities firms?
2. Why, according to the authors, do banks want to get involved in risky securities dealings? Why do securities firms want to link up with banks?
3. What dangers do the authors see in allowing banks to diversify into the securities markets?

Herman Gold, "Don't Let Banks Play the Market," *The Nation*, July 30-August 6, 1988. Copyright © 1988 by The Nation Co., Inc. Reprinted with permission.

Banks desire to get into the securities business. Conversely, securities firms want to get into banking. Congress is working on new regulations that will grant both these wishes—and why not?

Deregulation has arguably been a success in lowering costs of trucking, air travel and long-distance telephone service. Banks and securities firms are private businesses too, and it seems only fair to let them and the rest of us profit by some competition. Unfortunately for the U.S. taxpayer, the matter is not quite so simple.

The first step toward understanding what's at stake is to recognize an important difference between banks and securities firms: Although both are private businesses trying to make a profit for stockholders, banks do business with a government guarantee. Bank depositors are insured against losses by the Federal Deposit Insurance Corporation. How banks came to have at least some of their liabilities insured by the taxpayer is an interesting piece of history.

The F.D.I.C. came into existence with the passage of the Glass-Steagall Act, on June 16, 1933. Congress enacted this legislation to end a wave of bank runs and, more generally, to encourage the public to entrust its money to U.S. banks. Even a sound and well-managed bank could be forced to close if rumors led a large portion of its depositors to demand their money in a short period of time. Bank closings were a loss to the community in which the bank operated and a threat to commerce.

Eliminating Risk

Glass-Steagall provided government insurance for deposits of up to $2,500 (now $100,000). In return for Federal support for their liabilities, banks were required to do business under government regulation. The regulations enacted were designed to save banks (and the taxpayer) from the frauds and risks of the securities markets. In the aftermath of the crash of 1929, Wall Street was seen as a kind of grand casino in which gamblers played with other people's money. Such disparate political figures as Democratic Senator Carter Glass and Republican Herbert Hoover agreed that banks should not risk taxpayers' money in this casino. Glass-Steagall and subsequent legislation allowed banks to buy and sell stocks and bonds for customers' demands and to make long-term investments in bonds for their own accounts, but it barred short-term trading of most securities, and explicitly forbade banks to underwrite corporate offerings.

What does it mean to underwrite a corporate stock or bond offering? Today, it means that one or a few large firms guarantee a certain price to the issuing company, and make a profit to the extent that they can sell (distribute) the offering at a price higher than the guaranteed one. If they cannot sell the entire offering, they swallow the loss. This kind of high-profile, high-risk, high-profit transaction is considered the apex of the securities business.

Wasserman © 1991, *Boston Globe*. Distributed by the Los Angeles Times Syndicate.
Reprinted with permission.

Until recent years banks were relatively uninterested in securities trading and corporate underwriting, but they are now racing to get into the action. The reason for the rush is a trend usually referred to as "securitization," which has brought about a change in the way credit is pumped through the body economic. In its narrow definition, securitization means pooling debt to be sold as a security—mortgages, for instance, are pooled and sold to pension funds rather than held by banks. More generally, securitization means lenders and borrowers meet directly in securities markets. Rather than raising money by borrowing from banks, large corporations sell bonds and short-term I.O.U.s directly to the public. The agents of these public offerings are securities firms, which can underwrite new issues. In 1986, U.S. corporations did almost 50 percent of their fund-raising in the securities markets. As recently as 1979 the proportion was less than 40 percent. The long-term implications of this trend are not yet clear, since corporations relied on the securities markets for 45 to 50 percent of their funding in the 1950s without driving their bankers out of business. Nevertheless, bankers are worried about the competition.

Securitization reduces corporate costs by cutting out the banker middleman between borrowing corporations and those with funds. From one point of view, this is good news for all of us. Lower transaction costs mean a lower cost of funds for the corporation, a better return for the provider of funds and a more efficient economic engine for the United States. Banks, however, would like to pursue their lost business into the securities markets. . . .

Bad Loans

Behind this rationale lies another one the banks don't like to talk about: They are in financial trouble because they loaned too many billions to Mexico, Brazil and other less-developed countries, which can afford to pay only a fraction of the interest on their huge debts. Most of these loans are carried on the banks' books as assets, thanks to the cooperation of Federal bank examiners and indeed the whole U.S. financial and political establishment. If these loans were recognized as losses, many of the largest banks in the country would have to declare bankruptcy. Thus, financial insiders quietly argue that banks should be allowed and even encouraged to go into the securities market so that income from the new business can help them recapitalize.

Banks, then, have two good reasons for wanting unlimited access to the securities markets. But why are securities firms so eager to go into banking? The answer becomes clear if one examines more closely what a banking charter is worth. In addition to access to the F.D.I.C., a bank has access to the payment clearinghouse that is connected to the Federal Reserve Bank as a lender of last resort. The clearinghouse (the Fedwire network, automated clearinghouses and check-clearing arrangements) enables a bank to pay checks and other claims against its accounts before it receives the corresponding payment from the account holder. A conclusive resolution of transactions at the end of each day (finality of payment) is a boon to commerce, but occasionally requires a bank to draw overnight loans of large size from one of the Federal Reserve Banks to cover the difference between claims paid and accounts due. In emergencies this access to the Federal Reserve as lender of last resort can become very important indeed. When a computer system of the Bank of New York crashed in 1985, the bank borrowed $23 billion overnight from the Federal Reserve Bank of New York to settle its accounts.

Access to the payment clearinghouse and to the Federal Reserve, like access to the F.D.I.C., provides government support for the convenience and security of the banking business. So just as banks want to become universal financial institutions by adding securities trading and corporate underwriting, securities firms want to become universal financial institutions by buying banks or pieces of banks to gain access to the Federal Reserve payments mechanism.

Incompetent Bankers

[Bankers are] coming along saying, "We need to be deregulated so we can get into other industries such as securities and insurance and others." They're saying this at the same time that the banking industry has come in seeking $75 billion that they're going to need to bail out banks that have been incompetently managed. If you can't make money banking, where people come and give you money, then how are you going to make money where you actually have to deliver a product?

I think banking is too important to be left to bankers, much less that we should now turn over substantial other segments of our economy to bankers. These are people who have already been making a mess of it. Why should we turn them loose to make a bigger mess, following in line with the S&L executives?

Jim Hightower, *Multinational Monitor,* June 1991.

The competing ambitions of banks and securities firms are represented by powerful lobbying efforts orchestrated by the American Bankers Association (A.B.A.) and the Securities Industry Association (S.I.A.). . . .

Narrow Issues

Congressional concerns are focused on two relatively narrow issues. One is antitrust. Regulations are being drafted that will limit the size of the new universal financial institutions. Citicorp, for instance, will not be allowed to buy Merrill Lynch, or vice versa. The other issue is how to prevent the spread of government involvement in the whole financial system—the access to the F.D.I.C., the payments system and the discount window of the Federal Reserve—so that those who own banks cannot take government along with them into the risks of the securities business. It will not be easy to draw a line that will confine government support to only one part of a single financial institution.

Let us suppose, however, that clever drafting of new banking regulations can prevent monopolistic combinations and avoid a blanket taxpayer guarantee of the finances of full-service institutions. There remain two important long-term concerns not being adequately addressed in the Congress or elsewhere.

The first concern is the financial health of banks. Their troubles are real but the proposed solution—letting them compete without trammel in the securities markets—is an illusory one. Big-bank exposure from bad loans (for empty shopping centers and mothballed drilling rigs, as well as loans to Brazil and Mexico) exceeds $100 billion. The potential income from the securities business is not nearly large enough to wipe out these bad debts on bank balance sheets. As a rough estimate of the additional revenues and profits available, consider the earnings of the large investment firms and the national full-line securities houses. Underwriting revenues for them in 1986 (their best year ever) reached almost $5 billion, and trading revenues about $10 billion. With other revenues, these produced a pretax profit of less than $4 billion. Clearly, even a substantial portion of this profit would not take the banks very far toward covering their bad loans. And it is by no means clear that banks can count on making a profit. Newcomers in any business tend to drive profits down, and hiring personnel with the skills required to handle the new business would be a serious up-front cost for the banks.

And while profits may be less than anticipated, the risks may prove higher. Securities firms have been taking greater risks of late to keep their bottom line growing. The four U.S. underwriters of the British government's stake in British Petroleum lost almost $100 million each when the market collapsed in October 1987, even after the British government intervened (reportedly under prodding from the U.S. Treasury) to limit losses. The U.S. underwriters were victims of bad timing, of course, but the size of the bet each made was in line with the current market practice of concentrating risk and return in underwriting.

Doing the Banks a Favor

Concern for the financial health of banks unleashed to find new types of business should also be sharpened by a recent experiment. Between 1980 and 1982, Savings and Loan Associations (S&Ls) in the United States were caught between rising interest rates, which had to be paid to keep their depositors, and much lower yields of mortgages they had already locked in. Their crisis was successfully represented to Congress, which, after due deliberation, offered guarantees of solvency and liberalized the laws that had largely limited S&Ls to mortgage financing. While the intention of the Garn-St. Germain Act of 1982 was to help the thrifts get through their earnings crisis, the result, unfortunately, was much different. Some S&Ls turned themselves around and returned to profitability, but many went from crisis to disaster in trying to compete in unfamiliar kinds of business. Most of the failing thrifts across the nation have been bailed out by state and Federal insurance—that is, at the expense of the taxpayer. The same result is likely to occur on an even greater scale if banks are encouraged to enter the corporate securities markets.

Nor can it be argued that the securities business is on its way to much greater revenues and profits that could in the future save the banks. In fact, the recent downturn in business for securities firms has led them to fire many of the younger people so recently recruited on $100,000 salaries. Booming profits for securities firms between 1982 and 1986 may have been the upside of a cycle rather than the stable trend that many took it to be. Regulators may do the banks a favor by keeping them out of the securities market until it is clearer what the future holds for this business.

Evaluating Sources of Information

When historians study and interpret past events, they use two kinds of sources: primary and secondary. Primary sources are eyewitness accounts. For example, a man's personal account of losing his home because of a bank failure would be a primary source. An economist's report which incorporates the man's account in an analysis of the banking system would be a secondary source. Primary and secondary sources may be decades or even hundreds of years old, and often historians find that the sources offer conflicting and contradictory information. To fully evaluate documents and assess their accuracy, historians analyze the credibility of the documents' authors and, in the case of secondary sources, analyze the credibility of the information the authors used.

Historians are not the only people who encounter conflicting information, however. Anyone who reads a daily newspaper, watches television, or just talks to different people will encounter many different views. Writers and speakers use sources of information to support their own statements. Thus, critical thinkers, just like historians, must question the writer's or speaker's sources of information as well as the writer or speaker.

While there are many criteria that can be applied to assess the accuracy of a primary or secondary source, for this activity you will be asked to apply three. For each source listed on the following page, ask yourself the following questions: First, did the person actually see or participate in the event he or she is reporting? This will help you determine the credibility of the information—an eyewitness to an event is an extremely valuable source. Second, does the person have a vested interest in the report? Assessing the person's social status, economic interests, professional affiliations, nationality, and religious or political beliefs will be helpful in considering this question. By evaluating this you will be able to determine how objective the person's report may be. Third, how qualified is the author to make the statements he or she is making? Consider what the person's profession is and how he or she might know about the event. Someone who has spent years being involved with or studying the issue may be able to offer more information than someone who simply is offering an uneducated opinion; for example, a politician or layperson.

Keeping the above criteria in mind, imagine you are writing a report on whether recent bank failures have hurt average Americans. You decide to cite an equal number of primary and secondary sources. Listed below are several sources that may be useful for your research. *Place a P next to those descriptions you believe are primary sources. Place an S next to those descriptions you believe are secondary sources.* Next, based on the above criteria, *rank the primary sources, assigning the number (1) to that which appears the most valuable, (2) to the source likely to be the second-most valuable, and so on, until all the primary sources are ranked. Then rank the secondary sources, again using the above criteria.*

<table>
<tr><td>*P or S*</td><td></td><td>*Rank in Importance*</td></tr>
<tr><td>_____</td><td>1. Five accounts by people who have lost their homes because of bank failures.</td><td>_____</td></tr>
<tr><td>_____</td><td>2. A government document that reviews reports of all bank failures in the twentieth century and their impact on the economy.</td><td>_____</td></tr>
<tr><td>_____</td><td>3. A report written by the president of a failed bank, detailing the amount of money corporations and individuals have lost as a result of his bank's closing.</td><td>_____</td></tr>
<tr><td>_____</td><td>4. A newspaper article that uses statistics from the American Bankers Association to show that bank customers have nothing to worry about.</td><td>_____</td></tr>
<tr><td>_____</td><td>5. The viewpoint in this chapter by Lowell L. Bryan.</td><td>_____</td></tr>
<tr><td>_____</td><td>6. An article in a scholarly economics journal entitled "The Impact of Recent Bank Closings on the Nation's Economy."</td><td>_____</td></tr>
<tr><td>_____</td><td>7. A television documentary called "The Banking Crisis in America."</td><td>_____</td></tr>
<tr><td></td><td>8. A speech by the president that states that although America's banks are in a strong position, Congress has a plan to bail out any that should fail.</td><td></td></tr>
<tr><td>_____</td><td>9. An article in *Forbes*, a business magazine, that quotes small business owners on how the banking situation has affected them.</td><td>_____</td></tr>
<tr><td>_____</td><td>10. A book called *The Future of Banking* that pulls together the predictions of several banking experts.</td><td>_____</td></tr>
<tr><td>_____</td><td>11. The viewpoint in this chapter by Herman Gold.</td><td>_____</td></tr>
</table>

Periodical Bibliography

The following articles have been selected to supplement the diverse views presented in this chapter.

Jonathan Brown	"Risk, Regulation, and Responsibility: Reforming the Banks," *Multinational Monitor*, June 1991.
James B. Burnham	"Deposit Insurance: The Case for the Narrow Bank," *Regulation*, Spring 1991. Available from the Cato Institute, 224 Second St. SE, Washington, DC 20003.
Ron Chernow	"Why Save the Banks?" *The American Prospect*, Summer 1991. Available from PO Box 7645, Princeton, NJ 08543.
John J. Curran	"Does Deregulation Make Sense?" *Fortune*, June 5, 1989.
L.J. Davis	"The Problem with Banks? Bankers," *Harper's Magazine*, June 1991.
John Steele Gordon	"Understanding the S&L Mess," *American Heritage*, February/March 1991.
William Greider	"Bailout Now, Pay Later: Will Big Banks Go the Way of S&Ls?" *Rolling Stone*, June 13, 1991.
Ronald Grzywinski	"The New Old-Fashioned Banking," *Harvard Business Review*, May/June 1991. Available from Harvard Business School Publishing Division, Boston, MA 02163.
Gary Hector	"Bank Reform Won't Save the Banks," *Fortune*, April 8, 1991.
Jonathan R. Macey and Geoffrey P. Miller	"The Once and Future American Banking Industry," *The American Enterprise*, September/October and November/December 1991.
John Miller	"The Banks Came Tumbling Down," *Dollars & Sense*, October 1991.
John Miller	"Hard Times for Bankers," *Dollars & Sense*, September 1991.
Matthew Miller	"The 100 Grand Illusion," *The Washington Monthly*, July/August 1990.
Ralph Nader	"No More Bailouts!" *Mother Jones*, September/October 1990.
Robert J. Samuelson	"Who's Being Protected?" *Newsweek*, February 19, 1990.
Walker F. Todd	"Time to Stop Bailing Out the Banks," *The Nation*, September 16, 1991.
Catherine Yang and Mike McNamee	"Reform, or a Crackdown on Banking?" *Business Week*, July 15, 1991.

What Is the Future of American Labor?

ECONOMICS IN AMERICA

Chapter Preface

Dramatic changes are occurring in America's workplaces. As the U.S. population ages and shifts in ethnic makeup, minorities, women, part-time workers, and older workers are a growing percentage of the working population. As the economy moves away from heavy industry, service and white-collar positions are increasing. As America finds tougher competition from its worldwide trading partners, companies strive for more ways to cut costs. According to a 1991 article in *The Futurist*, a bimonthly magazine that analyzes future economic, social, and political trends, all of these factors will "bring sweeping changes" to American labor. Among these changes, many predict, will be the demise of trade unions.

The union movement rose in the 1930s after an era of extreme exploitation of workers by employers. Unions formed to fight for workers' rights and for their economic improvement. Union strength reached its height in the 1950s, when one in four workers belonged to unions. Labor experts maintain that union strength has been gradually declining ever since. Today, an economy that seems to be shrinking rather than growing leaves less room for unions to negotiate. With industries such as automobile manufacturing collapsing, and others merging and then reducing their size, workers are glad simply to be employed and are less willing to make demands that might threaten their jobs.

Perhaps even worse for the future of labor unions, many corporations have become "smarter" in the way they treat employees. They offer desirable benefits and good working conditions, sometimes on tacit condition that workers forego belonging to a union. Another major management trend that may be causing union decline is the move to increase worker involvement. This movement has allowed workers to feel that they have more say in company decision making and so no longer need unions to speak for them.

Union advocates, however, say that despite these positive changes, unions are still needed. For instance, the *Minority Trendsletter*, a quarterly journal that focuses on social justice issues, points to a strong need for union representation among workers who have little power over their employment conditions. These workers are minorities, women, and unorganized service employees—secretaries, health-care workers, and teachers, for example. As union representation in these industries grows, say union advocates, unions will again become a vital force.

Union strength is one of the issues debated in the following viewpoints as the authors consider the status of American workers today and in the future.

"Unions have little if anything to contribute to America's progress."

Unions Are Obsolete

Anthony Harrigan and William R. Hawkins

Anthony Harrigan, president of the U.S. Industrial Council Educational Foundation, is a newspaper columnist and author of seventeen books. William R. Hawkins is an economics consultant, professor, and author. In the following viewpoint, Harrigan and Hawkins claim that unions do not meet the needs of working people and contribute little to American progress. The authors believe that unions cause higher prices on consumer goods, decreased productivity, and unemployment.

As you read, consider the following questions:

1. Why do the authors say that unions do not deserve their old reputation for helping downtrodden workers?
2. List two examples of the harmful burdens the authors say unions impose on business?
3. According to Harrigan and Hawkins, why is the push by unions to increase the minimum wage a deceptive tactic?

Excerpted from *American Economic Preeminence: Goals for the 1990s* by Anthony Harrigan and William R. Hawkins, 1989. Reprinted with permission of the U.S. Industrial Council Educational Foundation, Washington, D.C.

Unionism has been defended on the grounds that it helps poor, downtrodden workers gain a larger piece of the pie. Yet the history of unions in America does not support this notion. Unions have generally only been successful in industries with high productivity and which used skilled labor and/or were in strategic fields with economic "leverage." This is because a union cannot gain for its members wages and benefits out of thin air. It can only be successful in a field that is prosperous. But the union acts to erode the prosperity of the industry it has penetrated, leading eventually to the decline of both the industry and the union. It does this with higher wages that raise prices, lower output and reduce employment; with work rules that decrease productivity; and with resistance to innovation. Princeton labor economist Albert Rees has concluded:

> If the union is viewed solely in terms of its effect on the economy, it must in my opinion be considered an obstacle to the optimum performance of our economic system. It alters the wage structure in a way that impedes the growth of employment in sectors of the economy where productivity and income are naturally high and that leaves too much labor in low-income sectors of the economy like southern agriculture and the least skilled service trades . . . and while some of this gain may be at the expense of the owners of capital, most of it must be at the expense of consumers and the lower-paid workers. . . .

The decline of the American rail system has been a national tragedy. There has been a small revival in recent years in the form of new shortline railroads. However, the rail workers unions are seeking to cripple these new small rail lines, many operated in conjunction with local governments, by saddling them with the same labor rules and practices imposed on larger, long-haul lines. These short lines are vital to many small communities, but they cannot bear the imposition of unreasonable costs, delays and disruptions, and other inefficiencies created by unions. The Railway Labor Act, passed in 1926, permits featherbedding and holds railroads to other outdated work practices while also burdening them with excessive financial requirements. The Act should be amended so that progress in the railroad industry is no longer considered illegal.

Labor Law Reforms

The burdens imposed on the trucking industry are of the same basic characteristic as those imposed on the railroads. Trucking companies have to deal with the Teamsters Union which is rightly regarded as one of the most corrupt and hoodlum-dominated unions in the country.

Labor law has tended to support unions, giving them a power they would not otherwise be able to exercise on their own. One can argue that the modern union movement in the United States was created when the government established the National Labor Relations Board (the Wagner Act) in 1935. Ironically, the NLRB was upheld by the Supreme Court in 1937 on the grounds that it would *decrease* the disruption of the economy by unions. The idea was that once unions were recognized and made secure, they would be less militant. That strikes increased by an order of magnitude during the decade following the NLRB's establishment proves that the effect was just the opposite.

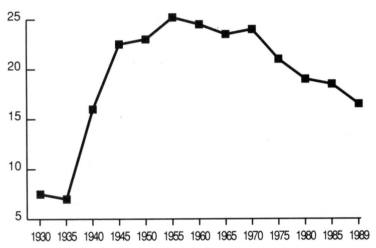

Union Membership Declines
(membership as a percent of the total labor force)

Source: U.S. Department of Labor, Bureau of Labor Statistics.

Public reaction to union abuses led to the amendment of the NLRB in 1947 (the Taft-Hartley Act). Most of the reforms were made to protect workers from coercion by union bosses. Among the changes was an attempt to strengthen the rights of workers not to join a union if they so desired. This "right to work" provision was made conditional, however, by the inclusion in Section 7 of the phrase "except to the extent that such right may be effected by an agreement requiring union membership as a condition of employment." In other words, if the union can gain a closed ship by contract with a firm, the individual worker loses his rights. This is an intolerable infringement on the civil liberties of every employee. The right of an individual not to join a union should be considered as well-protected under the Constitution and the labor laws as the right of a worker to join a union. Though several states have enacted right to work laws, a true national right to work must become the law of the land.

Unions are the main driving force behind efforts to increase the minimum wage law, not because union members are paid the minimum wage set by statute (union members make far more than this), but because the unions know that the minimum wage is used as the "floor" upon which entire negotiated wage structures are built. By raising the floor, unions hope to raise the levels they are on as well. If such a tactic is successful it will represent another income transfer from lower-paid workers to union members, as well as increased unemployment throughout the economy.

It is an elementary principle of economics that raising the price of any commodity by fiat means that less of it will be used. Applied to labor, this means that wage increases unrelated to productivity increases will lead to higher unemployment. The distinguished economist Thomas Sowell has written:

> The term "minimum wage" law defines the process by its hoped for results. But the law itself does not guarantee that any wage will be paid, because employment remains a voluntary transaction. All that the law does is reduce the set of options available. . . . What is perhaps most surprising is the persistence and scope of belief that people can be made better off by reducing their options. In the case of the so-called minimum wage law, the empirical evidence has been growing that it not only increases unemployment, but that it does so most among the most disadvantaged workers.

This is because employment depends on a comparison of wages with productivity. Those who are least productive, due to lack of skills, experience or work discipline, will be those who lose their jobs as mandated wage rates move beyond what their labor is worth to prospective employers. The effect of a higher real minimum wage will be to expand the "unemployable" underclass with the predictable effects on welfare costs and crime rates. . . .

Unions Growing Desperate

As unions have retreated in recent years, a new strategy has been devised by union militants. This is the so-called "corporate campaign" whereby a local dispute is transformed into a national issue. The union targets outside directors on a company's board and endeavors to bring financial and media pressure on these directors' own companies. Here and there this strategy has worked, but it has also failed, most conspicuously against the Hormel Company in Minnesota. The "corporate campaign" is enormously disruptive to the workers involved and to the communities where the targeted plants are hit. Communities and the citizens are whipped into a frenzy, with emotional confrontations that leave lasting divisions. Since media attention is crucial to this union strategy, violence is often used to attract national press coverage. This strategy is fresh evidence of the labor movement's lack of concern for the public interest.

A more subtle campaign, an effort to deal with the serious image problem unions have acquired for themselves over the years, is to move into more middle class and "family" issues. Unions have focused attention on parental leave, mandated social benefits and various health issues. This strategy has been much more successful. However, the old economic realities persist. Whether unions aim for higher wages or high benefits, the result is the same: fewer jobs and weaker industries. Unions are exhibiting, in overt form, the same malady that has infected most of an American society hooked on instant consumption, leisure and debt: the desire to consume more than is being produced. This is a dead end.

Unions Are Obsolete

As the union movement shrinks, its radical fringe comes to assume greater influence on the remains. Though traditional union leaders are pushing middle-class and family values in an attempt to lure back workers, particularly women, they are losing ground within the labor movement to left-wing activists with an anti-family political agenda that includes joint campaigns with lesbian and "gay rights" groups and an anti-American foreign policy agenda of U.S. disarmament and support for communist regimes. As we move into the 1990s, it will become increasingly apparent that unions have little if anything to contribute to America's progress.

"Unions . . . can provide an important support for the maintenance of political democracy."

Unions Are Vital

Thomas C. Kohler

Thomas C. Kohler, associate professor of law at Boston University, wrote the following viewpoint for *Crisis*, a monthly journal of social and religious thought. In this viewpoint, Kohler argues that despite many predictions of the demise of trade unions, these organizations are still vital and deserve support. He asserts that unions provide important forums for direct citizen involvement in government, a function Kohler believes is essential to the health of American democracy.

As you read, consider the following questions:

1. Kohler calls collective bargaining "a private law-making system." What does he mean?
2. According to the author, how do unions enhance the status of the individual?
3. Why does Kohler believe the loss of trade unions would harm American society?

Thomas C. Kohler, "In Praise of Unions," *Crisis*, October 1989. Reprinted by permission of *Crisis*, PO Box 1006 Notre Dame, IN 46556.

Unions are in a rather odd position today. Once the subject of intense controversy, they have become one of the few things about which both conservatives and liberals generally agree. And, as the common view has it, there is precious little about unions worth praising.

As conservatives tend to think and to speak of them, unions are economic institutions, plain and simple, whose main purpose is to exact higher wages for fewer hours than the market would otherwise permit. Unions accomplish this goal through acting as cartels, i.e. they function as alliances of resource suppliers whose control over job opportunities permits them to influence the outcomes of the market process in favor of their members. By so impeding the functioning of the market, conservatives frequently argue, unions decrease overall social welfare by imposing costs that everyone else has to bear.

Conservative Criticisms of Unions

These costs assume a variety of forms. Unions, as their critics point out, tend to be more prevalent in sectors of the economy where productivity and income are naturally high. By altering the wage structure, unions induce firms to hire fewer workers. This results in too much labor being employed in the lower-paid sectors of the economy where the least-skilled service occupations tend to predominate. The gains enjoyed by the "barons of labor" (who were relatively well-off to begin with) come primarily at the expense of the nonunionized. Thus, their critics often argue, unions increase inequalities in the distribution of income. Moreover, through work rules and other restrictions they impose, unions also lower the productivity of labor and capital. In all, as many conservatives see it, unions leave all but their members less well-off by obstructing the most efficient allocation and use of resources.

Whether—and the extent to which—this picture of the economic impact of unions is accurate remains a subject of debate among professional economists, and at least one recent, major empirical study has called much of it into question. But, a negative opinion of unions is hardly unique to conservatives and free-market advocates. Liberals themselves increasingly have come to regard unions as archaic left-overs of an earlier era whose value (to the extent it existed) has long since passed.

Liberal Criticisms of Unions

The standard liberal critique of unions is founded on the view that majorities pose a constant threat to individuals and their rights and cannot be trusted. Thus, many liberals are as profoundly skeptical of unions as they are of legislatures and other institutions of majority rule, and for the same reason. In this view, individuals are safest when insulated from the venalities and biases that majoritarian institutions so frequently express. Consequently, as this framework has it, functions traditionally performed by autonomous employee associations (unions) can be undertaken more reliably and equitably by some arm of the state.

Thus, for example, disputes over employee discharges—which in the unionized setting typically are adjusted through a private grievance arbitration process that the union and the employer jointly administer—are seen by many liberals as better adjudicated before courts or state administrative boards. Similarly, other aspects of the employment relationship are regarded as being more fairly and effectively established through uniform, statutorily set standards than is possible when they are privately arranged through the terms of a union contract. In this view, fairness is a function of procedure, the formality and regularity of which the state best can guarantee. Indeed, as many liberals see it, the union movement itself simply represents a sort of historical way station in the evolving recognition of rights that majorities may not infringe.

Distrust of Majority Rule

The distrust of majority rule that underlies many liberals' misgivings about unions also describes the point at which the views of left and right often converge. Like their liberal colleagues, many conservatives, particularly those with a libertarian orientation, also distrust majorities. Though their starting points differ, their jointly-held suspicion about majoritarian institutions frequently leads liberals and conservatives to the same conclusions. Thus, left and right alike condemn unions on the same grounds they sometimes employ to argue that the judiciary's power to review and overturn legislation is necessary if individual rights are to be protected. Government through non-representative institutions, they agree, is safer and more stable than reliance upon majority rule. What chiefly separates them, of course, are the types of policies they think these non-representative bodies (primarily courts) should adopt. Skepticism about the capacity of the common person to exercise reason and self-restraint joins many on the right and left in the view that democracy itself is a utopian ideal.

In the popular mind, unions do not seem to fare much better. The idea of a union not infrequently tends to be vaguely associated with Archie Bunker characters and cartoon versions of autocratic and possibly corrupt "boss" leadership. To many, unions as institutions seem a feature of smokestack industries, and thus appear inappropriate to the needs of the (hopefully envisioned) high-tech economy of the future. These views seem to be borne out in union membership trends. Though the reasons for it are complex and controversial, the fact is that private sector union-ism has been in decline since the mid-1950s. Today, in the private sector, unions lose more than half of the elections to which employees are asked to vote to signify their desire for representation. . . .

Reasons to Support Unions

Unions and the practice of bargaining can provide an important support for the maintenance of political democracy. To understand how this is so, it is necessary to understand something about the nature of collective bargaining.

© Gary Huck/*People's Weekly World*. Reprinted with permission.

As people tend to think of it, collective bargaining is simply a process through which wage and benefit rates are set. While this is a part—and an important part—of collective bargaining, it hardly captures its essence. Collective bargaining is best understood as a private law-making system. As the Supreme Court has described it, the collective bargaining agreement is "more than a contract; it is a generalized code" which represents "an effort to erect a system of industrial self-government" through which the employment relationship may be "governed by an agreed-upon rule of law."

This rule is one that the parties alone are responsible for promulgating and administering. And it is in the activity of deciding the character and application of this rule that the importance of collective bargaining rests. For it is through their involvement in the process that average citizens can become engaged in deciding the law that most directly determines the details of their daily lives. Thus, unions and the practice of collective bargaining can act as schools for democracy where the habits of self-governance and direct responsibility are instilled.

Sharing in decisions on matters like eligibility for promotions and advanced training, education and health benefits, the discipline of fellow employees or the most fair way to handle a novel employment matter, may appear to lack the cachet that attaches to Supreme Court decisions or to legislative elections. But, it is a mistake to regard such issues as too mundane for serious attention. As Tocqueville so clearly understood, individuals and society alike become self-governing only through repeatedly and regularly engaging in acts of self-government. It is when a people no longer have direct responsibility for making the day-to-day decisions about the order of their lives, Tocqueville correctly warned, that a democracy encounters the greatest danger of becoming perverted.

Unions Mean Citizen Involvement

As things now stand, the town meeting, the neighborhood ward, grassroots political clubs, and the other local institutions that once characterized American democracy have largely disappeared. Though often overlooked, unions are one institution that can stand in their stead as a means for direct citizen involvement in the activities of self-governance. Collective bargaining represents the only alternative to the pervasive state regulation of a primary social relationship—the relationship of employment. It is no coincidence that as the practice of collective bargaining has declined, the state, through legislation and the judiciary, has assumed an increasingly prominent role in employment relations issues. In a society in which one's job is generally both a primary form of wealth and a determinant of status, the significance of direct citizen involvement in deciding the law of employment cannot be discounted.

Unions have another characteristic important to the habits that sustain a democracy. They are autonomous associations, independent of the government and of the institutions on which their members are economically reliant. Consequently, the activities unions undertake, whether at the workplace or in the form of the many (and often unnoticed) social welfare programs unions sponsor, occur as a result of self-decision and self-organization. Thus, unions can help to overcome the sorts of indifference and unthinking dependence that corrode the habits of self-direction on which democracy is based. By mediating the relationship between employees, the state, and their employers, unions also act to diffuse the power these institutions exercise over individuals. In so doing, unions serve to enhance individual status.

A Forum for Moral Consensus

If it is to be successful, the course of action a union follows on any matter is dependent upon the "rank and file" having reached a consensus about it. Like any group decision, such consensus represents the product of a discussion. The opportunities unions provide to engage people in such discussions is another achievement [we] should especially value.

Unions Teach Democracy

A strong trade union movement, with widespread collective bargaining, can strengthen all of society. A recent U.S. government report showed that union workers earn $2 more an hour in wages and $3 more in benefits than unorganized workers. Because of their higher pay and better security, they are less likely to need government-provided welfare or health benefits. Union workers are also more likely to have a voice in workplace decisions and local affairs. Strong democratic unions can be the training grounds for community leaders. That is one reason unions have been resisted by totalitarian regimes and why they should be fostered in democratic societies.

Joseph Sullivan, *Origins*, August 31, 1989.

By providing a forum to discuss, deliberate over, and decide what is to be done here and now about practical affairs, unions can involve people both in an inquiry into, and in the development of, a rational consensus over what ought to be valued and why. Such discussions truly are normative, and participation in them engages people in the most distinctly human of activities: reflection and choice. What is so crucial about such discussions is that they require people to decide for themselves the kind of people they will be. In a society increasingly dominated by large institutions and in which opinions are so pervasively shaped by the media, such opportunities are indeed rare. . . .

In short, the human voice is normative. As Aristotle points out in the *Politics*, while the utterances of other types of animals are restricted to expressions of pleasure or pain, human conversation exhibits some apprehension of the good and the hurtful, the just and the less desirable. Typical of human discussion about needs or things wished for is the effort to justify them by reference to some hierarchy of values and notions of fairness. As humans, our potential for authentic self-rule comes through our involvement in such conversations. . . .

A third reason that [we] should care about the fate of unions pertains to the general dissolution of mediating groups as a whole. No single "mediating structure," whether in the form of families, religious congregations, neighborhoods, civic organizations and service associations, or unions, is likely to survive in the absence of other such bodies. All of them require and can inculcate the same habits: decision, commitment, self-rule, and direct responsibility. When people lose these habits, no single institution alone can restore them. In brief, the existence and decline of such bodies is mutually conditioning; the loss or deformation of any one of them threatens the rest.

"They are still pushing the 1930s issues."

Unions Must Change Outmoded Methods

James Risen

In the following viewpoint, James Risen, a staff writer for the *Los Angeles Times*, asserts that unions are in trouble because they are still operating as though it were the 1930s, when the desperation of workers caught in the Great Depression allowed unconscionable exploitation by employers. In order to be a power in the future, Risen states, unions must open their eyes to the causes of declining membership and address the issues important to today's workers, issues such as child care, flexible work schedules, and health insurance.

As you read, consider the following questions:

1. Why does Risen consider the unions' traditional organizing and bargaining methods out of date?
2. List two of the reasons given in this viewpoint for the decline in union membership.
3. Does Risen believe unions are dead? Why or why not?

James Risen, "Unions' Future Questioned After Summer of Setbacks," *Los Angeles Times*, August 15, 1989. Copyright, 1989, Los Angeles Times. Reprinted with permission.

The crisis atmosphere was palpable around the Drake Hotel as top union officers found themselves muttering under their breaths as they walked out of the closed 1989 summer meeting of the AFL-CIO's executive council.

The AFL-CIO's leadership had just been listening to the worsening reports coming back from labor's front lines: one presentation on the disastrous Eastern Airlines strike, followed by an equally grim update on the coal miners' strike against Pittston Co.'s eastern mines.

The news was all bad. . . .

Out-of-Date Methods

Many labor specialists believe that the union movement's traditional organizing and bargaining methods—forged in the crucible of the Great Depression—seem badly out of date to workers raised in an era of a highly mobile work force, international competition and managements that have become far more sophisticated in the ways they deal with employees.

"A lot of people just feel that labor unions can't do anything for them any more," said Raymond Hilgert, a labor analyst at Washington University in St. Louis.

"What unions are not offering is up-to-date concepts that appeal to workers," added Homer Deakins, an anti-union labor lawyer whose firm helped Nissan defeat the UAW in Smyrna.

"They are still pushing the 1930s issues."

American labor leaders, of course, dispute that unions are in the throes of a permanent decline. They argue that key demographic trends—including the growth in the number of women and Latinos in the work force, groups that tend to be far more pro-union than white males—bode well for increased unionization in the future. They point also to a 1988 poll by the Gallup Organization that found public approval of unions to be at its highest points since 1981.

"In my view, we are in the early stages of a labor renaissance in the United States," asserted Philip Comstock, executive director of the Wilson Center for Public Research, which conducts union-sponsored polls of workers during organizing drives.

"Every poll I've seen shows that many millions more workers want to join labor unions than are members today," AFL-CIO President Lane Kirkland added in a news conference. "And we want to take advantage of that."

Kirkland and others counsel patience; they note that organizing drives are rarely successful on the first vote. It took years, for example, for the UAW to organize Ford and General Motors in the 1930s.

"We are not short of breath," he insisted.

Yet, outside observers see little evidence to support the AFL-

CIO's optimism. In fact, almost every available statistic shows that the labor movement has been unable to reverse the erosion in its membership and influence that began in the late 1950s and early 1960s.

Unions now represent just 16.8% of American workers, down from 30% just 20 years ago, and union membership has stagnated at about 17 million during a decade in which the labor force has undergone explosive growth, climbing over the 100 million mark for the first time.

Old Style Still Reigns

Even the most unreflective union leaders finally recognized in the '80s that labor had its own internal problems. Yet the bureaucratic business, or service, model of unions still reigns: officials act on behalf of a passive membership, negotiating and servicing contracts and possibly plugging for a Democratic candidate around election time.

David Moberg, *In These Times*, November 7-13, 1990.

Such a dramatic loss of economic and bargaining clout has further convinced workers today that unions can do little to help—especially when they see labor forced to agree to steep wage concessions or risk disastrous strikes such as those at Eastern or Pittston.

Even AFL-CIO officers concede that many workers now believe that the potential benefits of joining a union do not outweigh the risk that management will simply shift its work overseas or to a non-union site. At the same time, union leaders charge, federal labor regulators move so slowly that workers feel they have little protection against companies that seek to delay or ignore union victories.

"I think there is a heightened fear among workers today of management retribution" for attempting to unionize, said Dick Wilson, director of organizing for the AFL-CIO. "There's no question that is a major obstacle to organizing."

In fact, unions now mount only about half as many organizing elections as they did a decade ago, according to the National Labor Relations Board.

Irrelevant Unions

"Non-union workers today see unions as almost irrelevant to them," said David Sirota, chairman of Sirota, Alper & Pfau, an independent New York-based consulting firm that does extensive polling and survey work among employees of major corporations.

219

Improved labor relations at many corporations also have lessened worker interest in unions, Sirota and other researchers have found. As employee involvement programs have spread throughout American industry, management has been able to usurp one of the traditional functions of the labor union—providing a channel through which workers can voice their grievances.

Although in some industries—most notably the domestic auto industry—workers have rebelled against such employee involvement programs, they have generally led to reduced tension in the workplace, Sirota said.

"Most non-union workers we interview say they don't need a union, in part because management has gotten better and more clever in their basic policies of how they treat workers," Sirota said.

Treats Workers Well

"There is a reason, after all, that a company like IBM has 200,000 workers in this country that are all non-union," he added. "IBM is not a vicious company with union busters. Their game is treating people well."

Such practices clearly worked at Nissan. The popularity of the company's Japanese-style worker-involvement programs, including an employee peer review process for workers threatened with being fired, helped turn the tide against the UAW.

During the organizing drive, Nissan successfully mounted an internal media campaign that sought to convince workers that they were part of "one team" that would only be splintered into two by a union. The pitch found a receptive audience—Nissan, following a practice gaining increasing acceptance among large corporations, had screened its employees before hiring them to determine their attitudes on labor unions.

"The company is giving me everything I need," Nissan assembly line worker Farron Hendrix said at the time of the election in Smyrna. "I get a leased car, they've got an employee recreation center and a swimming pool. They treat me like a movie star."

Indeed, treating employees fairly seems to be paying off much better than head-busting for companies interested in getting rid of unions.

"Pepsi has changed, they are more of a people-oriented company now," said Gary Peshle, a route salesman for Pepsi-Cola, who voted to decertify his Teamsters local and revert to non-union status. "It used to be that management cracked a whip, and we had nothing but turmoil for five year with the union. But now management has more of an attitude where they ask us about things first."

"The only people that were nasty here were the union people," added Joan Bayan, a credit union loan officer who recently voted to decertify the UAW.

"If people have been through a fair and honestly run community-held election . . . it is harder for the unionbusters to create . . . hysteria."

Unions Must Enlist Community Support

Amy Newell interviewed by *Multinational Monitor*

Amy Newell, the first woman elected to national office in an American basic manufacturing union, is secretary-treasurer of the United Electrical, Radio, and Machine Workers of America (UE). In the following viewpoint, she is interviewed by *Multinational Monitor*, a monthly journal of political and social opinion. Newell asserts that businesses set out to "bust," or destroy, unions. The only way to circumvent this, she believes, is to establish fair community-based labor boards as alternatives to the present government-run labor boards that tend to be biased in favor of employers.

As you read, consider the following questions:

1. According to Newell, why is U.S. union membership declining?
2. Why does Newell believe community leaders can be effective labor board members?
3. According to Newell, what is the purpose of enlisting community members in a "fair election committee"?

Amy Newell, interviewed by *Multinational Monitor*, "Building the Nation, an interview with Amy Newell." This article first appeared in the April 1991 issue of *Multinational Monitor*, PO Box 19405, Washington, DC 20036; subscriptions, $22/year. Reprinted with permission.

Multinational Monitor: What are the main reasons that union membership in the United States is declining?

Amy Newell: Well, there are structural questions having to do with changes in the economy. The mass production industries in this country were organized in the big CIO tidal wave in the 30s and 40s. A lot of newer industries that have developed since that time have not been organized in a mass way.

Also, the difficulties in organizing are really a tremendous obstacle not only to unions, but to workers who would like to organize to join unions.

No Meaningful Penalties for Corporations

MM: What sort of difficulties do you specifically mean?

Newell: The way the National Labor Relations law and enforcement is structured, it really pays for most bosses to break the law. That is the simple fact of the matter. There are no meaningful penalties for those who violate the law, and the procedures for enforcing it are incredibly time-consuming and slow.

For example, we organized a shop in Chicago in October 1987. The workers voted by a 2 to 1 margin to join the union. The employer filed objections to the conduct of the election. Those objections were investigated by the [National Labor Relations] Board and dismissed. The employer appealed to the full Board in Washington, D.C., which certified the UE as the collective bargaining agent.

[Still], the boss refused to bargain. The company simply said, "Make us; make us bargain." So it dragged on. It took three years before the Seventh Circuit Court of Appeals finally ordered the company to sit down and bargain with the union under threat of some sort of penalty, a fine. And after three years of stalling, that was all the employer had to do—sit down and bargain—even though they had been in violation of the law for almost three years.

It is the same thing when workers are fired because of their union activities. It is difficult to present a case—you practically need a smoking gun to have the Board agree that someone was fired because of union activities. But even when it is crystal clear, it can take years and years, and all the employer is obligated to do then is offer reinstatement and, at most, pay back wages minus any interim earnings of the worker. Most working people, when they are fired, have to get another job or somehow support themselves and their families. And if they should luck out, let's say, and actually get a better paying job than the one they were illegally fired from, the employer faces absolutely no penalty even though they clearly broke the law.

I heard Richard Trumka, [president of the United Mine Workers], give a speech a few years ago. He said, here we have these tomes, these thick, thick books of labor laws and the last rule is: the union loses. The workers lose because of the way the whole thing is set up.

IN THIS AGE OF SLEAZE AND FINANCIAL SCANDAL, I'M PROUD TO SAY THAT I MADE MY MONEY THE OLD FASHIONED WAY— BY THE EXPLOITATION OF LABOR.

© Goldberg/*People's Weekly World*. Reprinted with permission.

MM: How can the labor movement and individual unions overcome these legal impediments?

Newell: Well, I can tell you one thing we have been trying to implement in our organizing work. At least as long as I have been with the union, the UE has organized on the basis that we aren't just going to win a Labor Board election, we are going to build a union among the workers in a given plant with a Labor Board election at some point to ratify that, to prove it, to win legal bargaining rights in that shop. But we have taken that to a whole other stage in trying to bypass the procedures of the Labor Board to the extent possible. It is very difficult to just completely bypass the Board because the bottom line is that it is the mechanism which governs labor relations in the United States.

Our experiences petitioning for Labor Board elections [have shown] the very extensive ability of companies to delay the elections, to use that time to intimidate people and fire people and try to [destroy] the unity of workers.

We have been trying to set up a community-based alternative to the Labor Board. We organize fair election committees of community leaders—people from the religious community, elected public officials, people of stature in whatever community we are trying to organize—who will conduct a fair, secret-ballot election. They are non-partisan people with a voting list, with observers and all the normal mechanisms of the Labor Board. After the community election is held, they certify that a majority of workers have designated the union as their representative. And that can be accomplished in a week, with a fair and secret ballot and a monitored election.

Then when the company proceeds to make a mockery of the Labor Board procedure, stalling it for months and months, it really drives home to people how biased the government set-up is.

Community Boards

We try to work to make these community labor boards monitor other aspects of what is going on at that particular plant, such as firings because of union activity and unilateral changes that companies might make to discourage union activity, even though it is unlawful. The idea is to use the mechanisms of public support and public denunciations to demystify the process from the Labor Board election down to the real life of the plant and the community in which it is located.

We also try to install the union in the plant. They have had their community-held election. If the majority of the plant has voted for the union, then we try to go ahead and put the union in that plant: elect a grievance committee, elect shop stewards. We try to develop a functioning local union even though we do not have legal certification from the Labor Board as the collective bargaining representative at that point. Then people can see that they have their union. They have voted, people of stature in the community have said, "The majority has decided, you have a union now," they elect their stewards and shop officers and so forth and proceed to function as a union. Then when we have to go to a Labor Board election to get official legal bargaining rights, it is really demystified a lot for people. They have already had the experience of building the union in their shop.

MM: When you do that—hold an election and build a union—how have the companies you have organized responded?

Newell: It is really interesting. These employers come back and they say, "Go to the Labor Board." They know that that is the arena where the advantages accrue to them in terms of very cumbersome bureaucratic procedures. I can't recall an employer yet who said, "The mayor has certified the election. Well, then we will bargain with the union." I don't think we have had one case like that. They always say go to the Labor Board. And they hire their high-priced consultants, their unionbusters, to bring in their dog-and-pony show to scare people and buy them and deceive them and fire them and intimidate them and hope that the 6 or 8 or 12 or 15 weeks of delay that they get under Labor Board procedures will give them the time they need to wreck [our organizing efforts]. . . .

The unionbusters try to create a feeling of hysteria in the plant on election day. [They say], "The plant may close and move overseas. You are signing a blank check. You are turning your future over to outsiders. . . ." But if people have been through a fair and honestly run community-held election and have begun trying to have a local union function in that shop, it is harder for the unionbusters to create that kind of hysteria. It is easier for the workers to keep their perspective.

"Participation . . . [holds] the key to future productivity increases, even apart from the human value to be gained. "

Increased Employee Participation Would Benefit Labor

Charles Heckscher

Charles Heckscher, author of *The New Unionism*, is associate professor of human resources management at the Harvard Business School in Cambridge, MA. In the following viewpoint, he argues that old-style management, in which the manager decrees and the workers obey, is ineffective. A better way, and the way of the future, he says, is a democratic arrangement in which workers and managers labor together on an equal basis, each individual contributing his or her intelligence to the common task of making the business succeed.

As you read, consider the following questions:

1. What shortcomings does Heckscher see in the old-style, bureaucratic method of labor-management relations?
2. According to Heckscher, what are some of the ways workers' roles at the General Motors Saturn plant differ from those at traditional manufacturing companies?
3. What does the author say is the particular advantage of democratic organization in business?

Charles Heckscher, "Can Democracy Build Competitiveness?" This article appeared in the October 1991 issue of, and is reprinted with permission from, *The World & I*, a publication of The Washington Times Corporation, © 1991.

Democracy is widely believed to be *good* in human terms: that is, it appears to maximize the values of justice, freedom, and human development. My claim, however, is that it is also *effective*: that the way to competitiveness now lies through employee involvement. The reason is that democracy is the best structure for mobilizing intelligence.

This runs against common sense—or at least one aspect of common sense. Everyone "knows" that democracy is messy and inefficient: Factional battles, endless debates, and special-interest claims all conspire to delay and distort. We see this every day reading the morning papers. How often does it happen that we see what obviously needs to be done about some dire problem; how frustrating it is to watch this patently sensible solution sidetracked by expedient indulgence of vocal and self-interested minorities. How often do we say to ourselves, "If only I were running things, I would take care of it!"

Managers in a Bureaucracy

Managers, who *do* run things, cannot tolerate this kind of incompetence. Their job is to make good decisions, and to implement them quickly and decisively to meet competitive challenges. They are not in the business of debating, nor of pleasing employees. As a result, they turn to the basic principles of bureaucracy, which Max Weber outlined a century ago and which remained unsurpassed for decisive implementation. A clear hierarchy of accountability, defined roles, rewards tied to performance—these are the ways to get the maximum effective effort from a large group of people. If you have the right answer, this is the way to go.

Yet there is a critical problem with this approach: A lot of the time, no one has the right answer. With the growing complexity of markets and technologies, strategy increasingly has to be pieced together. Those at the "top" of the organization, for example, have a wide view of competitors and long-term trends, but they generally are not in close touch with customers. This weakness has led many companies to grief. On the other hand, those at the "bottom" may know the customers better, and they may have a much better feel for operational inefficiencies; but they cannot implement change without knowledge of other parts of the organization.

In complex organizations there is no way to gather all relevant data into the head of one person, or even a few persons, for successful strategic decision making. If that is true, then good strategy must be determined by something else: by the presence of an effective process for building consensus among differing viewpoints. Such a process constitutes both a fundamental challenge to the effectiveness of bureaucratic authority and a foundation for an increase in employee involvement.

Such ideas are not, as they often have been in the past, the mere fancy of intellectuals. The last thirty years increasingly have produced the astonishing sight of hard-nosed managers preaching worker participation. Consider, for example, Jack Welch, often known as "Neutron Jack," the leader who took General Electric and shook it until there were no loose parts left, who laid off thousands of managers and shucked off whole divisions. What is his view of participation? "The idea of liberation and empowerment of our work force," he says, "is not enlightenment—it's a competitive necessity."

"One of the robots went out and he said somebody threw a monkey wrench in the works. What's a wrench?

Stayskal. Reprinted by permission: Tribune Media Services.

Welch is far from alone in using the language of empowerment: In major corporations from AT&T to Xerox, the word has become common coin. This is, moreover, merely the latest manifestation of a long-term growth in employee participation efforts. Thirty years ago these companies were experimenting with adding responsibilities to individual jobs; twenty years ago they started setting up problem-solving groups of workers to make recommendations to management; ten years ago they began giving teams power to make managerial decisions like scheduling and ordering of materials. Today several hundred plants have pushed out to the leading edge, eliminating direct supervision altogether so that groups of workers can run large portions of the operation. Behind them come over 80 percent of the largest one hundred companies, all of which have implemented some substantial form of employee involvement.

I cite these events to show that the notion of worker participation in management is no longer an "outsider's" concept tied in with the idea of limiting management power. On the contrary, participation is itself becoming an accepted form of management—one that its advocates see as holding the key to future productivity increases, even apart from the human value to be gained. . . .

The transformation I am focusing on . . . does not formally *contest* corporate power, but it *transforms* the nature of management authority. It comes from within, as large corporate organizations search for ways to go beyond the clear lines and settled relations of traditional forms. The advantages of hierarchy—the clarity of accountability, the predictability of performance—have lost their luster; now bureaucracy instead seems ponderous and unresponsive.

The idealistic reasons for the critique of bureaucracy have been heard for centuries; what is new is the development of *pragmatic* reasons that promise to improve the performance of organizations. It is from these that the effective drive for change is produced.

Elements of the Transformation

Many strands are being woven together to make the new pattern. The old model was that developed at the turn of the century by Frederick Taylor, the apostle of mistrust: He mistrusted workers, whom he believed would always shirk if given the chance, and he also mistrusted managers, whom he saw as inconsistent and given to unscientific assumptions. Taylor's solution was to determine in detail the best way of doing a job, and then to enforce absolute adherence to that way on the part of both workers and managers.

In this command structure, workers were neither expected nor given the tools to think intelligently beyond their immediate jobs. Though in practice the scope of action was never as narrow as Taylor would have liked it, it was narrow enough. Workers might think of a slightly better way to tweak the machine, or they might instead think of a clever way to slow it down to spite management; many battles were fought over these boundaries of discretion. But the notion that workers might rethink the very organization of the operational system, or take responsibility for scheduling and ordering materials, was completely out of bounds.

Taylorism embodied the core principle of bureaucracy: that people should stick to their own personal knitting. . .

Today the Taylorist paradigm is clearly in major retreat at the shop-floor level. The success of Japanese "quality circles," imported to the United States during the 1970s, demonstrated the astonishing fact that blue-collar workers were capable of contributing intelligently to decisions about issues beyond their particular job performance. When they sat down to think about product quality, for example, they could make enormous improvements—if they were given information and allowed to discuss problems with the managers and engineers, who were nominally responsible for quality.

Labor-Management Teams Produce Quality

More often than not, workers who are part of teams find their jobs more rewarding and stimulating than fragmented, production-line work. . . .

[In addition,] studies indicate that work-team systems that allow workers real participation in decision-making . . . can produce better quality cars more efficiently than do auto plants with traditional work organizations.

John Hoerr, *Business Week*, February 20, 1989.

From this insight grew a trend of wide-ranging discussion groups with names such as "quality of work life" or "employee involvement." Ford and General Motors, the birthplaces of the assembly line and other key structures of industrial bureaucracy, quickly became among the most aggressive in moving away from these principles in their factories. Thousands of shop-floor teams were set up for discussions not only of quality but of work structure in general.

At the other end of the organization, seemingly unconnected, yet converging, events were taking place as the ranks of management began to dismantle their walls. In the sixties and seventies there was a gradual growth of cross-functional committees; under the conditions of the eighties, the process became less gradual. Cost pressures led to sudden and drastic reductions in middle-management layers: At least 15 percent of all management jobs in the *Fortune* 500 were cut during the decade. The result was an immediate need for more flexible and spontaneous cooperation. "Parallel structures"—task forces and flexible planning groups—gained more weight in relation to the traditional hierarchy.

Only in the last few years have some companies started to pull these strands together. A good example is Saturn, the new car company created by General Motors to compete head-to-head with Japanese imports. At the shop-floor workers are organized in self-managing teams with a high level of responsibility for scheduling, hiring, inventory control, and quality; following a Japanese lead, any worker can shut the line down for quality problems.

Perhaps the most extraordinary aspect of Saturn is the degree of worker sophistication about matters far outside the normal purview: car design, organizational structure, and competitive strategy. When teams discover design flaws that interfere with the assembly process, for example, they call a meeting with an engineer who is known as a "resource." The teams argue the point, and frequently they win. What do they do if they reach an impasse? "We might do a cause-and-effect analysis"—a complex and effective technique for structuring discussion.

And everyone, from the shop-floor through the middle of the organization, can talk spontaneously like a business analyst about the market positioning of the product, the future prospects, what the competition is doing. They learned this in their initial training, and it is reinforced constantly in the corporate culture. Problems and disagreements at all levels are dealt with by reference to the business strategy. . . .

Key Traits of Teamwork

From these cases, and from many others that tend in the same direction, one can draw a set of key characteristics that form a model of *post-bureaucratic* organization:

1. *Extensive consensus-building mechanisms.* These companies have developed an extraordinary array of *structures* that work to create consensus among different parts of the organization. Though it remains possible to go to a "boss" for a resolution of issues, this route is used far less frequently than in bureaucracies. A typical response, instead, is to form a committee of people with knowledge of the problem to generate a consensus solution. . . .

2. *Reliance on principles rather than rules.* Each of these organizations has developed a few formal principles in place of many rules. . . .

3. *Thorough information sharing.* Shell-Sarnia's workers have access to the computer system used by management; they can and do get information on productivity, costs, pricing, and sales. At Saturn, union leaders sit on the top-level management council.

4. *Focus on overall goals.* Some have described these post-bureaucratic firms as "task-driven": All employees are expected to relate their work to the goals of the whole. Corporate strategy is the common coin of discussion, linking people from diverse areas. The mechanisms of integration and information keep this strategic perspective alive and familiar in day-to-day operations.

5. *Professional ethic.* Though often hard to describe, a company's basic ethic is of critical importance in providing a framework for trust and communication. In corporate bureaucracies

the idea is the "organization man," conscientious in performing tasks and *loyal* to the organization. There is a strong element of dependence in the corporate ethic: Identities and prospects are tied to progress through the ranks of a single company, and employees shape themselves to fit.

Professional Perspective

In the more participatory systems the employees—from shop-floor to the top levels—have a more independent and professional perspective. They do not necessarily expect to remain loyal to the company; more exactly, the question seems irrelevant. They expect to stay as long as they have challenging work and can make a meaningful contribution, but no longer. The notion of "hanging on" and looking for something to do is abhorrent to them. The participatory ethic emphasizes outside relationships—professional societies, training programs, networks—as much as inside.

Participation by Workers Increases Productivity

Employee participation, if done right, can and does raise productivity. . . .

It now seems a good bet that some form of institutionalized participation by workers can raise productivity as well as increase the effectiveness of other productivity-enhancing measures such as profit-sharing. And it costs little.

Which participatory programs work best? The sketchy evidence points . . . toward substantive shop-floor consultation—something that goes beyond the suggestion box and engages workers in a meaningful way.

Alan S. Blinder, *Business Week*, April 17, 1989.

This ethic is not the "cold" one of the free agent ready to jump to whatever firm will offer the most money. These employees are committed to the mission and task of the firm, and they value the relationships they build, but they are not attached to the company as an entity. Nor are they attached to a person: In all the cases with which I am directly familiar, the organization leader is seen not as a revered hero but as merely a respected mortal. This ethic, as I perceive it, has a maturity that surpasses the dependent aspect of loyalty.

These elements have been brought to perhaps their highest current level in the firms I have mentioned, but the trends go much further. Most large companies with which I am familiar are, for example, sharing vastly greater amounts of information with employees at all levels than they did a decade ago, and they are greatly increasing the range of consensus-based committees. There is reason to believe, then, that the cases I have chosen are on the leading edge rather than off on their own track. . . .

Utilizing Intelligence of All

What is the particular advantage of a participatory system? Ideally, it makes more complete use of the *intelligence* of its employees.

In a bureaucracy—even an enlightened one—employees are expected to think only within the boundaries of their job descriptions. The health of the organization depends on the clarity of these boundaries; those who try to go further are actually destructive, because they create confusion and irresolvable problems. "That's not my job," is the classic identifying line of a bureaucrat; and those who try to break these constrains are likely to be *told*, "That's not your job.". . .

A bureaucracy is therefore limited by the capacities of the head and by the degree of rigidity introduced down the hierarchy. These limitations are manageable as long as information remains in a certain range of complexity and change is not too fast, so that the head can absorb it all. Once actual demands surpass those dictated by job descriptions, the need for effective decision making transcends the abilities of individual leaders. Technological and market changes have brought the economy as a whole to that point, inspiring the widespread (and relatively recent) drive to "debureaucratize" organizations.

In a participatory system, by contrast, members are expected to think creatively beyond their own areas—the line worker to question the mechanical engineer, the mechanical engineer to challenge the purchasing manager, and everyone to take on the strategic planners. It is from this mixing of perspectives that the energy for innovation and creativity develops.

"Nowhere is there any indication of where accountability and authority can be placed for work or competitive effectiveness in any of these [democratic] arrangements."

Increased Employee Participation Would Harm Labor

Elliott Jaques

A visiting research professor of management science at George Washington University, Elliott Jaques is also the author of several books on business management. In the following viewpoint, he argues that the trend toward democratic management, in which workers and managers work together on an equal basis, will ultimately be harmful to business and to workers. In such systems, he states, accountability is weak if not nonexistent, resulting in disorganized and ineffective business organizations.

As you read, consider the following questions:

1. Why does the author think democratic management systems are harmful?
2. On what three false premises does Jaques say proponents of workplace democracy base their ideas? How does Jaques respond to these premises?
3. What does Jaques believe makes for good worker-manager relations?

Elliott Jaques, "Managerial Leadership, the Key to Good Organization." This article appeared in the October 1991 issue of, and is reprinted with permission from, *The World & I*, a publication of The Washington Times Corporation, © 1991.

There is a seriously disruptive movement afoot in American management. It bids fair to undermine our business competitiveness steadily and relentlessly. This movement is centered around the general idea of workplace democracy and worker involvement. These aspirations towards a better and more humane workplace are admirable; they cannot be gainsaid. The difficulty is that the steps proposed for fulfilling these aspirations are unrealistic and self-defeating. They demoralize the managerial system and take the heart out of the innovativeness of individual contributors.

These current ideas center upon replacing the managerial hierarchy, which is considered undemocratic, with so-called democratic group practices of various kinds. But the issue is not one of democracy versus hierarchy. What is required is to leave democracy and democratic voting to the political field where they belong and to find ways of transforming the managerial hierarchy into systems of accountable, human, value-adding managerial leadership.

To try to eliminate the managerial hierarchy in order to eliminate managerial autocracy is to throw out the baby with the bathwater. For the exercise of authority tied properly to accountability is one of the most constructive of all human activities. The real task—and the difficult one—is to replace autocratic management with accountable authoritative management. It can be done. I propose here to show how.

Background

For some years now there has been a constant stream of publications by human resource experts and academics foreseeing the end of the managerial hierarchy and its replacement by some vague and unspecified new form or forms of organization. Peter Drucker, Tom Peters, Rosabeth Moss Kanter, Ed Lawler, Warren Bennis, Quinn Mills, Michael Hammer, Shoshana Zuboff, Barker and Ghoshal, Stan Davis, and countless others have forecast the end of the industrial age and the entrepreneurial age, and the coming of what has been called variously the information age, the services age, or the post-modern age.

This new age will supposedly require a transformation of the managerial hierarchy into an extraordinary array of "new" organizations—all of them democratic in tone. Thus we see arguments in favor of: workplace democracy, the company without boundaries or walls, cluster organizations, self-managing teams, corporate hubs, global matrix networks, symphony-orchestra-type systems, groups that grow spontaneously around information flows and just as spontaneously dissolve, quality circles, continuous improvement councils, substitution of leaders for managers at higher levels, and even the replacement of organization altogether by the inculcation of everyone into "a matrix frame of mind." But, ominously, nowhere is there any indication of where accountability and authority can be placed for work or competitive effectiveness in any of these arrangements.

© Goldberg/*People's Weekly World*. Reprinted with permission.

These ideas have influenced the outlook of many senior executives. Thus, for example, James Houghton, chairman of Corning, Inc., endorses the idea of Ralph Kilmann that we need organizational networks with a corporate hub that acts as negotiator, facilitator, broker, or think tank to a "global network of people and information, each exerting an influence on the other." Gone are accountable chief executive officers, and accountable presidents of subsidiary companies spread throughout the world connected to the corporate CEO and to their own subordinates through an accountable management hierarchy.

Managers as Facilitators

Similarly, experienced and successful CEOs such as Robert Haas, chairman and CEO of Levi Strauss, has picked up the idea that managers are no longer to direct and "control" their subordinates, but rather to function as facilitators to help them arrive at effective group decisions. And Jack Welch extols the GE workout program of corporatewide town meeting discussion groups led by academics to identify unnecessary practices, letting managers off the hook for inefficiencies.

The trouble with these ideas is that they are based upon unrealistic fantasies about what the managerial hierarchy should be. None of them gets rid of the managerial hierarchy, nor can they do so, despite Tom Peters' unfounded notion that the managerial hierarchy at Citicorp, Federal Express, and other corporations has begun to disappear. For the reality of the ubiquitous employment systems by which modern societies mainly get their work done today is that people are employed as individuals in hierarchies in which some individuals—managers—are held *accountable for the work of other individuals*—their subordinates. This individual managerial accountability does not, and cannot, disappear merely by the introduction of groupthink. Boards of directors are in gross dereliction of duty if they allow their corporate CEO's to abandon their individual accountability and thereby abdicate. Nor can any other appointed manager be allowed to do, whatever his or her level in the organization.

Accountability Is Essential

Organizations need to be able to employ individual people who are accountable, and clearly accountable, for getting work done. I challenge any protagonist of these "new" organizational styles to identify where accountability lies in their systems: In fact, they are organizational monstrosities tailor-made for buck passing. And by *accountability*, I am referring to accountability for new designs, for bringing new products rapidly to market, for establishing new world markets, for maintaining quality, for reducing costs, for developing the executive talent pool, for acquisitions and new ventures—in short, accountability for all the work at all levels and in all functions that make an organization competitively effective.

Can so many human resource practitioners, academics, and

consultants be wrong? Unfortunately, yes. This has happened because they have bought three misleading notions.

• First is the impression that managers are coercive autocrats who lord it over subordinates and that more democratic group decision making is needed. This is incorrect. Autocratic managers are symptoms not of the managerial system per se but of badly organized managerial systems—for example, with too many layers and with people breathing down each other's necks—that are almost universal.

• Second is the supposition that the Japanese competitive miracle was achieved by quality circles, continuous improvement councils, and other kinds of democratic teams and groupthink. Those procedures were peripheral. The . . . miracle in Japan was achieved by building quality, just-in-time working, and continuous improvement into the process, that is, instituting accountability in the managerial system, where these ideas flourish to this day.

• Third is the naive assumption that the new information technology will make managers redundant. None of the proponents of this idea has so far given any indication even of having considered where accountability would lie for ensuring that action was taken and for the quality of that action.

"Participative Management"

Along with this disruptive attempt to put "democratic teams" in place of good management is the idea of "participative management," as though ordinary good management were not necessarily based upon effective two-way working relationships between effective managerial leaders and their subordinates. Indeed, the very phrase "participative management" suggests the possibility of something called "nonparticipative management"! But surely "nonparticipative" management is not management at all; it is coercion and should not be associated with the concept of management.

In the same vein is the currently popular idea of *empowerment*. This is a direct reflection of the failure to establish a satisfactory hierarchical organization in which the right amount of accountability and the accompanying authority are allocated to each layer in the hierarchy. We do not need "less layers and power down," we need the *correct* number of layers, and the *correct* authority at each level, as I shall describe below.

We also go wrong with vague ideas like "networking"—an aspiration with no indication of how to get it. And we go equally wrong with the fallacious and damaging idea of employees dealing with each other like suppliers and customers. It is the duty of effective value-adding managers to mediate between subordinates in a constructive, human way. Letting subordinates fight it out like suppliers and customers is an abdication from this duty, and, in fact, can be shown to dehumanize working relationships, as false propositions always do.

Reinforcing the overriding falseness of these ideas of democratic teams and processes within the managerial hierarchy, two other equally misleading and disruptive ideas have been promoted by the experts.

The first is that personality conflicts have a large part to play in the problems that beset hierarchy. Personality inventories like the Myers-Briggs test are said to match personalities so as to get groups that have just the right amount of aggressiveness, sociability, proactive initiative, risk taking, reflectiveness, and so on distributed among the members. The members of such groups theoretically take into account their knowledge of each other's personality makeup and so avoid conflict.

A History of Hostility

U.S. manufacturers . . . have also borrowed Japanese techniques of forming work teams and quality discussion groups to tap the innovative potential of their employees. But there is still a great deal of resistance on both sides, and it remains to be seen whether the suspicion and hostility of generations can be overcome.

Financial World, June 25, 1991.

This emphasis upon personality actually focuses upon serious psychopathology. For if members are not disturbed to the point where they are unable to control their behavior, if they are able to leave their psychopathology at home, then they should be left to express their personalities freely. If the organization is requisitely established and the working relationships clearly specified, then nothing but good comes from leaving their "personalities" alone.

Finally we have the unfortunate contribution of wage and salary economics and motivation theory. Economists tell us that human labor is a commodity and its value should be determined by the marketplace like any other commodities. Wrong! Real human beings have an inherent relative value determined by their level of capability. They seek levels of work in which they can exercise their capability to the full—and feel justly and fairly treated as human beings when they are paid on a scale that pays differentially for varying levels of work.

Given an equitable differential pay system and opportunities for work at levels consistent with one's capability, people do not need to be motivated by bonus incentives. We are humans, not pigeons. Whereas political equality is basic to political democracy, people do not really seek equality at work, nor do they seek to be judged either as groups or by groups. In our work, we seek accountable, value-adding managers with the right degree of higher capability to judge our effectiveness, assess our capabilities, and recognize our merit. That is what good management ought to be about—and can be about.

One of the hallmarks of a truly democratic free enterprise society is to ensure that each and every citizen really does have the opportunity for work in which he or she can utilize his or her full potential capability as that potential unfolds and matures throughout life to levels higher in capability. Our employment organizations should have the bounden duty to contribute to that process, not by hollow fads and practices and denial of authoritative management, but by the hard work of establishing requisite organization structure and requisite managerial leadership practices.

Recognizing Statements That Are Provable

We are constantly confronted with statements and generalizations about social and moral problems. In order to think clearly about these problems, it is useful if one can make a basic distinction between statements for which evidence can be found and other statements that cannot be verified or proved because evidence is not available, or the issue is so controversial that it cannot be definitely proved.

Readers should be aware that magazines, newspapers, and other sources often contain statements of a controversial nature. The following activity is designed to allow experimentation with statements that are provable and those that are not.

The following statements are taken from the viewpoints in this chapter. Consider each statement carefully. *Mark P for any statement you believe is provable. Mark U for any statement you feel is unprovable because of the lack of evidence. Mark C for any statements you think are too controversial to be proved to everyone's satisfaction.*

If you are doing this activity as a member of a class or group, compare your answers with those of other class or group members. Be able to defend your answers. You may discover that others will come to different conclusions than you do. Listening to the reasons others present for their answers may give you valuable insights into recognizing statements that are provable.

P = provable
U = unprovable
C = too controversial

1. A United States government report showed that union workers earn $2 more an hour in wages and $3 more in benefits than unorganized workers.

2. In the popular mind, unions tend to be vaguely associated with Archie Bunker characters and cartoonish, corrupt bosses.

3. Union membership has been declining since the mid-1950s.

4. Unions, by raising the wage structure, impede the growth of employment and increase prices for consumers.

5. The decline of the American rail system has been a national tragedy.

6. IBM has 200,000 non-union workers in this country.

7. Studies indicate that allowing workers to participate in decision making can produce better quality products more efficiently.

8. The reason democracy is effective is that it is the best structure for mobilizing intelligence.

9. The old style of management was to determine in detail the best way of doing a job, and then to enforce absolute adherence to that way.

10. United States manufacturers have borrowed Japanese management techniques.

11. Democratic management techniques seriously undermine America's business competitiveness.

12. People do not really seek equality at work; they seek fair pay and good managers who value them.

13. By mediating the relationship between employees, the state, and their employers, unions act to diffuse the power these institutions exercise over individuals.

14. A union can only be successful in a prosperous industry.

15. Unions support minimum wage increases.

Periodical Bibliography

The following articles have been selected to supplement the diverse views presented in this chapter.

Norm Alster — "What Flexible Workers Can Do," *Fortune*, February 13, 1989.

Charles W. Baird — "Solidarity and Labor Law Reform in the 1990s," *The Freeman*, June 1990. Available from The Foundation for Economic Education, Inc., 30 S. Broadway, Irvington-on-Hudson, NY 10533.

Aaron Bernstein — "Do More Babies Mean Fewer Working Women?" *Business Week*, August 5, 1991.

Jeremy Brecher and Tim Costello — "Labor Goes Global," *Z Magazine*, part I: January 1991; part II: March 1991.

Business & Society Review — "Symposium: Are Unions Dead?" Summer 1990. Available from Management Reports, Inc., 25-13 Old Kings Highway North, Suite 107, Darien, CT 06820.

Joseph F. Coates, Jennifer Jarratt, and John B. Mahaffie — "Future Work," *The Futurist*, May/June 1991.

Gary Delgado — "Independent Labor Organizations Go Their Own Way," *The Minority Trendsletter*, Summer 1991.

Bill Dennison — "Where Stands the Trade Union Movement?" *Political Affairs*, July 1989.

Jaclyn Fierman — "Shaking the Blue-Collar Blues," *Fortune*, April 22, 1991.

Financial World — "Managing American Labor," June 25, 1991. Available from 1328 Broadway, New York, NY 10001.

Thomas Geoghegan — "Glory Days," *The New Republic*, May 29, 1989.

William Greider — "Down but Not Out: Labor Struggles to Find Its Voice," *Rolling Stone*, October 17, 1991.

Dwight R. Lee and Robert L. Sexton — "Patience and Property: Corporate vs. Union Management," *The Freeman*, August 1990.

Michael Maccoby — "Productivity with a Human Face," *The Washington Monthly*, March 1991.

Michael Maccoby — "Unions and the Democratic Vision," *The World & I*, October 1991.

Glossary of Terms

bond a loan to a government or corporation; when people buy bonds, they earn a specified rate of interest for lending the seller money for a specified period of time.

budget deficit the amount of money a government spends that exceeds the amount of money taken in.

bureaucracy a form of management of government with a large degree of specialization; that is, each department (bureau) has its own functions, and, usually, rigid rules regulate how departments interact.

capital gains tax a tax on income from the sale of a personally owned asset that has increased in value.

capitalist class term used by socialists and others for the members of society that control the use of capital (money and equipment); usually, high government and corporate officials.

CDs (certificates of deposit) money deposited for a specified amount of time; the deposit often has a locked-in amount of interest; the certificate describes the amount of the deposit as well as the time span and interest rates.

collective bargaining negotiations between labor (usually represented by unions) and management.

commercial paper similar to bonds, but these are short-term loans to corporations, issued with no **security**.

consumer price index an index measuring the change in the cost of typical purchases of goods and services.

currency money used by consumers (e.g., paper money) to buy and sell goods and services; the amount spent reflects the value of the product or service purchased.

deficit the amount by which the money spent by a company or country exceeds its income.

demand-side economics economic theory stressing the demand side of the **supply-and-demand** equation; idea that an increased demand for goods creates markets and the need to supply those markets; according to demand-side theorists, taxing and redistributing corporate profits and maintaining wage protections enables a much larger segment of the population to buy goods, thereby stimulating economic growth.

depression a prolonged period with little or no economic growth characterized by low employment, low productivity, low interest rates, low profits, and high inflation.

deregulation the removal of laws that restrict certain business activities; typically, the regulations that are removed have in effect allowed certain companies to gain a monopoly; deregulation removes the monopoly by allowing other types of companies to participate in the same business; deregulation also allows highly regulated industries, such as banks, to enter new fields of business, such as risk-laden investment concerns.

diversification increasing the number of activities a business is involved in or the number of ways a person invests money; for example, a bank that diversifies may branch out from dealing strictly with savings and loans to issuing credit cards and investing in stocks.

FDIC (Federal Deposit Insurance Corporation) the government agency that insures bank deposits up to a limit of $100,000 per account.

federal debt the total amount of money a government owes.

"the Fed" (Federal Reserve Banking System) the central bank of the United States; the Fed sets interest rates and regulates the money supply.

finance companies companies that specialize in making loans to individuals.

fiscal policy actions taken by the federal government to stabilize the economy by increasing or decreasing federal spending, increasing or decreasing taxes, and increasing or decreasing the deficit or surplus in the federal budget.

flat rate tax a tax system in which all persons are taxed the same percentage regardless of earnings.

foreign deficit the amount of debt a country owes to foreign countries.

FSLIC (Federal Savings and Loan Insurance Corporation) the federal agency that offers insurance to savings and loan associations.

GATT (General Agreement on Tariffs and Trade) established as an agency of the United Nations in 1948, its members are pledged to work together to reduce tariffs and other barriers to international trade and to eliminate discriminatory treatment in international commerce.

GDP (Gross Domestic Product) the value of all goods and services produced within a country over a given period regardless of who owns the facilities.

GNP (Gross National Product) the value of all goods and services produced within a country over a given period (usually a year); the production facilities must be owned by residents of the nation.

Great Depression in the 1930s, an extended depression in the United States in which millions of people were unemployed and thousands of companies failed.

inflation a relatively large increase in the prices of goods and services, usually caused by a shrinking supply of goods or an increase in the amount of currency beyond the needs of trade; usually steep inflation like that of pre-World War II Germany (2500 percent in one month) leaves currency virtually worthless and can lead to economic collapse.

junk bonds extremely high-risk bonds issued by companies that may not be able to repay them; because of the high risk, they usually offer a high rate of interest.

Keynesian economics named after its major proponent, John Maynard Keynes, this approach calls for limited government interference in an essentially capitalist system to ensure a healthy economy (high employment, low inflation).

LBO (leveraged buyout) a group of individuals takes control of a company by purchasing the majority of its stock with borrowed money; the individuals then hope to pay off these huge loans with the future profits of the purchased company.

monopoly complete control of a product by one seller or producer.

national debt similar to **federal debt**; some define it as including *all* debt owed in a country by individuals, companies, and the government.

NLRB (National Labor Relations Board) the federal agency that oversees and often mediates labor disputes.

private sector that part of the economy made up of privately owned business.

privatization having the private sector do things currently done by government; for example, some cities have eliminated garbage pickup by city employees, turning over that service to private companies.

progressive tax a tax system in which those with higher incomes pay a higher percentage of their income to taxes.

protectionism policies designed to protect a country's industries from foreign competition; such policies might include import **tariffs** or quotas or **subsidies** for domestic products.

public sector the government; that part of the economy made up of federal and other organizations that are the shared responsibility of the public.

Reaganomics another name for **supply-side economics**, so-called because it was the economic philosophy of the Reagan administration.

real wages wages expressed in terms of what today's dollar will buy; a common way of determining buying power is through the **consumer price index**.

recession a period of reduced economic activity.

recovery the period following a **recession** during which the economy begins to grow again.

refinancing debts new loans granted to help pay off current debts.

rescheduling debts changing or postponing the dates on which debt payments are due in order to create additional time to repay a debt.

SEC (Securities and Exchange Commission) the federal agency that regulates the securities industry.

securities stocks and bonds.

security the collateral that guarantees a loan; for example, to get a car loan, a person puts up the car for collateral; if the borrower defaults on the loan, he or she is liable to lose the car.

S&Ls (savings and loan associations) organizations similar to banks in that they accept savings deposits and offer loans, but are more limited in their activities and are subject to different regulations than banks; in the late 1980s, thousands of S&Ls failed, leaving the government and ultimately the taxpayers to cover the customers' losses.

stagflation a period of high unemployment and inflation and low consumer demand.

subsidy grant by a government to a private person or company to assist an enterprise.

supply and demand the core concepts of old-style (market) economics; supply is the quantity of a good that would be *offered* by producers, while demand is the quantity of a particular good that would be *purchased* by consumers; the law of supply and demand holds that the cost of goods is determined by the ratio of supply to demand.

supply-side economics an economic theory that contends that a supply of goods creates demand for such goods and that the proper role for government is to stimulate production; or the supply side of the **supply-and-demand** equation; reducing tax rates and providing incentives for corporate development are two things most supply-siders favor to stimulate the economy.

tariff a duty imposed by a government on imported or in some cases exported goods.

tax shelter an investment or tax code provision that reduces one's tax burden.

trade credits short-term loans granted to finance the purchase of specific goods.

trade deficit the amount of money that is lost when a country imports more goods than it exports.

transnationals companies that do business abroad as well as in their home country.

Organizations to Contact

The editors have compiled the following list of organizations that are concerned with the issues debated in this book. All have publications or information available for interested readers. For best results, allow as much time as possible for the organizations to respond. The descriptions below are derived from materials provided by the organizations. This list was compiled upon the date of publication. Names, addresses, and phone numbers of organizations are subject to change.

American Bankers Association
1120 Connecticut Ave. NW
Washington, DC 20036
(202) 663-5000

The association is comprised of commercial banks and trust companies. It furthers education on the banking industry and promotes relationships with government. It maintains a 500,000-volume library on banking, money, economics, and finance. The association publishes the monthly *Banking Journal* and *Consumer Banking Digest* and the newspaper *Bankers Weekly*.

American Enterprise Institute (AEI)
1150 17th St. NW
Washington, DC 20036
(202) 862-5800

The institute sponsors research on a wide range of national and international issues. AEI issues policy studies on government regulation, economics, energy, and taxes. It publishes the bimonthly journal *The American Enterprise* as well as books on economic issues, including *After the Crash: Linkages Between Stocks and Futures, Balancing Act: Debt, Deficits, and Taxes,* and *Crisis in the Budget Process: Exercising Political Choice.*

**American Federation of Labor/Congress
of Industrial Organizations (AFL/CIO)**
815 16th St. NW
Washington, DC 20006
(202) 637-5000

The AFL/CIO, made up of 95 labor unions, 51 state federations, and 742 city bodies, is the largest federation of labor unions. It works to promote labor unions throughout the United States. Its publications include the weekly *AFL/CIO News.*

The Brookings Institution
1775 Massachusetts Ave. NW
Washington, DC 20036
(202) 797-6220

The institution, founded in 1927, is a liberal research and education organization that publishes material in the fields of economics, government, and foreign policy. The institution publishes the quarterly *Brookings Review* and various books and reports.

Cato Institute
224 Second St. SE
Washington, DC 20003
(202) 546-0200

The institute is a libertarian public policy research organization that works to limit government intervention in the economy. The institute publishes the *Cato Journal* and various books and reports.

Center on Budget and Policy Priorities
777 N. Capitol St. NE, Suite 705
Washington, DC 20002
(202) 408-1080, Fax (202) 408-1056

The center is a public policy research organization that promotes policies to help low- and moderate-income Americans. It fights for tax credits for the working poor and against federal budget cuts that would reduce aid to low-income families. It publishes a monthly newsletter and a variety of reports, including *Shortchanged: Recent Developments in Hispanic Poverty* and *Still Far from the Dream: Recent Developments in Black Poverty*.

Citizens for a Sound Economy Foundation
470 L'Enfant Plaza SW
East Building #7112
Washington, DC 20024
(202) 488-8200

The foundation works primarily to reduce government interference in the economy and to improve America's economy by reducing the budget deficit. It maintains that by freezing government spending, the deficit will decline without requiring any tax increases. The foundation publishes position papers including *Tax Increase or Spending Restraint: A Citizen's Guide to Deficit Reduction*.

Citizens for Tax Justice (CTJ)
1311 L St. NW
Washington, DC 20005
(202) 626-3780

CTJ works to change America's tax policies, arguing that reducing inequities between the rich and the poor will improve America's economy. It believes that the rich should pay a greater share of the tax burden than the middle class and the poor. Its publications include *Inequality & The Budget Deficit*.

The Committee for Economic Development (CED)
477 Madison Ave.
New York, NY 10022
(212) 688-2063

The committee is a research and education organization whose goal is to study and seek solutions to social and economic issues that affect the long-term health of the U.S. economy. Composed of business and academic leaders, it publishes reports and statements on the U.S. economy.

Eagle Forum
Box 618
Alton, IL 62002
(618) 462-5415

The Eagle Forum promotes free-market principles and contends that decreases in taxes and government spending can improve America's economy. It publishes the monthly *Phyllis Schlafly Report*.

Economic Policy Institute (EPI)
1730 Rhode Island Ave. NW, Suite 812
Washington, DC 20036
(202) 775-8810

The institute was founded in 1986 by a group of economic policy experts. The goal of the institute is to encourage scholarship on a variety of economic issues and to broaden the public debate about strategies to improve America's economy. It generally opposes government deregulation of industries and capital-gains tax cuts. EPI publishes a variety of position papers on economic issues, including *Reducing the Deficits: Send the Bill to Those Who Went to the Party* and *A Progressive Answer to the Fiscal Deficit*.

Economic Strategy Institute (ESI)
1100 Connecticut Ave. NW, Suite 1300
Washington, DC 20036
(202) 728-0993

The institute is a research center that focuses on the links between economic policies, global security, and international trade. It argues that the United States needs a comprehensive strategy that will reduce America's trade deficit and improve U.S. technological leadership. It publishes books and monographs on America's economy, including *Powernomics: Economics and Strategy After the Cold War, Investment: The Fast Track to a Strong Recovery*, and *Foreign Direct Investment in the United States: Unencumbered Access*.

The Foundation for Economic Education, Inc. (FEE)
Irvington-on-Hudson, NY 10533
(914) 591-7230

FEE publishes information and commentary in support of private property, the free market, and limited government. It frequently publishes articles on taxation, the budget deficit, and other economic issues in its monthly magazine *The Freeman*.

The Heritage Foundation
214 Massachusetts Ave. NE
Washington, DC 20002
(202) 546-4400

The Heritage Foundation is a well-known conservative think tank that supports free enterprise and supply-side economic theories. In 1990, the foundation issued a detailed proposal for reducing the budget deficit by cutting excessive government spending. The Heritage Foundation's publications include the periodic *Backgrounder*, the monthly *Policy Review*, and the *Issues Bulletin*.

Institute for Research on the Economics of Taxation (IRET)
1331 Pennsylvania Ave. NW, Suite 515
Washington, DC 20004-1774
(202) 347-9570

IRET is a public policy and economics research organization dedicated to economic growth through free-market tax and fiscal policies. It promotes tax cuts to increase the growth of America's economy. IRET publishes a variety of books, as well as its periodicals *Congressional Advisory, Byline, Bulletin, Money Memo,* and *IRET News.*

National Bureau of Economic Research (NBER)
1050 Massachusetts Ave.
Cambridge, MA 02138-5398
(617) 868-3900

NBER, founded in 1920, is a research organization dedicated to analyzing the major issues confronting America's economy. NBER publishes the monthly *NBER Digest* and the quarterly *NBER Reporter,* as well as a variety of position papers and books. It has recently published *Reducing the Risk of Economic Crisis, National Savings and Economic Performance,* and *Tax Policy and the Economy.*

Reason Foundation
3415 South Sepulveda Blvd., Suite 400
Los Angeles, CA 90034
(213) 391-2245

The foundation promotes individual freedoms and free-market principles. In its monthly magazine, *Reason,* it has published articles advocating tax reductions to stimulate the economy and government spending reductions to reduce the budget deficit.

Union for Radical Political Economics (URPE)
Department of Economics
University of California
Riverside, CA 92521
(714) 787-3538

URPE seeks, through political economic analysis, to present a continuing critique of the capitalist system while helping to construct a progressive social policy and increase socialist alternatives. URPE publishes a quarterly journal, *Review of Radical Political Economics.*

United Auto Workers (UAW)
Solidarity House
8000 E. Jefferson Ave.
Detroit, MI 48214
(313) 926-5000

The UAW is the international union of automobile, aerospace, and agricultural implement workers of America. Among its publications are *Solidarity,* a newspaper, and the quarterly journal *Skill.*

Bibliography of Books

James R. Barth et al. — *Banking Industry in Turmoil: A Report on the Condition of the United States Banking Industry and the Bank Insurance Fund.* Washington, DC: U.S. Government Printing Office, 1990.

William J. Baumol, Sue Anne Batey Blackman, and Edward N. Wolff — *Productivity and American Leadership: The Long View.* Cambridge, MA: MIT Press, 1991.

George J. Benston, R. Dam Brumbaugh, and others — *Blueprint for Restructuring America's Financial Institutions: Report of a Task Force.* Washington, DC: The Brookings Institution, 1990.

Samuel Bowles, David M. Gordon, and Thomas E. Weisskopf — *After the Waste Land: A Democratic Economics for the Year 2000.* Armonk, NY: M.E. Sharpe, Inc., 1990.

Denny Braun — *The Rich Get Richer: The Rise of Income Inequality in the United States and the World.* Chicago: Nelson-Hall, 1990.

Lowell L. Bryan — *Bankrupt: Restoring the Health and Profitability of Our Banking System.* New York: HarperCollins, 1991.

Lowell L. Bryan — *Breaking Up the Bank: Rethinking an Industry Under Siege.* Homewood, IL: Dow Jones-Irwin, 1988.

Timothy J. Conlan, Margaret T. Wrightson, and David R. Beam — *Taxing Choices: The Politics of Tax Reform.* Washington, DC: Congressional Quarterly, Inc., 1990.

James Dale Davidson and William Rees-Mogg — *The Great Reckoning: How the World Will Change in the Depression of the 1990s.* New York: Summit Books, 1991.

Robert Eisner and and Paul J. Pieper — *How Real Is the Federal Deficit?* New York: The Free Press, 1989.

Catherine England and Thomas F. Huertas, eds. — *The Financial Services Revolution.* Washington, DC: The Cato Institute, 1988.

Thomas Geoghegan — *Which Side Are You On?* New York: Farrar, Straus & Giroux, 1991.

John B. Gilmour — *Reconcilable Differences? Congress, the Budget Process, and the Deficit.* Berkeley: University of California Press, 1990.

Robert Hamrin — *America's New Economy: The Basic Guide.* New York: Franklin Watts, 1988.

Robert Heilbroner and Peter Bernstein — *The Debt and the Deficit: False Alarms, Real Possibilities.* New York: W.W. Norton, 1989.

Wei-Chiao Huang, ed. — *Organized Labor at the Crossroads.* Kalamazoo, MI: W.E. Upjohn Institute for Employment Research, 1989.

Paul Krugman — *The Age of Diminished Expectations: U.S. Economic Policy in the 1990s.* Cambridge, MA: The Cambridge Press, 1990.

Dan LaBotz — *Rank-and-File Rebellion: Teamsters for a Democratic Union.* New York: Verso Books, 1990.

Lawrence B. Lindsey	*The Growth Experiment.* New York: Basic Books, 1990.
R.E. Litan	*What Should Banks Do?* Washington, DC: The Brookings Institution, 1987.
Alfred L. Malabre Jr.	*Understanding the New Economy.* Homewood, IL: Dow Jones-Irwin, 1989.
Philip Mattera	*Prosperity Lost: How a Decade of Greed Has Eroded Our Standard of Living and Endangered Our Children's Future.* Reading, MA: Addison-Wesley, 1991.
Mike Parker and Jane Slaughter	*Choosing Sides: Unions and the Team Concept.* Boston: South End Press, 1988.
Robert A. Pastor	*Integration with Mexico: Options for U.S. Policy.* Washington, DC: The Brookings Institution, 1991.
Joseph A. Pechman	*Tax Reform, the Rich, and the Poor.* Washington, DC: The Brookings Institution, 1989.
Kevin Phillips	*The Politics of Rich and Poor.* New York: Random House, 1990.
James L. Pierce	*The Future of Banking.* New Haven, CT: Yale University Press, 1991.
Clyde V. Prestowitz Jr., Ronald A. Morse, and Alan Tonelson, eds.	*Powernomics: Economics and Strategy After the Cold War.* Washington, DC: Economic Strategy Group, 1991.
Alice M. Rivlin	*Reviving the American Dream: The Economy, the States, and the Federal Government.* Washington, DC: The Brookings Institution, 1992.
Richard Rosecrance	*America's Economic Resurgence: A Bold New Strategy.* New York: Harper & Row, 1990.
Laurence S. Seidman	*Saving for America's Economic Future.* Armonk, NY: M.E. Sharpe, Inc., 1990.
Arthur B. Shostak	*Robust Unionism: Innovations in the Labor Movement.* Ithaca, NY: ILR Press, 1991.
Herbert Stein, ed.	*Tax Policy in the Twenty-First Century.* New York: John Wiley & Sons, 1988.
George Strauss, Daniel G. Gallagher, and Jack Fiorito, eds.	*The State of the Unions.* Madison, WI: Industrial Relations Research Association, 1991.
Lawrence H. Summers	*Tax Policy and the Economy.* Cambridge, MA: MIT Press, 1990.
U.S. Department of the Treasury	*Modernizing the Financial System: Recommendations for Safer, More Competitive Banks.* Washington, DC: U.S. Government Printing Office, 1991.
Paul Weiler	*Governing the Workplace.* Cambridge, MA: Harvard University Press, 1990.
Joseph White and Aaron Wildavsky	*The Deficit and the Public Interest.* Berkeley: University of California Press, 1989.
Lawrence H. White	*Competition and Currency: Essays on Free Banking and Money.* Washington, DC: The Cato Institute, 1989.
Lawrence J. White	*The S&L Debacle: Public Policy Lessons for Bank and Thrift Regulation.* New York: Oxford University Press, 1991.

Index